Harlof and Vanna B. Olsen
Business Collection

# PRICING DERIVATIVES

**Other Titles in the McGraw-Hill Library of Investment and Finance**

*Convertible Securities* by John P. Calamos

*Pricing and Managing Exotic and Hybrid Options* by Vineer Bhansali

*Risk Management and Financial Derivatives* by Satyajit Das

*Valuing Intangible Assets* by Robert F. Reilly and Robert P. Schweihs

*Managing Financial Risk* by Charles W. Smithson

*High-Yield Bonds* by Theodore Barnhill, William Maxwell, and Mark Shenkman

*Valuing Small Business and Professional Practices* by Shannon Pratt, Robert F. Reilly, and Robert P. Schweihs

*Implementing Credit Derivatives* by Israel Nelken

*The Handbook of Credit Derivatives* by Jack Clark Francis, Joyce Frost, and J. Gregg Whittaker

*The Handbook of Advanced Business Valuation* by Robert F. Reilly and Robert P. Schweihs

*Global Investment Risk Management* by Ezra Zask

*Active Portfolio Management* by Richard Grinold and Ronald Kahn

*The Hedge Fund Handbook* by Stefano Lavinio

*Pricing, Hedging, and Trading Exotic Options* by Israel Nelken

*Equity Management* by Bruce Jacobs and Kenneth Levy

*Asset Allocation* by Roger Gibson

*Valuing a Business* by Shannon P. Pratt, Robert F. Reilly, and Robert Schweihs

*The Complete Arbitrage Deskbook* by Stephane Reverre

*Quantitative Business Valuation* by Jay Abrams

*Applied Equity Analysis* by James English

*Exchange Rate Determination* by Michael Rosenberg

*Dynamic Portfolio Theory and Management* by Richard Oberuc

*Building Financial Models* by John Tjia

*Modeling Financial Markets* by Benjamin Van Vliet and Robert Hendry

*The Handbook of Business Valuation and Intellectual Property Analysis* by Robert Reilly and Robert Schweihs

# PRICING DERIVATIVES

## The Financial Concepts Underlying the Mathematics of Pricing Derivatives

**AMBAR N. SENGUPTA**
*Department of Mathematics*
*Louisiana State University*
*Baton Rouge, Louisiana*

**McGraw-Hill**
New York Chicago San Francisco Lisbon London
Madrid Mexico City Milan New Delhi San Juan
Seoul Singapore Sydney Toronto

The McGraw-Hill Companies



1 2 3 4 5 6 7 8 9 0 DOC/DOC 0 9 8 7 6 5

ISBN 0-07-144588-9

This book is printed on recycled, acid-free paper containing a minimum of 50% recycled, de-inked fiber.

**Library of Congress Cataloging-in-Publication Data**

Sengupta, Ambar, 1963-
Pricing derivatives : the financial concepts underlying the mathematics of pricing derivatives / by Ambar N. Sengupta.
p. cm.
ISBN 0-07-144588-9 (hardcover : alk. paper)
1. Derivative securities—Prices—Mathematics. I. Title.
HG6024.A3S44 2005
332.64'57—dc22

2004028196

# CONTENTS

LIST OF TABLES xi

PREFACE xiii

PART ONE

## FUNDAMENTALS

Chapter 1

### Price and Probability 3

An Option Pricing Formula 5

Chapter 2

### The Market Equilibrium Measure 9

Chapter 3

### Price as Expectation 13

Chapter 4

### Changing Numeraires 15

Chapter 5

### Changing Numeraires: Examples 19

Fixed Exchange Rate 19

The Log-Normal Case 20

Chapter 6

### No-Arbitrage and the Min-Max Argument 23

No-Arbitrage and the Pricing Measure 24

Proof of Theorem 6.1.1 26

*Uniqueness / Nonuniqueness of the Measure Q* 29
*The Central Idea: The Max–Min Argument* 30
A Formal Framework 30

**Chapter 7**

**Conditional Price as Conditional Expectation: The Martingale Principle** 39

Conditional Probabilities and Expectations 39
The Generalized Martingale Principle 41
The Discounted Price Process as a Martingale 41
Change of Numeraire Revisited 43

**PART TWO**

**PRICES OF BASIC INSTRUMENTS**

**Chapter 8**

**Bonds and Interest** 47

Zero-Coupon Default-Free Bond Prices 48
Assets with Default Risk 50
Credit Default Swaps: CDS 53

**Chapter 9**

**Forward Prices** 55

**Chapter 10**

**Futures Prices** 61

The Futures Agreement 62
Futures Prices in the Discrete Case 62
Futures Prices in the Continuous Case 63

**Chapter 11**

**Calls and Puts** 67

Options: A Closer Look 69
Call Price 72

Put Price 75
Put-Call Parity 76
Another Proof of the Option Price Formula 76
Option Price Inequalities 77
The American Call Option 81

Chapter 12
**Forward Rate** 85

Chapter 13
**Swaps and the Swap Rate** 91
The Floating Leg 92
The Swap Rate 93
Swap Rates and Forward Prices 95

Chapter 14
**Natural Time Lag and the Convexity Adjustment** 97

Chapter 15
**Swaption Price** 99

Chapter 16
**Volatility and Hedging** 101
Volatility 101
Hedging 103
"The Greeks" 104

PART THREE
**MODEL PRICES**

Chapter 17
**Option Prices in the Log-Normal Case** 111
The Option Price Formula 111
Derivation of the Formula 112
Another Proof of the Formula 115

Chapter 18

**The Black-Scholes Model** 117

Derivation of the Black-Scholes Formula 118
The Black-Scholes Stochastic Differential Equation 121
Black-Scholes Parameters 122

Chapter 19

**The State Space and Evolution** 125

The State Space 125
Markov Evolution of Market States 126
Green's Functions for Markov Models 128
Green's Functions and Feynman-Kac 129

Chapter 20

**Gaussian Models** 135

The Model Fundamentals 135
One-Factor Gaussian Model 137
Multifactor Gaussian Model 141
Volatility and Correlations 144
Convexity Adjustment 148

Chapter 21

**The $\chi^2$ Model** 151

Model Fundamentals 151
Green's Functions 153
*The Forward Green's Function* 154
*The Nondiscounted Green's Function* 155
*The Shifted Green's Function* 156

Chapter 22

**Derivation of Green's Functions** 159

The One-Factor Gaussian Model 163
*The Forward Green's Function* 163
*The Nondiscounted Green's Function* 167
*The Green's Function $G^{\text{shifted}}$* 167

One-Factor Chi-Squared Cox-Ingersoll-Ross Model 169
The Multifactor Gauss Model 176

## PART FOUR

# MATHEMATICAL TOOLS

Chapter 23

**Elements of Measure and Integration** 185

Measures, Sigma-Algebras, Functions 185
Integration 189
Interchanging Limit and Integration 191
Generated $\sigma$-Algebras 191
Product Spaces and Fubini's Theorem 194
Complex Measures 195
The Radon-Nikodym Theorem 196
The Distribution Measure 197
Lebesgue Measure and Some Integrals 198
The $\pi - \lambda$ Theorem and Uniqueness of Measures 200

Chapter 24

**Probability Theory** 201

The Framework 201
$\sigma$-Algebras 204
Independence 205
Independence and $\sigma$-Algebras 206
Conditional Expectations 207
The Characteristic Function 211
Recovering $Q$ from its Characteristic Function 213
Convergence Notions 215

Chapter 25

**Stochastic Processes** 219

Some Basic Notions 219
Processes and Filtrations: The Usual Conditions 220
Martingales 221

Construction of Stochastic Processes 222
Brownian Motion 226
Markov Processes 229
The Stochastic Integral 232
The Algebra of Stochastic Differentials 232

**Chapter 26**

**Probability and Differential Equations** 237

The SDE and the PDE 238
Discretizing the PDE: A Numerical Scheme 240
The Difference Scheme: A Probabilistic Interpretation 243
From the Difference Scheme to the SDE 246

**Chapter 27**

**The Hahn-Banach Theorem** 249

The Geometric Setting 249
The Algebraic Formulation 251
The Hahn-Banach Theorem 255
A Geometric Interpretation 259

END NOTES 263
BIBLIOGRAPHY 269
INDEX 273

# LIST OF TABLES


6.1 A Formal Market Model 33

11.1 Google Call Options at 9:17am ET on September 17, 2004, with Expiration December 17, 2004. Stock Price: $117.49. 69

11.2 Google Call Options, with strike $110, at 9:17am ET on September 17, 2004. Stock Price: $117.49. 71

11.3 Google September Call Options on Expiration Date September 17, 2004. Stock Price: $117.49. 72

16.1 Summary of General Price Formulas I 106

16.2 Summary of General Price Formulas II 108

19.1 Green's Functions and Numeraires 129

19.2 Summary of Modeling Concepts 133

20.1 Summary of Gaussian Models 150

22.1 Properties of the Gaussian and $\chi^2$ Distributions 182

25.1 Itô Multiplication Table 234

# PREFACE

The purpose of this book is to present the conceptual foundations for pricing derivatives and other financial instruments. We proceed as far as possible in a model-independent way. For example, *with just a minimum of mathematical apparatus we show in Chapter 1 how the structure of the celebrated Black-Scholes option price formula can be understood.* The standard presentation of this formula makes this structure appear to be a by-product of a calculation involving the normal distribution rather than as a fundamental feature of option prices. We mention this particular example here to illustrate what we mean by the term "conceptual approach" as well as to underline its power.

The ideas presented in this book go back, in essence, to Arrow [3] and Debreu [12]. Here is a cartoon-style summary of the central idea of our approach:

| Price = Probability = Green's function |
|---|

The first equality sign is indicative of the fundamental relationship between price and probability, which we explore in the first part of this book. The second equality sign is indicative of the relationship between the relevant probabilities and fundamental solutions, called Green's functions, to certain differential equations. We are using the term "Green's function" here as it is often used in quantum physics to denote the fundamental function that describes the propagation of a state in time.

We begin in Part One by analyzing the fundamental relationship between price and probability: how price and probability measure each other. A market in equilibrium has its own "view" of how likely different events are, and this determines and is determined by the prevailing prices of all market instruments. This *market equilibrium measure* of probabilities of events is by no means coincident with the views of all market players, but rather a measure that emerges through the trading process that ensures market equilibrium.

We then proceed in Part Two to determine *model-independent* pricing formulas for certain standard market instruments such as forwards, futures, bonds, options, and swaps. These general formulas can be specialized to specific market models to yield more concrete pricing formulas.

In Part Three, we first set up a general framework of state spaces and Green's functions for markets. Then we compute explicit price formulas assuming some specific forms of the market state space and market equilibrium measure. Here we study the multifactor form of a model introduced by Hull and White and then a single-factor model due to Cox, Ingersoll, and Ross. We work out the Green's functions, which determine prices in these models.

Part Four presents the principal mathematical concepts, results, and techniques used in the earlier parts.

Let us state what this book *does not* aim to provide. It is not our goal to present a technical monograph on stochastic processes motivated by finance. It is also not our goal to present a compendium of trading techniques for the derivatives trader. There are many valuable works available for both of these worthy needs.

This book arose from a long series of discussions the author had with Greg Lieb. The context for those discussions was the immediate need to develop numerical tools for calculating prices of a variety of interest-rate derivatives. This book is not concerned with numerical procedures or specific trading techniques. However, the conceptual issues addressed in this book were motivated by those discussions.

I have benefited from conversations with far too many people to attempt compiling a fair list of names of those I should thank. At a personal level, I am deeply thankful to Ingeborg Wald, and I am also thankful for the encouragement I have received from friends and family to complete this project.

**Ambar N. Sengupta**

# PRICING DERIVATIVES

# PART ONE

# Fundamentals

*Trading* is the process of exchange of assets, the fundamental step towards deciding what different assets are worth relative to each other. In a *market* where extensive trading takes place, a *consistent pricing* of assets is generated. Consistency here means that if $A$ can be exchanged for $B$, and $B$ for $C$, then $A$ can be exchanged for $C$. This principle makes it possible for a mathematician producing theorems to buy coffee (and other necessities of life).

There is an intangible entity for which an immensely active market exists. This entity is *risk*. Risk, of course, is an undesirable commodity and so its price is negative. A person who buys risk from another receives a payment, the *premium*, from the seller of risk. An extensive market in risk, or risky products, also serves a social function: it spreads risk out over a larger community and cushions the economic blow a small entity might face due to misfortune.

For financial markets, risk is not traded as an asset in itself but rather as a quality imbedded in various instruments, and it is the pricing of these risky instruments that we shall be concerned with. In Part One we explore the relationship between probability and price, and in Part Two we use this to build a model–independent formalism for pricing risky complex instruments.

CHAPTER 1

# Price and Probability

There is a fundamental relationship between price and probability that lies at the foundation of the mathematical theory of asset pricing. In this chapter we study this relationship and see how price and probability measure each other.

Consider an event $B$. We examine how the probability of event $B$ can be measured through the price of a special financial instrument $I_B$. The instrument $I_B$ is specified in terms of the event $B$:

> $I_B$: if the event $B$ occurs, then the owner of the instrument receives one Euro. If event $B$ doesn't occur, there is zero cash flow, and the owner receives nothing and pays nothing.

How much is the instrument $I_B$ worth to you? Surely it depends on how likely you judge the event $B$ to be. Indeed, *how much you judge $I_B$ to be worth is an excellent measure of how likely you judge the event $B$ to be.*

If you believe for sure that $B$ will occur, then the instrument is worth one Euro. If you know that $B$ is definitely not going to occur, then the instrument is worthless. If you think there is one chance in 10 that $B$ will occur, then you would consider 1/10th of a Euro as a fair price for the instrument. In fact, how much (in terms of Euros) the instrument is worth to you is precisely your estimate of how likely it is for the event $B$ to occur. Thus:

- *The price of the instrument $I_B$, measured in Euros, you would pay is your estimate of the probability $Q(B)$ of the event $B$.*

This is how price measures probability, and probability measures price. We will call the measure $Q$ of probabilities a *pricing measure*.

Probability is judged by you (by whatever means you choose), the person who is deciding the worth of the instrument $I_B$. In this example, the role of the Euro is that of a measuring unit for price. Such a measuring unit is called a *numeraire*.

The numeraire plays a subtle but crucial role here: the probability $Q(B)$ of the event $B$ *depends on the choice of numeraire*.

We will return to this possibly nonintuitive issue later. For the moment we note that the payoff for the instrument $I_B$ in terms of a different numeraire might be quite complex: the event $B$ itself might be specified by a range in which the exchange rate between the two numeraires is required to lie.

There are two standard useful numeraires:

**(i)** One unit of cash (in a given currency) today;

**(ii)** One unit of cash at a future date $t$.

Note that *a numeraire has a time stamp*, which we did not make explicit in the illustration above.

However, other numeraires are also useful in theoretical analysis used to derive price formulas. For example, numeraires of the following type are useful in deriving stock or bond option prices:

**(iii)** One share of a particular stock to be delivered in 3 months;

**(iv)** A particular 30-year bond to be delivered in 1 year.

**Example** We start at a certain initial date $t_0$. A stock is trading at \$40 a share. Let $B$ be the event that on a future date $t$, the price will rise to \$45 or more.

Consider an instrument $J$, which entitles the holder to 100 shares of the stock on date $t$ if event $B$ occurs but is worthless if $B$ does not occur.

Take the numeraire to be 1 share of the stock to be exchanged on date $t$.

How much of the numeraire would you pay for the instrument $J$ on date $t_0$?

Clearly, $J$ is equivalent to 100 times $I_B$, the instrument that pays 1 share on date $t$ if $B$ occurs and is worthless otherwise.

Thus the price you would pay for $J$ is $100Q(B)$ units of the numeraire. For example, if you assess the probability $Q(B)$ to be .75 (i.e. there is a 75% chance that the stock will trade at or above \$45 on date $t$), then as fair exchange for receiving the instrument $J$ on date $t_0$ you would be willing to make a commitment, on date $t_0$, to pay 75 shares on date $t$.

## AN OPTION PRICING FORMULA

Options are the most basic derivative instruments. Let us see how the ideas we have examined lead to a general formula for pricing certain types of options.

A typical option is a contract between two parties, the holder and the writer, which gives the holder the right to buy/sell a certain asset at an agreed-upon price at an appropriate time. We shall derive a formula for the price of such an option in terms of the behavior of the price of the underlying asset.

A European *call option* on an asset $\mathcal{A}$ gives the holder of the option the right to buy this asset at an agreed-upon price on an agreed-upon date in the future. For instance, the holder might have the right to buy 100 shares of a particular stock 3 months in the future at \$50 a share. If at the expiration date of this option the share is trading below \$50 then, of course, the holder will not exercise the call. On the other hand, if the stock is trading above

\$50, the holder profits by exercising the option. The fundamental task now is to determine how much this option is worth at any given time (prior to expiration).

Consider then a European call option on an asset $\mathcal{A}$, with strike $K$ dollars and expiration date $t$. We can view this as a combination of two instruments I and II:

- Instrument I entitles the holder to receive 1 unit of the asset on date $t$ if the price of the asset on date $t$ is more than $K$ dollars
- Instrument II requires the holder to pay $K$ dollars on date $t$ if the price of the asset on date $t$ is more than $K$ dollars

Let $[S_t > K]$ denote the event that the price $S_t$ of $\mathcal{A}$ on date $t$ is more than $K$ dollars.

Let $q_1$ be your estimate of the probability of the event $[S_t > K]$ using 1 unit of $\mathcal{A}$ to be delivered on date $t$, as numeraire. In other words, you consider it fair to promise to pay $q_1$ units of the asset on date $t$ in return for an agreement that you would be given one unit of the asset on date $t$ if its price then exceeds $K$, but you would receive nothing if the price is at or below $K$. This probability $q_1$ may be symbolically denoted as

$$q_1 = Q_1([S_t > K]),$$

where $Q_1$ is your measure of probabilities of events using the given asset, deliverable on date $t$, as numeraire.

Next suppose $q_2$ is your estimate of the probability of the event $[S_t > K]$, using one dollar to be delivered on date $t$ as numeraire. In other words, you consider it fair to promise to pay $q_2$ dollars on date $t$ in return for an agreement that you would be given one dollar if the asset price exceeds $K$ on date $t$ but would receive nothing if the price stays at or below $K$. Again, we can write $q_2$ as

$$q_2 = Q_2([S_t > K]),$$

where $Q_2$ is your measure of probabilities of events using one dollar deliverable on date $t$ as numeraire.

Now let $FS_t$ be the *forward price* for the asset $\mathcal{A}$, i.e., it is the price you would pay, in dollars to be paid on date $t$, but agreed upon initially, for 1 unit of $\mathcal{A}$ to be delivered on date $t$.

Then the forward price of Instrument I is

$$(FS_t)q_1.$$

On the other hand, the forward price of Instrument II is

$$-Kq_2.$$

Thus the forward price of the call option, measured in date $t$ dollars, is:

$$\boxed{(FS_t)Q_1([S_t > K]) - KQ_2([S_t > K])} \tag{1.1}$$

This is the amount, in dollars deliverable on date $t$, you would consider the call option to be worth.

The pricing formula (**1.1**) is essentially a very general form of the *Black-Scholes formula*. We have here, in essence, a conceptual proof of this general formula.

We will return later to more details concerning option pricing formulas. In particular, we shall see that if the asset price $S_t$ is assumed to have a log-normal distribution with respect to $Q_2$, then it will have a log-normal distribution also with respect to $Q_1$, and this leads to a more computationally explicit form (1.1) called the Black-Scholes formula.

CHAPTER 2

# The Market Equilibrium Measure

A market is in equilibrium if all market participants agree on a *common price* for each asset.

In market equilibrium, if an asset A can be traded for an asset B, and B can be traded for C, then A should be tradeable with C. If this transitivity property does not hold, then an astute market participant can accumulate large quantities of a desired asset (such as a particular currency) by going through appropriate buying and selling. This is the essence of *arbitrage*. A market at equilibrium has no arbitrage opportunities.

Of course, in real life markets are never fully at equilibrium because different people attach different values to an asset. *Trading* is the process by which a common price is agreed upon by buyer and seller. So it is reasonable to suppose that a market where extensive trading takes place is near equilibrium.

Recall the instrument $I_B$ considered in Chapter 1. It pays off 1 unit of currency if the event $B$ occurs and pays nothing if $B$ does not occur. We have seen that the fair price for $B$ according to any one individual is a measure of how likely the event $B$ is according to that individual. In market equilibrium all traders will agree on what the instrument is worth, i.e., the price (= probability) $Q(B)$

is the same for all persons involved in the market. Clearly, this measure of probability is very special and reflects the *market's view* of likelihoods of events.

Let us not forget that a particular *numeraire* (Euros in the example in Chapter 1) is being used to measure prices/probabilities.

The probabilities $B \mapsto Q(B)$ in market equilibrium constitute the *market-equilibrium measure* or *risk-neutral measure* for the given numeraire, at the market equilibrium. It is the pricing measure implied by market prices (more precisely, it is a pricing measure consistent with market prices).

The use of the term "risk-neutral" reflects the point of view that each instrument/asset carries some risk and $Q(B)$ is the right price, as determined by the market, to exchange one risk for another.

Thus, assuming the market is at equilibrium:

| The market-equilibrium measure $Q$ models the market's view of likelihoods of events. |
|---|

Note that the market's assessment of the likelihood of an event is:

**a.** The result of trading consensus and might be quite different from what a particular individual assesses the likelihood to be;

**b.** Not the same as the real-life probability of the event.

Indeed, "real-life probability" is far murkier a concept than the price-based notion of probability. Real-life probabilistic quantities are estimated using historical statistical data. Market-equilibrium probabilistic quantities are implied from market prices.

For any instrument, the bid prices will at first be less than the ask prices; trade will occur at an intermediate price. The trade price could thus have a range of values, between the highest initial bid and the lowest initial ask. Thus, in principle, it is possible that all traders might also simultaneously agree on a different price $Q'(B)$ for the instrument $I_B$, and so *it is possible that in a particular market there is more than one possible market-equilibrium measure.*

CHAPTER 3

# Price as Expectation

Consider an instrument $J$ whose payoff depends on certain events $B_1, \ldots, B_N$.

The instrument $J$ will pay the owner $c_1$ Euros if event $B_1$ occurs, $c_2$ Euros if event $B_2$ occurs,..., $c_N$ Euros if event $B_N$ occurs. If none of the events $B_i$ occur, then the instrument pays nothing.

Let us call such an instrument a *simple instrument*.

Clearly, $J$ is equivalent (in worth) to $c_1$ number of instruments $I_{B_1}$, $c_2$ number of instruments $I_{B_2}, \ldots,$ and $c_N$ units of instrument $I_{B_N}$; formally,

$$\text{payoff of } J = c_1 1_{B_1} + \cdots + c_N 1_{B_N}$$

where $1_B$ is the payoff for the instrument $I_B$, i.e. a payoff of 1 unit if event $B$ occurs, and 0 otherwise.

Now recall that for $I_{B_1}$ the price you will pay is $Q(B_1)$ (in Euros, of course). For $I_{B_2}$ the price is $Q(B_2)$, and so on. So

$$\text{price of } J = c_1 Q(B_1) + c_2 Q(B_2) + \cdots + c_N Q(B_N)$$

Mathematically,

$$\text{price of } J = \int (\text{payoff from } J)\, dQ = E_Q[\text{payoff from } J]$$

were $E_Q[\cdots]$ means *expected value* with respect to the probability measure $Q$. The integration $\int \cdots dQ$ is just another notation for the expected value (Chapter 23 describes the mathematical theory of integration).

Indeed, this formula makes perfect intuitive sense and we may safely say that if $J$ is any instrument (simple or not)

$$\text{price of } J = \int (\text{payoff from } J)\, dQ = E_Q[\text{payoff from } J] \quad (3.1)$$

The price here is again in terms of Euros, i.e., in terms of the numeraire. The measure $Q$ is the one used to determine prices. It may be the market equilibrium measure.

The definition of the expectation $E_Q[X]$, equivalently the integral $\int X\, dQ$, for a general payoff $X$ is obtained by a sequence of approximations of the instrument $J$ by simple instruments. The mathematical definition is given in Chapter 23.

Formula (3.1) just says that the price you would consider fair to pay for the instrument $J$ is your expected payoff from $J$.

cenario prevailing over the time period $[0, T]$. De- $Q_T$ and $Q_Y$ by just $Q$. Then we have the change-of- formula

$$dQ_T = \frac{p(0,T)dQ}{P(0,T)} \tag{4.7}$$

$$P(0,T) = E_Q[p(0,T)] \tag{4.8}$$

much you would pay today to receive 1 dollar on the fu- date $T$, without knowing which market scenario will prevail time $[0, T]$. This is the *bond price* for a bond maturing on $T$ and is also called the *discount factor*. Note that $p(0,T)$ random quantity depending on the market scenario prevail- g over the time period $[0, T]$, while $P(0,T)$ is the bond price etermined totally by knowledge available at the initial date 0.

## EXERCISE

Let $Q$ and $Q_T$ be as in the example. Suppose that the interest rates over the period $[0, T]$ are known at the outset with certainty, i.e. $p(0,T)$ is a fixed nonrandom quantity (having the same value no matter what the market scenario). Show that then $Q = Q_T$.

CHAPTER 4

# Changing Numeraires

We have observed in our earlier discussions the role played by a *numeraire*. A numeraire is an asset used as a measuring unit for valuation of instruments.

As we have seen earlier, a numeraire is used in specifying the pricing measure $Q$. If $I_B$ is the instrument that pays off one unit of the numeraire when event $B$ happens and nothing otherwise, then the price of $I_B$ is $Q(B)$ units of the numeraire.

In this chapter we examine how the pricing measure $Q$ is affected when passing from one numeraire to another.

Consider the following numeraires:

**(i)** One dollar today,

**(ii)** One dollar at a future date $t$,

**(iii)** One share of a particular stock to be delivered in 3 months,

**(iv)** A particular 30-year bond to be delivered in 1 year.

Observe that different numeraires can be *risky* relative to each other. For example, how much one share of a stock will be worth in 3 months, as measured in dollars at that time, is not a certain quantity, i.e., it is a random variable.

Let $Q_X$ and $Q_Y$ be the probability measures corresponding to numeraires $X$ and $Y$, respectively. We will determine the relationship between $Q_X$ and $Q_Y$.

Let $v_X^Y$ be the "exchange-rate" for $X$ in terms of $Y$, i.e.

$$\text{1 unit of } X \text{ is worth } v_X^Y \text{ units of } Y. \tag{4.1}$$

In general, $v_X^Y$ is a *random* quantity, i.e. it *depends on the market scenario*. We will assume $v_X^Y$ is always positive.

An important special case is when $X$ is 1 unit of currency to be delivered at a future date $T$ and $Y$ is the unit of currency at time 0. In this case $v_X^Y$ is denoted $p(0, T)$:

$$p(0, T) = \text{worth today of a unit of currency to be paid at the future date } T.$$

The value $p(0, T)$ will, in general, depend on the market scenario prevailing over the future time period $[0, T]$ and so is a random quantity. It is the *scenario-dependent discount factor*.

Returning to the general situation, consider now an event $B$, and the instrument $I_B$ that pays off one unit of the numeraire $X$ if $B$ occurs and pays 0 otherwise. It is worth

$$Q_X(B)$$

units of the numeraire $X$.

Now the price, in units of $Y$, you would be pay for a unit of $X$ is

$$E_{Q_Y}[v_X^Y]$$

So

$$I_B \text{ is worth } Q_X(B)E_{Q_Y}[v_X^Y] \text{ units of } Y \tag{4.2}$$

Now look at $I_B$ from the point of view of $Y$. The payoff of $I_B$, measured in units of $Y$, is described by the random variable

$$v_X^Y 1_B$$



So its value is

$$E_{Q}$$

units of $Y$.

Equating the two answers (4.

$$Q_X(B) = \frac{E_{Q_Y}[v_X^Y 1_B]}{E_{Q_Y}[v_X^Y]} =$$

Thus we have obtained a formula yielding $Q$ terms of the $Q_Y$ measure.

More generally, by the same reasoning, if we ment $J$ whose payoff is denoted $f$ then:

$$\int f\,dQ_X = \frac{\int f v_X^Y\,dQ_Y}{\int v_X^Y\,dQ_Y}$$

This can be expressed symbolically as

$$dQ_X = \frac{1}{E_{Q_Y}[v_X^Y]} v_X^Y dQ_Y \tag{4.6}$$

This is another way to express the conversion formula connecting the two numeraires.

**Example** Let $Y$ be 1 dollar today, and $X$ be 1 dollar at a future date $T$. In this case the exchange rate $v_X^Y$ is denoted $p(0, T)$ and will, in general, be a random variable depending on the market scenario (interest rates over the period $[0, T]$). Thus, 1 dollar to be delivered on date $T$ is worth $p(0, T)$ dollars today, given

CHAPTER 5

# Changing Numeraires: Examples

Continuing our study of change of numeraire, we work out two examples: (i) when the two numeraires bear a fixed ratio to each other; (ii) when the exchange rate between the two numeraires has a log-normal distribution.

## FIXED EXCHANGE RATE

Consider two numeraires $X$ and $Y$ such that the exchange rate between the two is nonrandom—i.e., the same in all scenarios. Thus, basically, $Y$ is a definite multiple of $X$ such as $Y = 5X$.

Formally, this means that $v_X^Y$ is a constant, the same in all market scenarios. Here, and always, $v_X^Y$ is the worth of 1 unit of $X$ in terms of $Y$.

Then, using the conversion formula (4.4):

$$Q_X(B) = \frac{E_{Q_Y}\left[v_X^Y 1_B\right]}{E_{Q_Y}\left[v_X^Y\right]} = \frac{\int v_X^Y 1_B \, dQ_Y}{\int v_X^Y \, dQ_Y}, \tag{5.1}$$

we have

$$Q_X(B) = E_{Q_Y}(1_B) = Q_Y(B)$$

for all events $B$, because the constant value $v_X^Y$ can be taken out of the integrals in numerator and denominator in (5.1). Thus, in this case,

$$Q_X = Q_Y \tag{5.2}$$

This equality is intuitively clear: $X$ and $Y$ bear a fixed relation to each other, the same in all scenarios, and so assessments of probabilities according to $X$ and $Y$ should be the same.

## THE LOG-NORMAL CASE

Consider an asset $X$ whose price $S = v_X^Y$, at some given time, relative to a numeraire $Y$ has a log-normal distribution with respect to the pricing measure $Q_Y$, i.e., $\log S$ is a Gaussian variable relative to the measure $Q_Y$. We shall prove the remarkable fact that *$S$ is also log normally distributed with respect to the measure $Q_X$.* This is a very important observation.

**Theorem 5.2.1** *Let $S$ be the price of an asset $X$ relative to a numeraire $Y$, and suppose that* $\log S$ *has Gaussian distribution with mean $m$ and variance $\sigma^2$, relative to the measure $Q_Y$. Then* $\log S$ *is Gaussian with mean $m + \sigma^2$ and variance $\sigma^2$, relative to $Q_X$.*

Notice the *shift in the mean* caused by the change of the reference measure.

The theorem above follows by using the conversion-of-numeraires relation (4.4) and taking $L = \log S$ and $P = Q_B$ in the following result:

**Lemma 5.2.2** *Let $L$ be a random variable that is Gaussian with mean $m$ and variance $\sigma^2$ with respect to a probability* *measure $P$. Let $P'$ be the measure specified by*

$$P'(B) = \frac{E_P(e^L 1_B)}{E_P(e^L)} \tag{5.3}$$

*for all events $B$. Then the distribution of $L$ with respect to $P'$ is Gaussian with mean $m + \sigma^2$ and variance $\sigma^2$.*

***Proof.*** The following is a very useful fact about Gaussian random variables : *a random variable $Z$ is Gaussian if and only if there are real numbers $a$ and $b$ such that*

$$E(e^{wZ}) = e^{aw + bw^2/2} \tag{5.4}$$

*for all real (or complex) numbers $w$.* For such a variable, it turns out that

$$a = E(Z) \text{ and } b = \sigma_Z^2, \text{ the variance of } Z.$$

So to determine the distribution of $L$ with respect to $P'$ it suffices calculate $E_{P'}(e^{wL})$. Equation (5.3) implies that

$$\int f\, dP' = \frac{\int f e^L\, dP}{E_P(e^L)}$$

for any measurable function for which either side makes sense. Taking the special case of $f = e^{wL}$, we then have

$$\begin{aligned} E_{P'}(e^{wL}) &= \frac{E_P(e^L e^{wL})}{E_P(e^L)} \\ &= \exp\left[(w+1)E_P(L) + (w+1)^2\sigma_L^2/2 - E_P(L) - \sigma_L^2/2\right] \\ &= \exp\left[w\left\{E_P(L) + \sigma_L^2\right\} + \frac{1}{2}w^2\sigma_L^2\right] \end{aligned}$$

Comparing with (5.4) we conclude that $L$ is indeed Gaussian with respect to $P'$ with mean $E_P(L) + \sigma_L^2$ and variance $\sigma_L^2$. QED

CHAPTER 6

# No-Arbitrage and the Min-Max Argument

A market in which extensive trading takes place creates a *consistent system of prices* or "exchange rates" for the instruments being traded: if instrument $A$ can be traded for $B$, and $B$ for $C$, then $A$ can be traded for $C$. If such a system of prices exists then the market is in a form of equilibrium. As we have noted earlier, price inconsistency would allow a trader to accumulate unlimited quantities of some asset, and this is not sustainable.

A real market is, of course, always fluctuating around equilibrium rather than in actual equilibrium. Visible price inconsistences arise but do not last very long because traders move quickly to take advantage of these inconsistencies or *arbitrage opportunities*.

However, markets may contain highly complex, subtle forms of arbitrage that go unexploited for long periods. Moreover, in a market where very complex nonstandardized instruments, tailor-made to the needs of particular buyers, are available there are often no universally agreed-upon ways to price such instruments. Pricing would be done by choosing a market model, but it might take some time before the market makes it clear if the pricing was done correctly.

Our goal in this chapter is to show how the hypothesis that a market is free of arbitrage opportunities gives rise to a pricing measure. The discussion of price and probability in Chapter 1 assumed the existence of instruments such as $I_B$, which, in a real market, will not generally exist. Yet, as we shall see in this chapter, prices for a certain set of traded instruments together with the nonexistence of arbitrage implies that a consistent set of prices exist for a much larger class of instruments, and this leads to the pricing probability measure $Q$.

Linking no-arbitrage and existence of a consistent set of prices is a *min-max argument*, a powerful idea that is useful in several ways in economic equilibrium theory and game theory. It also lies at the heart of the Hahn-Banach theorem in mathematics.

There are many ways to make precise the notion of arbitrage, and there are corresponding theorems linking no-arbitrage and existence of a pricing measure. We shall proceed at an intuitive level, but in the last section provide a more mathematically formalized discussion. Our objective is to stress the core idea of *the equivalence of price consistency with the existence of a pricing measure via a min-max argument*, and not any particular formalization of the idea. As is often the case in mathematics, it is possible to dress up this core idea in many sophisticated forms in a variety of technical settings.

## NO-ARBITRAGE AND THE PRICING MEASURE

We shall use the term *arbitrage opportunity* to mean the possibility of forming a portfolio of assets that provides a riskless profit opportunity. This means that the portfolio results in no loss, no matter which market scenario occurs and yields a profit in at least some market scenario. A trader who sees an arbitrage opportunity will seize upon it to lock in profit until demand-supply forces adjust prices in such a way as to make the arbitrage opportunity disappear. In a real market this process occurs often and helps ensure that the market stays near equilibrium. In ideal equilibrium, a consistent system of prices exists, and there is no arbitrage opportunity.

Let $\Omega$ be the set of all possible market scenarios, a typical *scenario* being denoted $\omega$. For the sake of focusing on the main ideas, as opposed to formalism, let us assume that $\Omega$ is finite.

Consider an asset $A$. Denote by

$$V^A(\omega)$$

the price of the asset $A$ in scenario $\omega$. All prices are with respect to some fixed numeraire. Our task is to determine the worth of $A$ when one does not know the particular scenario $\omega$ that will occur. Let us call this the *a priori price* of $A$; we denote it

$$V_0^A$$

For example, $A$ could be 1 share of a particular stock *at a particular time* in the future. Then $V_0^A$ could mean the present price of the future asset $A$.

Suppose the asset $A$ does not provide an arbitrage opportunity. What can we say about $V_0^A$? Clearly the *a priori* price $V_0^A$ must lie between the highest and least possible values of the $V^A(\cdot)$. Otherwise, holding or shorting the instrument $A$ would give an arbitrage opportunity.

Thus we already have an important observation: if $A$ does not provide an arbitrage opportunity, then $V_0^A$ *can be written as a weighted average (a convex combination) of all the possible values* $V^A(\omega)$:

$$V_0^A = \sum_{\omega \in \Omega} q^A(\omega) V^A(\omega) \tag{6.1}$$

where each $0 \le q^A(\omega) \le 1$ and $\sum_{\omega \in \Omega} q^A(\omega) = 1$. This must be valid for each asset $A$ if the entire market is arbitrage free.

This simple observation contains the kernel of a much deeper fact. To see this, notice that the no-arbitrage condition for the entire market is very strong:

> it is not possible to combine any set of assets into a portfolio so that the combined worth of the portfolio would be certain to yield a profit in at least one market scenario, and would result in no loss in all scenarios.

What does this say about the weights $q^A(\omega)$? It turns out that what it does say is this:

> *a single set of weights $q(\omega)$ must work simultaneously for all assets $A$!*

We will summarize this remarkable fact in Theorem 6.1.1.

**Theorem 6.1.1** *The following are equivalent:*

1. *There is no portfolio that gives an arbitrage opportunity;*
2. *There is a probability measure $Q$ on the market scenarios such that for any event $B$, the instrument $I_B$ has price $Q(B)$ units of the numeraire (recall that $I_B$ is the instrument that yields 1 unit of the numeraire when event $B$ occurs and nothing otherwise.)*

We are using the term "theorem" a bit loosely here because we have not completely formalized the framework. A more formal account is given later in this chapter.

## PROOF OF THEOREM 6.1.1

We shall assume that the set $\Omega$ of all market scenarios is finite.

We have already noted that the existence of a pricing measure implies the no-arbitrage condition: the price of any instrument being the average of all possible values in all possible scenarios must lie between the maximum and minimum of such values, thereby ensuring that no possibility of arbitrage profit exists.

Consider, for each particular scenario $\omega$, a special instrument $\delta_\omega$ whose value is 1 when the scenario $\omega$ occurs and is 0

CHAPTER 4

# Changing Numeraires

We have observed in our earlier discussions the role played by a *numeraire*. A numeraire is an asset used as a measuring unit for valuation of instruments.

As we have seen earlier, a numeraire is used in specifying the pricing measure $Q$. If $I_B$ is the instrument that pays off one unit of the numeraire when event $B$ happens and nothing otherwise, then the price of $I_B$ is $Q(B)$ units of the numeraire.

In this chapter we examine how the pricing measure $Q$ is affected when passing from one numeraire to another.

Consider the following numeraires:

**(i)** One dollar today,

**(ii)** One dollar at a future date $t$,

**(iii)** One share of a particular stock to be delivered in 3 months,

**(iv)** A particular 30-year bond to be delivered in 1 year.

Observe that different numeraires can be *risky* relative to each other. For example, how much one share of a stock will be worth in 3 months, as measured in dollars at that time, is not a certain quantity, i.e., it is a random variable.

Let $Q_X$ and $Q_Y$ be the probability measures corresponding to numeraires $X$ and $Y$, respectively. We will determine the relationship between $Q_X$ and $Q_Y$.

Let $v_X^Y$ be the "exchange-rate" for $X$ in terms of $Y$, i.e.

$$1 \text{ unit of } X \text{ is worth } v_X^Y \text{ units of } Y. \tag{4.1}$$

In general, $v_X^Y$ is a *random* quantity, i.e. it *depends on the market scenario*. We will assume $v_X^Y$ is always positive.

An important special case is when $X$ is 1 unit of currency to be delivered at a future date $T$ and $Y$ is the unit of currency at time 0. In this case $v_X^Y$ is denoted $p(0, T)$:

$$p(0, T) = \text{worth today of a unit of currency to be paid at the future date } T.$$

The value $p(0, T)$ will, in general, depend on the market scenario prevailing over the future time period $[0, T]$ and so is a random quantity. It is the *scenario-dependent discount factor*.

Returning to the general situation, consider now an event $B$, and the instrument $I_B$ that pays off one unit of the numeraire $X$ if $B$ occurs and pays 0 otherwise. It is worth

$$Q_X(B)$$

units of the numeraire $X$.

Now the price, in units of $Y$, you would be pay for a unit of $X$ is

$$E_{Q_Y}\left[v_X^Y\right]$$

So

$$I_B \text{ is worth } Q_X(B) E_{Q_Y}\left[v_X^Y\right] \text{ units of } Y \tag{4.2}$$

Now look at $I_B$ from the point of view of $Y$. The payoff of $I_B$, measured in units of $Y$, is described by the random variable

$$v_X^Y 1_B$$

So its value is

$$E_{Q_Y}\left[v_X^Y 1_B\right] \tag{4.3}$$

units of $Y$.

Equating the two answers (4.2) and (4.3), we see that

$$Q_X(B) = \frac{E_{Q_Y}\left[v_X^Y 1_B\right]}{E_{Q_Y}\left[v_X^Y\right]} = \frac{\int v_X^Y 1_B \, dQ_Y}{\int v_X^Y \, dQ_Y} \tag{4.4}$$

Thus we have obtained a formula yielding $Q_X$–probabilities in terms of the $Q_Y$ measure.

More generally, by the same reasoning, if we have an instrument $J$ whose payoff is denoted $f$ then:

$$\int f \, dQ_X = \frac{\int f v_X^Y \, dQ_Y}{\int v_X^Y \, dQ_Y} \tag{4.5}$$

This can be expressed symbolically as

$$dQ_X = \frac{1}{E_{Q_Y}\left[v_X^Y\right]} v_X^Y dQ_Y \tag{4.6}$$

This is another way to express the conversion formula connecting the two numeraires.

**Example** Let $Y$ be 1 dollar today, and $X$ be 1 dollar at a future date $T$. In this case the exchange rate $v_X^Y$ is denoted $p(0, T)$ and will, in general, be a random variable depending on the market scenario (interest rates over the period $[0, T]$). Thus, 1 dollar to be delivered on date $T$ is worth $p(0, T)$ dollars today, given the market scenario prevailing over the time period $[0, T]$. Denote $Q_X$ by $Q_T$ and $Q_Y$ by just $Q$. Then we have the change-of-numeraire formula

$$dQ_T = \frac{p(0, T)dQ}{P(0, T)} \tag{4.7}$$

where

$$P(0, T) = E_Q[p(0, T)] \tag{4.8}$$

is how much you would pay today to receive 1 dollar on the future date $T$, without knowing which market scenario will prevail over time $[0, T]$. This is the *bond price* for a bond maturing on date $T$ and is also called the *discount factor*. Note that $p(0, T)$ is a random quantity depending on the market scenario prevailing over the time period $[0, T]$, while $P(0, T)$ is the bond price determined totally by knowledge available at the initial date 0.

## EXERCISE

Let $Q$ and $Q_T$ be as in the example. Suppose that the interest rates over the period $[0, T]$ are known at the outset with certainty, i.e. $p(0, T)$ is a fixed nonrandom quantity (having the same value no matter what the market scenario). Show that then $Q = Q_T$.

CHAPTER 5

# Changing Numeraires: Examples

Continuing our study of change of numeraire, we work out two examples: (i) when the two numeraires bear a fixed ratio to each other; (ii) when the exchange rate between the two numeraires has a log-normal distribution.

## FIXED EXCHANGE RATE

Consider two numeraires $X$ and $Y$ such that the exchange rate between the two is nonrandom—i.e., the same in all scenarios. Thus, basically, $Y$ is a definite multiple of $X$ such as $Y = 5X$.

Formally, this means that $v_X^Y$ is a constant, the same in all market scenarios. Here, and always, $v_X^Y$ is the worth of 1 unit of $X$ in terms of $Y$.

Then, using the conversion formula (4.4):

$$Q_X(B) = \frac{E_{Q_Y}\left[v_X^Y 1_B\right]}{E_{Q_Y}\left[v_X^Y\right]} = \frac{\int v_X^Y 1_B \, dQ_Y}{\int v_X^Y \, dQ_Y}, \qquad (5.1)$$

we have

$$Q_X(B) = E_{Q_Y}(1_B) = Q_Y(B)$$

for all events $B$, because the constant value $v_X^Y$ can be taken out of the integrals in numerator and denominator in (5.1). Thus, in this case,

$$Q_X = Q_Y \tag{5.2}$$

This equality is intuitively clear: $X$ and $Y$ bear a fixed relation to each other, the same in all scenarios, and so assessments of probabilities according to $X$ and $Y$ should be the same.

## THE LOG-NORMAL CASE

Consider an asset $X$ whose price $S = v_X^Y$, at some given time, relative to a numeraire $Y$ has a log-normal distribution with respect to the pricing measure $Q_Y$, i.e., $\log S$ is a Gaussian variable relative to the measure $Q_Y$. We shall prove the remarkable fact that *$S$ is also log normally distributed with respect to the measure $Q_X$.* This is a very important observation.

**Theorem 5.2.1** *Let $S$ be the price of an asset $X$ relative to a numeraire $Y$, and suppose that* $\log S$ *has Gaussian distribution with mean $m$ and variance $\sigma^2$, relative to the measure $Q_Y$. Then* $\log S$ *is Gaussian with mean $m + \sigma^2$ and variance $\sigma^2$, relative to $Q_X$.*

Notice the *shift in the mean* caused by the change of the reference measure.

The theorem above follows by using the conversion-of-numeraires relation (4.4) and taking $L = \log S$ and $P = Q_B$ in the following result:

**Lemma 5.2.2** *Let $L$ be a random variable that is Gaussian with mean $m$ and variance $\sigma^2$ with respect to a probability*

*measure $P$. Let $P'$ be the measure specified by*

$$P'(B) = \frac{E_P(e^L 1_B)}{E_P(e^L)} \tag{5.3}$$

*for all events $B$. Then the distribution of $L$ with respect to $P'$ is Gaussian with mean $m + \sigma^2$ and variance $\sigma^2$.*

***Proof.*** The following is a very useful fact about Gaussian random variables : *a random variable $Z$ is Gaussian if and only if there are real numbers $a$ and $b$ such that*

$$E(e^{wZ}) = e^{aw + bw^2/2} \tag{5.4}$$

*for all real (or complex) numbers $w$.* For such a variable, it turns out that

$$a = E(Z) \text{ and } b = \sigma_Z^2, \text{ the variance of } Z.$$

So to determine the distribution of $L$ with respect to $P'$ it suffices calculate $E_{P'}(e^{wL})$. Equation (5.3) implies that

$$\int f\, dP' = \frac{\int f e^L\, dP}{E_P(e^L)}$$

for any measurable function for which either side makes sense. Taking the special case of $f = e^{wL}$, we then have

$$\begin{aligned} E_{P'}(e^{wL}) &= \frac{E_P(e^L e^{wL})}{E_P(e^L)} \\ &= \exp\left[(w+1)E_P(L) + (w+1)^2\sigma_L^2/2 - E_P(L) - \sigma_L^2/2\right] \\ &= \exp\left[w\left\{E_P(L) + \sigma_L^2\right\} + \frac{1}{2}w^2\sigma_L^2\right] \end{aligned}$$

Comparing with (5.4) we conclude that $L$ is indeed Gaussian with respect to $P'$ with mean $E_P(L) + \sigma_L^2$ and variance $\sigma_L^2$. QED

CHAPTER 6

# No-Arbitrage and the Min-Max Argument

A market in which extensive trading takes place creates a *consistent system of prices* or "exchange rates" for the instruments being traded: if instrument $A$ can be traded for $B$, and $B$ for $C$, then $A$ can be traded for $C$. If such a system of prices exists then the market is in a form of equilibrium. As we have noted earlier, price inconsistency would allow a trader to accumulate unlimited quantities of some asset, and this is not sustainable.

A real market is, of course, always fluctuating around equilibrium rather than in actual equilibrium. Visible price inconsistences arise but do not last very long because traders move quickly to take advantage of these inconsistencies or *arbitrage opportunities*.

However, markets may contain highly complex, subtle forms of arbitrage that go unexploited for long periods. Moreover, in a market where very complex nonstandardized instruments, tailor-made to the needs of particular buyers, are available there are often no universally agreed-upon ways to price such instruments. Pricing would be done by choosing a market model, but it might take some time before the market makes it clear if the pricing was done correctly.

Our goal in this chapter is to show how the hypothesis that a market is free of arbitrage opportunities gives rise to a pricing measure. The discussion of price and probability in Chapter 1 assumed the existence of instruments such as $I_B$, which, in a real market, will not generally exist. Yet, as we shall see in this chapter, prices for a certain set of traded instruments together with the nonexistence of arbitrage implies that a consistent set of prices exist for a much larger class of instruments, and this leads to the pricing probability measure $Q$.

Linking no-arbitrage and existence of a consistent set of prices is a *min-max argument*, a powerful idea that is useful in several ways in economic equilibrium theory and game theory. It also lies at the heart of the Hahn-Banach theorem in mathematics.

There are many ways to make precise the notion of arbitrage, and there are corresponding theorems linking no-arbitrage and existence of a pricing measure. We shall proceed at an intuitive level, but in the last section provide a more mathematically formalized discussion. Our objective is to stress the core idea of *the equivalence of price consistency with the existence of a pricing measure via a min-max argument*, and not any particular formalization of the idea. As is often the case in mathematics, it is possible to dress up this core idea in many sophisticated forms in a variety of technical settings.

## NO-ARBITRAGE AND THE PRICING MEASURE

We shall use the term *arbitrage opportunity* to mean the possibility of forming a portfolio of assets that provides a riskless profit opportunity. This means that the portfolio results in no loss, no matter which market scenario occurs and yields a profit in at least some market scenario. A trader who sees an arbitrage opportunity will seize upon it to lock in profit until demand-supply forces adjust prices in such a way as to make the arbitrage opportunity disappear. In a real market this process occurs often and

helps ensure that the market stays near equilibrium. In ideal equilibrium, a consistent system of prices exists, and there is no arbitrage opportunity.

Let $\Omega$ be the set of all possible market scenarios, a typical *scenario* being denoted $\omega$. For the sake of focusing on the main ideas, as opposed to formalism, let us assume that $\Omega$ is finite.

Consider an asset $A$. Denote by

$$V^A(\omega)$$

the price of the asset $A$ in scenario $\omega$. All prices are with respect to some fixed numeraire. Our task is to determine the worth of $A$ when one does not know the particular scenario $\omega$ that will occur. Let us call this the *a priori price* of $A$; we denote it

$$V_0^A$$

For example, $A$ could be 1 share of a particular stock *at a particular time* in the future. Then $V_0^A$ could mean the present price of the future asset $A$.

Suppose the asset $A$ does not provide an arbitrage opportunity. What can we say about $V_0^A$? Clearly the *a priori* price $V_0^A$ must lie between the highest and least possible values of the $V^A(\cdot)$. Otherwise, holding or shorting the instrument $A$ would give an arbitrage opportunity.

Thus we already have an important observation: if $A$ does not provide an arbitrage opportunity, then $V_0^A$ *can be written as a weighted average (a convex combination) of all the possible values* $V^A(\omega)$:

$$V_0^A = \sum_{\omega\in\Omega} q^A(\omega) V^A(\omega) \tag{6.1}$$

where each $0 \le q^A(\omega) \le 1$ and $\sum_{\omega\in\Omega} q^A(\omega) = 1$. This must be valid for each asset $A$ if the entire market is arbitrage free.

This simple observation contains the kernel of a much deeper fact. To see this, notice that the no-arbitrage condition for the entire market is very strong:

> it is not possible to combine any set of assets into a portfolio so that the combined worth of the portfolio would be certain to yield a profit in at least one market scenario, and would result in no loss in all scenarios.

What does this say about the weights $q^A(\omega)$? It turns out that what it does say is this:

> *a single set of weights $q(\omega)$ must work simultaneously for all assets $A$!*

We will summarize this remarkable fact in Theorem 6.1.1.

**Theorem 6.1.1** *The following are equivalent:*

1. *There is no portfolio that gives an arbitrage opportunity;*
2. *There is a probability measure $Q$ on the market scenarios such that for any event $B$, the instrument $I_B$ has price $Q(B)$ units of the numeraire (recall that $I_B$ is the instrument that yields 1 unit of the numeraire when event $B$ occurs and nothing otherwise.)*

We are using the term "theorem" a bit loosely here because we have not completely formalized the framework. A more formal account is given later in this chapter.

## PROOF OF THEOREM 6.1.1

We shall assume that the set $\Omega$ of all market scenarios is finite.

We have already noted that the existence of a pricing measure implies the no-arbitrage condition: the price of any instrument being the average of all possible values in all possible scenarios must lie between the maximum and minimum of such values, thereby ensuring that no possibility of arbitrage profit exists.

Consider, for each particular scenario $\omega$, a special instrument $\delta_\omega$ whose value is 1 when the scenario $\omega$ occurs and is 0

otherwise. Let

$$q(\omega) = \text{the market price of the special asset } \delta_\omega \text{ in the absence of any knowledge of which market scenario will occur.} \tag{6.2}$$

By the no-arbitrage condition, $q(\omega)$ must lie between the maximum and minimum of the possible values of the asset $\delta_\omega$, i.e. $0 < q(\omega) < 1$.

Now consider the portfolio consisting of one unit of each of the assets $\delta_\omega$, with $\omega$ running over all possible scenarios. *This has value* 1 *in all possible scenarios*. So, by the no-arbitrage condition, its price should be 1. But the price of this portfolio is

$$\sum_{\omega \in \Omega} q(\omega)$$

Thus $\sum_{\omega \in \Omega} q(\omega)$ must be equal to 1:

$$\sum_{\omega \in \Omega} q(\omega) = 1$$

which says that $q(\cdots)$ specifies a *probability* measure $Q$ on the set of scenarios, the probability $Q(B)$ of an event being

$$Q(B) = \sum_{\omega \in B} q(\omega)$$

Notice that this is indeed the price of the asset $I_B$, for the latter is equivalent to one unit each of the instruments $\delta_\omega$, with $\omega$ running over $B$.

The only trouble with the preceding argument is that the market might be so small that there is no actual traded instrument that has value 1 in scenario $\omega$ and 0 in all other cases, i.e., the asset $\delta_\omega$ might not exist. To deal with this kind of situation we could simply *create*, for each $\omega$, the asset $\delta_\omega$. This would do it, as long as we can prove that it is *possible* to assign some initial price to the asset $\delta_\omega$ such that the no-arbitrage condition still holds.

Let us say there are $N$ possible market scenarios, $\omega_1, \ldots, \omega_N$:

$$\Omega = \{\omega_1, \ldots, \omega_N\}$$

Denote by $a_i$ the price of an existing asset $A$ in scenario $\omega_i$; and, for convenience, let us denote by $a_0$ the *a priori* price of $A$. We use the terms "asset," "instrument," and "portfolio" interchangeably.

We are going to create the asset $\delta_{\omega_1}$. All we need to do is specify its *a priori* price $c_0$ (of course, $c_0$ is going to be $q(\omega_1)$), but we must do so in a way that the no-arbitrage condition continues to hold.

Thus, $c_0$ must be such that for any asset $A$, the *a priori* price of the portfolio consisting of the asset $A$ along with the instrument $\delta_{\omega_1}$ lies between the minimum and maximum of the possible values of this portfolio in all scenarios. Thus, $a_0 + c_0$ must be between the maximum and minimum values among $a_1 + 1$, $a_2, \ldots, a_N$.

So it will suffice to choose $c_0$ to be any number that lies between $\min\{a_1 + 1 - a_0, a_2 - a_0, \ldots, a_N - a_0\}$ and $\max\{a_1 + 1 - a_0, a_2 - a_0, \ldots, a_N - a_0\}$, for all existing assets $A$.

The only obstacle we now have to overcome is showing that such a choice is possible, i.e., we must show that for any assets $A$ and $B$ (from the existing set of assets),

$$\begin{aligned}&\text{the value } \min\{a_1 + 1 - a_0, a_2 - a_0, \ldots, a_N - a_0\} \text{ is}\\ &\text{less or equal to } \max\{b_1 + 1 - b_0, b_2 - b_0, \ldots, b_N - b_0\}\end{aligned} \tag{6.3}$$

for then we could choose $c_0$ to be between the highest of the $\min\{a_1 + 1 - a_0, \cdots\}$ and the lowest of the $\max\{b_1 + 1 - b_0, \ldots\}$:

$$\max_A \min\{a_1 + 1 - a_0, \ldots\} \le c_0 \le \min_B \max\{b_1 + 1 - b_0, \ldots\} \tag{6.4}$$

If (6.3) were not the case, then there would exist assets $A$ and $B$ such that $\min\{a_1 + 1 - a_0, a_2 - a_0, \ldots, a_N - a_0\}$ is greater than $\max\{b_1 + 1 - b_0, b_2 - b_0, \ldots, b_N - b_0\}$:

$$\min\{a_1 + 1 - a_0, a_2 - a_0, \ldots, a_N - a_0\} \\ > \max\{b_1 + 1 - b_0, b_2 - b_0, \ldots, b_N - b_0\}$$

This would imply that

$$a_1 + 1 - a_0 - (b_1 + 1 - b_0) > 0, \\ a_2 - a_0 - (b_2 - b_0) > 0, \ldots, a_N - a_0 - (b_N - b_0) > 0$$

i.e., $a_0 - b_0$ is $<$ all the numbers $a_1 - b_1, \ldots, a_N - b_N$. But this would mean that the asset $A - B$ (long $A$ and short $B$) would provide an arbitrage opportunity.

Thus we can adjoin the asset $\delta_{\omega_1}$ to the market, associating with it an *a priori* price in such a way that the no-arbitrage condition continues to be valid.

Doing this with all the other assets $\delta_{\omega_2}, \ldots, \delta_{\omega_N}$, one by one, we are finally done. With these new assets $\delta_\omega$, one for each scenario $\omega$, adjoined to the market, the no-arbitrage condition continues to be valid for the extended market, and we can use the argument described earlier to prove the existence of the weights $q(\omega)$. QED

## Uniqueness/Nonuniqueness of the Measure Q

If the assets $\delta_\omega$ exist, in themselves or as combinations of other assets, in the market then the proof above shows that the weights $q(\omega)$ are *uniquely determined*. In fact, as we have already seen, the probability $q(\omega)$ is simply the price of the asset $\delta_\omega$.

If the $\delta_\omega$'s don't exist in the market (i.e., cannot be expressed in any way as a combination of the existing instruments) then, from the reasoning used in the proof above, it is clear that there is a range of choices for each weight $q(\omega)$, i.e., the market equilibrium measure $Q$ is not unique.

The nonuniqueness is also apparent by looking at the simple case where there is only one asset and three possible future secenarios: the same number (the asset price) can be expressed as an average of three or more distinct numbers (possible values of the asset) in many ways.

If the prices of traded instruments in the market imply a unique pricing measure, we say that the market is *complete*.

### The Central Idea: The Max–Min Argument

The core idea, the *max-min argument* used above, works in many settings, even when the number of scenarios is infinite. The max–min method forms the crux of the proof of the *Hahn-Banach theorem*, a result that is used to prove versions of Theorem 6.1.1.

Not surprisingly, the same max–min method is also used in game theory for optimum strategies. Taking a very brief look at this, consider two persons, A and B, playing a game in which each has a choice of moves, and B has to pay A the amount $f(a, b)$ if A has chosen move $a$ and $B$ has made move $b$. Then, A will chose the move $a$ to maximize the minimum possible gain $\min_b f(a, b)$ when choice $a$ has been made; thus, A would then be sure to gain at least

$$\max_a \min_b f(a, b).$$

Similarly, we can look at B's desire to minimize the maximum loss, to the amount

$$\min_b \max_a f(a, b).$$

## A FORMAL FRAMEWORK

Here we shall formalize the ideas of no-arbitrage and pricing measures in a particular framework.

The concepts we are formalizing are:

**(i)** A market that can exist in a certain set of scenarios;

**(ii)** assets that have prices, in units of a particular numeraire, in each market scenario;

**(iii)** traders who, without exact information about the market scenario, associate *a priori* prices to the assets.

To keep things simple we work with a finite, though possibly very large, set

$$\Omega = \{\omega_1, \ldots, \omega_N\}$$

whose elements should be thought of as all the possible scenarios of the market.

Each traded asset has a specific price, in units of a chosen numeraire, in each market scenario $\omega$. Two assets that happen to always have exactly the same price will be viewed as being effectively the same asset. Thus, an asset can be modelled as a mapping

$$f : \Omega \to \mathbf{R} : \omega \mapsto f(\omega),$$

with $f(\omega)$ denoting the price of the asset $f$ in market scenario $\omega$.

Different assets may be combined to form portfolios and we also assume that each asset can be scaled in any way, with positive (long) and negative (short) multiples.

Thus, the set of assets forms a vector space $V$; indeed, $V$ is a subspace of $\mathbf{R}^\Omega$:

$$V \subset \mathbf{R}^\Omega,$$

where $\mathbf{R}^\Omega$ is the set of all maps $\Omega \to \mathbf{R}$.

Lastly, we have the set of traders. A trader $i$ is not assumed to know which market scenario $\omega$ actually prevails but, based on his/her understanding or estimate of which market scenario $\omega$ will be realized, associates to each asset $f$ a price $L_i f$ the trader is willing to pay or receive in exchange for the asset.

Clearly, $L_i f$ should be linear in $f$, i.e.

$$L_i(f + g) = L_i(f) + L_i(g) \text{ and } L_i(kf) = kL_i(f)$$

for any constant scaling $k$.

Of course, this linearity is also a form of no-arbitrage.

Thus, each trader $i$ has a pricing procedure given by a linear functional

$$L_i : V \to \mathbf{R} : f \mapsto L_i f$$

Moreover, if an asset is worth one unit of numeraire in every possible scenario, then clearly its price should be 1, i.e. $L_i(1) = 1$.

We have defined *market equilibrium* to be a situation where *all traders agree on common prices*, i.e., there is a common linear functional

$$L : V \to \mathbf{R}$$

used by all traders to decide prices:

*the price of asset $f$ is $L(f)$.*

Note that here we are talking of the market price before the actual scenario $\omega$ of the market is revealed. To stress this, sometimes we will use the term *a priori* price.

Now we formalize the notion of no-arbitrage. An asset $h$ provides an arbitrage opportunity for trader $i$ if the price $L_i h$ is strictly less than all possible values $h(\omega)$ or is strictly greater than all possible values $h(\omega)$. Thus, no-arbitrage means that $L_i$ has the property that

$$\min f \leq L_i f \leq \max f \text{ for all } f \in V \tag{6.5}$$

(The notion of arbitrage we are using here is slightly different from the one used in the previous section. We will return to this matter after the discussion that follows.)

Note that this implies in particular that if $f$ is constant, then $L_i f = f$ and so, specializing to $f = 1$:

$$L_i 1 = 1 \tag{6.6}$$

Here we have assumed that $1 \in V$.

**TABLE 6–1**

A Formal Market Model

| Mathematical Object | Interpretation |
|---|---|
| A finite set $\Omega$ | Elements of $\Omega$ correspond to market scenarios |
| A vector space $V$ of functions $\Omega \to \mathbf{R}$, with $1 \in V$ | a function $f : \Omega \to \mathbf{R}$ corresponds to an instrument, with $f(\omega)$ being the price of $f$ in market scenario $\omega$ |
| A linear functional $L_i : V \to \mathbf{R}$ for each trader $i$ | $L_i(f)$ is the *a priori* price associated to instrument $f$ by trader $i$ |
| $\min f \leq L_i f \leq \max f$ for all $f \in V$ | The no-arbitrage condition |
| All the $L_i$'s are equal to a common $L$ | The no-arbitrage condition across traders in the market |

Our model is summarized in Table 6.1.

The last condition above reflects the fact that market equilibrium corresponds to all traders using the same pricing functional $L$.

Note that the condition $\min f \leq L_i f \leq \max f$ for all $f \in V$ is equivalent to $L_i f \leq \max f$ for all $f \in V$ (just switch $f$ to $-f$ in the latter condition to obtain $L_i f \geq \min f$).

For the following, note that $\mathbf{R}^{\Omega}$, the set of all functions $\Omega \to \mathbf{R}$, is a linear space, being essentially $\mathbf{R}^N$ where $N$ is the number of market scenarios.

**Theorem 6.3.1** *Let $V$ be a subspace of $\mathbf{R}^{\Omega}$, where $\Omega$ is a non-empty finite set, and $L : V \to \mathbf{R}$ a linear functional satisfying the condition $Lf \leq \max f$ for all $f \in V$. Then there is a linear functional $L' : \mathbf{R}^{\Omega} \to \mathbf{R}$ which coincides with $L$ on the subspace $V$ and satisfies $\min f \leq L' f \leq \max f$ for all $f \in \mathbf{R}^{\Omega}$.*

***Proof.*** Consider an element $g \in \mathbf{R}^{\Omega}$ that is not in $V$, and let $W$ denote the subspace spanned by $g$ and $V$, i.e. $W = \mathbf{R}g + V$. It will suffice to show that $L$ can be extended to a linear functional $L_1$ on $W$ satisfying

$$L_1 F \leq \max F \text{ for all } F \in W,$$

for then the same argument applied step-by-step inductively produces the required linear functional $L'$ on $\mathbf{R}^{\Omega}$.

To define $L_1$ as a linear functional on $W$ agreeing with $L$ on $V$, it will be sufficient to specify the value of $L_1$ on the new element $g$; moreover, we must do so in such a way that

$$\min\{f+tg\} \leq Lf + tL_1 g \leq \max\{f+tg\} \tag{6.7}$$

holds for all $f \in V$ and real numbers $t$. Let $\alpha$ denote the proposed value for $L_1 g$.

It will suffice to produce a real number $\alpha$ such that

$$Lf + u\alpha \leq \max\{f+ug\} \text{ for all } f \in V \text{ and } u \in \mathbf{R}, \tag{6.8}$$

for switching $f$ to $-f$ and $u$ to $-t$ yields the first inequality in (6.7).

It is best to treat the cases $u > 0$ and $u < 0$ separately (if $u = 0$ then (6.8) is already given to be true). For $u = t > 0$ the condition (6.8) is equivalent to

$$\alpha \leq \max\{f+g\} - Lf \text{ for all } f \in V$$

(here we have used the fact that $tf$ runs over all of $V$ as $f$ does). For $u = -s < 0$, the condition (6.8) is equivalent to

$$Lh - \alpha \leq \max\{h-g\} \text{ for all } h \in V$$

Thus, (6.8) is equivalent to

$$Lh - \max\{h-g\} \leq \alpha \leq \max\{f+g\} - Lf \text{ for all } f, h \in V \tag{6.9}$$

Such an $\alpha$ can be found if and only if

$$Lh - \max\{h-g\} \leq \max\{f+g\} - Lf \text{ for all } f, h \in V \tag{6.10}$$

which can be put into a more obviously min-max looking form:

$$\sup_{h\in V} \min_{\omega\in\Omega} [Lh - \{h(\omega) - g(\omega)\}] \leq \inf_{f\in V} \max_{\omega\in\Omega} [\{f(\omega) + g(\omega)\} - Lf] \tag{6.11}$$

The condition (6.10) is equivalent to

$$L(h+f) \leq \max\{f+g\} + \max\{h-g\} \text{ for all } f, h \in V \quad (6.12)$$

All we have to do now is to establish this inequality. However, the original hypothesis on $L$ gives us

$$L(f+h) \leq \max\{f+h\} \text{ for all } f, h \in V$$

and we also have

$$\max\{f+h\} = \max\{f+g+h-g\} \leq \max\{f+g\} + \max\{h-g\}$$

and so the desired condition (6.12) holds. QED

The proof above is essentially the reasoning behind the *Hahn-Banach theorem*. When $\Omega$ is infinite Zorn's lemma is needed to finish off the argument.

Now we can prove the following fundamental result which provides the pricing measure:

**Theorem 6.3.2** *Let $V$ be a subspace of $\mathbf{R}^{\Omega}$, where $\Omega$ is a non-empty finite set, and $L: V \to \mathbf{R}$ a linear functional satisfying the condition $Lf \leq \max f$ for all $f \in V$. Then there is a probability measure $Q$ on the set of all subsets of $\Omega$ such that*

$$Lf = \int f\, dQ \quad (6.13)$$

*holds for all $f \in V$.*

***Proof.*** By the previous theorem $L$ extends to a linear functional $L': \mathbf{R}^{\Omega} \to \mathbf{R}$ satisfying $L'f \leq \max f$ for all $f \in \mathbf{R}^{\Omega}$. Switching $f$ to $-f$ this inequality leads to $L'f \geq \min f$ and so

$$\min f \leq L'f \leq \max f \text{ for all } f \in \mathbf{R}^{\Omega}. \quad (6.14)$$

Taking $f \geq 0$ shows that

$$L'f \geq 0 \text{ whenever } f \geq 0.$$

Taking $f$ to be the constant function 1 in (6.14) shows that

$$L'1 = 1$$

Because $\Omega$ is finite, the vector space $\mathbf{R}^\Omega$ has a basis consisting of the vectors $\delta_\omega$, with $\omega$ running over $\Omega$, with $\delta_\omega$ being the element of $\mathbf{R}^\Omega$, which has value 1 on $\omega$ and value 0 at all other points of $\Omega$. Any linear functional on $\mathbf{R}^\Omega$ is uniquely specified by its values on the basis elements $\delta_\omega$. Define

$$q_\omega = L'(\delta_\omega)$$

The properties of $L'$ noted earlier implies that $q_\omega \geq 0$ and

$$\sum_{\omega\in\Omega} q_\omega = L'\left(\sum_{\omega\in\Omega} \delta_\omega\right) = L'1 = 1$$

So the numbers $q_\omega$ specify a probability measure $Q$ on the subsets of $\Omega$:

$$Q(E) = \sum_{\omega\in E} q_\omega \text{ for all } E \subset \Omega \tag{6.15}$$

Then it follows that

$$\int f\,dQ = L'f$$

for all $f \in \mathbf{R}^\Omega$, because both sides are linear functionals of $f$, which agree on the basis elements $\delta_\omega$. In particular, specializing to elements $f \in V$ we have the representation (6.13). QED

When $\Omega$ is infinite, more structure is needed to construct the measure $Q$, which would live on a certain $\sigma$-algebra of subsets of (an extended version of) $\Omega$. We shall not pursue this task here.

The formalization of no-arbitrage we have used:

$$Lf \leq \max f$$

is not quite equivalent to what we worked with the preceding section, as we have noted earlier in the context of (6.5). We need to examine the case of a function $f$ for which $Lf$ is equal to max $f$ (or min $f$). Ideally, and to be consistent with the version from the preceding section, we would like to conclude that $f$ is constant. Having the representation of $Lf$ has $\int f\, dQ$ it follows that $f$ is indeed equal to the constant value max $f$, except on a set whose $Q$-probability is 0. This is satisfactory enough. However, if we insist on the stronger form of no-arbitrage:

$$Lf \leq \max f, \text{ with equality if and only if } f \text{ is constant}$$

then this would simply mean that all market scenarios $\omega$ do have positive probability of being realized.

CHAPTER 7

# Conditional Price as Conditional Expectation: The Martingale Principle

In this chapter we look at the mathematical method for incorporating market information into the framework for determining prices in terms of probabilities and expectations. In essence, the idea may be summarized as:

| Fair price of an instrument, given some information | = | Expected value of the price, conditional on the given information |
|---|---|---|

There are many situations where we need to assess the probability of an event subject to having additional information, such as the prices of a particular set of instruments. For example, a common situation is where we have to assess the likelihood of a future market event assuming we have all information of market instrument prices up to the present date.

## CONDITIONAL PROBABILITIES AND EXPECTATIONS

Consider a collection $\{Y_\alpha\}$ of market random variables. For example, the $Y_\alpha$ might be the prices of a set of assets at a certain time.

The probability of an event $C$, *given* the values taken by the variables $Y_\alpha$, ought to be a "function of" the $Y_\alpha$:

$$Q\,(C|\{Y_\alpha\}) = \text{probability of event } C\text{, given the values of all the } Y_\alpha \tag{7.1}$$

Plugging in specific values of $Y_\alpha$ would yield the probability of $C$, conditional on the $Y_\alpha$'s taking the specified values.

Correspondingly, there is also the notion of conditional expectation. If $X$ is a random variable, then the expected value of $X$, given the values of the variables $Y_\alpha$, is a "function of" the $Y_\alpha$'s:

$$E_Q\,[X|\{Y_\alpha\}] = \text{expectation of variable } X\text{, given the values of all the } Y_\alpha \tag{7.2}$$

This approach, though conceptually concrete, is technically awkward. To make any progress, it is best to use the notion of conditional expectation with respect to a *sigma-algebra*. Roughly speaking, a $\sigma$-algebra is the collection of all events specified through values of some collection of market variables. For instance, if $X$ and $Y$ are market variables (say, prices of two bonds), then the $\sigma$-algebra $\sigma(X, Y)$ consists of all events specified by values of $X$ and $Y$; for instance, the event that $Y$ exceeds $X$ by 50. For technical details and formal definitions, see Chapter 24.

Let $\mathcal{G}$ be a $\sigma$-algebra, a suitable collection of events. For instance, $\mathcal{G}$ may consist of all events that are determined by a family of variables $Y_\alpha$. Then for any event $C$, we have the conditional probability

$$Q\,(C|\mathcal{G}) = \text{probability of event } C\text{, conditional on the information } \mathcal{G} \tag{7.3}$$

This is a $\mathcal{G}$-measurable variable, i.e., it is a random variable determined by the information expressed by $\mathcal{G}$. If $\mathcal{G}$ is the $\sigma$-algebra generated by a given family of variables $Y_\alpha$, then for a variable to be $\mathcal{G}$-measurable effectively means that it is a "function of" the variables $Y_\alpha$.

If $X$ is a random variable, for which the expectation $E_Q(X)$ exists and is finite, there is also the conditional expectation

$$E_Q\,[X|\mathcal{G}] = \text{Expected value of } X \text{ conditional on the information } \mathcal{G} \qquad (7.4)$$

## THE GENERALIZED MARTINGALE PRINCIPLE

Consider a fixed numeraire and let $Q$ be the corresponding market equilibrium measure. Let

$$X$$

be the random variable giving the price, relative to the given numeraire, of a particular asset.

Thus $X(\omega)$ is the price of the asset in market-scenario $\omega$.

Let $\mathcal{F}$ be a $\sigma$-algebra of events representing a certain body of market information.

Then the conditional expectaton $E_Q[X|\mathcal{F}]$ should be the fair price $X_{\mathcal{F}}$ of $X$ under the information $\mathcal{F}$:

$$\textit{Fair price of } X\textit{, given the information } \mathcal{F}\textit{, is } X_{\mathcal{F}} = E_Q[X|\mathcal{F}] \qquad (7.5)$$

We shall call this the *generalized martingale principle* for prices. It holds relative to any market measure $Q$. The price $X_{\mathcal{F}}$ is fair as judged by the agent who is using the measure $Q$. In particular, $Q$ may be the market equilibrium measure, in which case $X_{\mathcal{F}}$ would be the fair price, as judged by the market, given the information $\mathcal{F}$.

## THE DISCOUNTED PRICE PROCESS AS A MARTINGALE

The argument given above for the fair price $X_{\mathcal{F}}$ being $E_Q[X|\mathcal{F}]$ might seem to be tautological, but the conditional expectation $E_Q[X|\mathcal{F}]$ has a precise mathematical definition, and so it is necessary to verify at some level that the claim that $X_{\mathcal{F}}$ equals $E_Q[X|\mathcal{F}]$ is reasonable. This may be done by rewording the max-min no-arbitrage argument in terms of conditional probabilities. Thus, now no-arbitrage should be understood in the sense that exists *no arbitrage opportunity under the information* $\mathcal{F}$.

A particular case of (7.5) is very useful. Let

$$X_T$$

be the random variable giving the price, relative to a given numeraire, of a particular asset at a time $T$. Thus $X_T(\omega)$ is the price at time $T$ of the given asset in market-state $\omega$. Now let $t < T$ be a time instant prior to $T$ and let

$$\mathcal{F}_t$$

be the sigma-algebra of all events specified by all market variables up till time $t$. Then, with $Q$ denoting the pricing-probability measure corresponding to the given numeraire,

$$E_Q[X_T|\mathcal{F}_t]$$

is the expected value of $X_T$, subject to the information available up till time $t$ (it is therefore a "function of" all asset prices up till time $t$). Thus it is reasonable to suppose that the agent who believes in the measure $Q$ will consider

$$X_t = E_Q[X_T|\mathcal{F}_t] \tag{7.6}$$

as the fair price for the asset at time $t$, as judged by all information available till time $t$. Thus the fair *price process*

$$t \mapsto X_t$$

for the asset has the *martingale* property (7.6). (Needless to say, we are talking about a real situation, for which the expectations for $X_t$ exist and are finite.)

The *same* numeraire is being used to measure the price at time $t$ and at time $T$. Thus, for example, the asset prices could be in terms of unit cash at time 0. This gives the *discounted price* of the asset and then (7.6) says that *the discounted price process is a martingale*.

## CHANGE OF NUMERAIRE REVISITED

Consider two numeraires $X$ and $Y$, related by the exchange rate $v_X^Y$:

$$1 \text{ unit of } X \text{ is worth } v_X^Y \text{ units of } Y. \tag{7.7}$$

In general, the quantity $v_X^Y$ depends on the market scenario $\omega$. Thus, $v_X^Y$ is really a random variable

$$v_X^Y : \Omega \to \mathbf{R}$$

taking positive values.

In Chapter 4 we saw that the pricing measures $Q_X$ and $Q_Y$ are related by

$$Q_X(B) = \frac{E_{Q_Y}\left[v_X^Y 1_B\right]}{E_{Q_Y}\left[v_X^Y\right]} = \frac{\int v_X^Y 1_B \, dQ_Y}{\int v_X^Y \, dQ_Y} \tag{7.8}$$

More generally, for an instrument whose payoff in market scenario $\omega$ is given by $f(\omega)$, the price relative to the numeraire $X$ is given by:

$$\int f \, dQ_X = \frac{\int f v_X^Y \, dQ_Y}{\int v_X^Y \, dQ_Y} \tag{7.9}$$

Going over the reasoning that led to these formulas suggests that these relations should continue to hold under the presence of additional information. More precisely, if $\mathcal{A}$ is a sigma-algebra of market events (say, for example, all events up till a certain time), then

$$\boxed{E_{Q_X}[f|\mathcal{A}] = \frac{E_{Q_Y}\left[f v_X^Y|\mathcal{A}\right]}{E_{Q_Y}\left[v_X^Y|\mathcal{A}\right]}} \tag{7.10}$$

This suggests, and follows from, the following purely mathematical result:

**Theorem 7.4.1** *Suppose $\mathcal{F}$ is a $\sigma$-algebra of subsets of a set $\Omega$, suppose $\mathcal{A}$ is a sub-$\sigma$-algebra, and suppose $Q_X$ and $Q_Y$ are probability measures on $\mathcal{F}$ related by*

$$Q_X(B) = \frac{E_{Q_Y}\left[v_X^Y 1_B\right]}{E_{Q_Y}\left[v_X^Y\right]} \tag{7.11}$$

*for all $B \in \mathcal{F}$, where $v_X^Y$ is an $\mathcal{F}$-measurable positive function on $\Omega$. Then*

$$E_{Q_X}[f|\mathcal{A}] = \frac{E_{Q_Y}\left[f v_X^Y|\mathcal{A}\right]}{E_{Q_Y}\left[v_X^Y|\mathcal{A}\right]} \tag{7.12}$$

*for all $\mathcal{F}$-measurable functions $f$ for which either side exists.*

We present the proof later in Chapter 24.

PART TWO

# Prices of Basic Instruments

Our objective in Part Two is to develop prices of certain fundamental financial instruments such as zero-coupon bonds, forwards, futures, options, and swaps. We proceed in a *model-independent* way, using the ideas of Part One to break down complex instruments into simpler ones that can be understood more directly in terms of the price-probability relationship.

Zero-coupon bonds are the basic instruments for the interest rate market. Most instruments we are concerned with involve certain future delivery dates, and we price such instruments by using the *forward pricing measure*. We shall go back and forth between different pricing measures in evaluating options and other more complex instruments.

The model-independent formulas we study in Part Two will be used in Part Three in the context of specific models to price instruments.

The general pricing formulas obtained in Part Two are summarized in Tables 16-1 and 16-2.

CHAPTER 8

# Bonds and Interest

A bond is a financial instrument that yields to the issuer an agreed-upon sum, the *face value*, at a chosen *maturity date*, and may also pay coupons prior to maturity if so agreed upon. Bond markets form the backbone of economic growth, allowing excess production from those who cannot consume the excess to those who can and need to, and allowing the productive capacities of the latter to repay the former. For the bond holder, the bond is a way of transferring wealth across time. Bonds finance investment activities of municipal, state, and national governments, multinational governmental agencies, as well as of all major corporations. Thus, the bond market is truly vast.

Virtually every major public or corporate project is financed through bonds. Even small projects sometimes get funds indirectly through global bonds. A tank for home water use in a small locality in India where this author grew up was financed in part by a low-interest World Bank loan. The World Bank, in turn, obtains funds for such loans through bond issues, bonds that carry low interest rates, reflecting the high degree of financial reliability the Bank enjoys. The tank could have been built by using local funds, either through tax revenues or through higher-interest loans drawing funds away from other needs, but the global market allowed funds to be obtained at low interest from far and distant places.

In this chapter, we study bonds in the framework developed in Part One. For expositional and conceptual simplicity, we focus mainly on zero-coupon bonds, i.e., bonds that pay no coupons and have only a final payoff on maturity.

To this end, we view a *bond* with *maturity date* $T$ as an instrument that makes only one payment, the payoff being 1 unit of currency paid at maturity.

A *coupon-bearing bond* makes several payments, at regular intervals, between the time of issue and maturity.

The first section below is devoted to the pricing of zero-coupon bonds that do not carry any risk of default (the formalism can also be applied, with some reinterpretation of terms, to the default case as well). These instruments mediate *intertemporal equilibirum* of markets, being essentially the *exchange rate between currency at one time with currency at another time*.

Most real bonds carry a risk of default. We shall study the pricing of such bonds in the second section.

## ZERO-COUPON DEFAULT-FREE BOND PRICES

For this section, we focus on bonds that have no risk of default and pay no coupons.

To analyze bond prices, we need to compare numeraires across time: We have to consider how much a unit of cash at one time is worth at another time. For any times $t < T$, let

$$p(t, T; \omega)$$

be the value (cash) at time $t$ of 1 unit of time-$T$ cash, assuming that market scenario $\omega$ occurs. We take this to mean the amount of cash at time $t$ that would evolve into 1 unit of cash at time $T$ if left to earn continuous interest at the prevailing short-term rates specified by scenario $\omega$. This is a somewhat abstract construct and not actually known at time $t$ because it depends on what occurs between time $t$ and time $T$.

As with any change-of-numeraire exchange rate, there is a natural consistency relation

$$p(s,t)p(t,u) = p(s,u) \tag{8.1}$$

whenever $s \leq t \leq u$.

It is convenient to analyze this multiplicative property by taking logarithms, to make it an additive property. To this end, let

$$\nu(s,t] = -\log_e p(s,t) \tag{8.2}$$

Of course, this is again a scenario-dependent quantity, i.e., it is a function of $\omega$.

Then, (8.1) is equivalent to

$$\nu((s,t]) + \nu((t,u]) = \nu((s,u])$$

Under mild conditions, it follows then that $\nu$ can be expressed as an integral:

$$\nu((s,t]) = \int_s^t r_x \, dx,$$

for a certain function $x \mapsto r_x$ (varying with $\omega$). Thus, putting everything back together we have

$$\boxed{p(s,t;\omega) = e^{-\int_s^t r_u(\omega)\,du}} \tag{8.3}$$

for all $0 \leq s \leq t$. This equation shows that $r_s(\omega)$ *is the instantaneous interest rate at time s in market state* $\omega$.

Note that in general $p(t,T)$ will depend on the *future* $[t,T]$. However, we make the eminently reasonable assumption that $r_t$ is $\mathcal{F}_t$-measurable. Indeed, we will always assume that

$$(t,\omega) \mapsto r_t(\omega)$$

is a stochastic process that has all the nice properties needed to make the mathematical technical work go through.

Let $Q_t$ be the pricing measure corresponding to 1 unit of cash at time $t$ as numeraire. Then the market *price for the bond* at time $t$, based on knowledge available up till time $t$, is

$$P(t, T) = E_{Q_t}[p(t, T)|\mathcal{F}_t], \tag{8.4}$$

where $\mathcal{F}_t$ is the $\sigma$-algebra determined by all market information available up till time $t$.

Thus, $P(t, T)$ is also a random variable, determined by all information available till time $t$.

Note the distinction between $p(t, T; \omega)$ and $P(t, T; \omega)$:

- $p(t, T; \omega)$ depends on the "future" $[t, T]$, but $P(t, T; \omega)$ is determined by the state of the market up till time $t$.

When $t = 0$ is the *initial moment*, we may treat the bond price $P(t, T)$ as a deterministic value because we assume that the market is initially in a fixed, known state.

The bond price $P(t, T)$ is also called a *discount factor* because it is the multiplier used to determine present value (i.e., value at time $t$) from the time-$T$ value of an asset.

The *interest rate over the period* $[t, T]$ is given by $R_{[t,T]}$, as specified by

$$P(t, T) = e^{-(T-t)R_{[t,T]}}, \qquad \text{i.e. } R_{[t,T]} = -\frac{\log P(t, T)}{T - t} \tag{8.5}$$

The *interest* over this period is the difference between the initial payment and the final receipt:

$$\text{Interest} = 1 - P(t, T) \tag{8.6}$$

## ASSETS WITH DEFAULT RISK

Common sense as well as experience tells us that a borrower who carries a higher risk of defaulting on a loan should pay a higher interest rate. The higher rate may be viewed as an insurance premium on the default risk. In this section we study the exact mathematical relationship between default risk and interest rate.

Consider an asset, such as a corporate bond, that carries default risk. We consider such an asset with a maturity date $T$ on which the asset price will be $S_T$ (which would be 1 for a bond). There is a random time $\tau$ at which this asset may default; we assume $0 \le \tau \le T$ except that if there is no default, we set $\tau = \infty$ as a matter of convenience. If there is a default at time $t$, we assume that an amount $R_t$ from the asset will be recovered.

Consider time instants $s \le t$. Let

$$\begin{aligned} p_1(s,t) &= \textit{probability of no default during } [s,t], \\ &\quad \textit{given that default hasn't occurred by time } s \\ &= Q\,[\tau > t \,|\, \tau > s]\,, \end{aligned}$$

where $Q$ is a pricing measure.

Then,

$$p_1(s,t)p_1(t,u) = p_1(s,u) \tag{8.7}$$

whenever $s \le t \le u$. *Notice the similarity with the property (8.1) of the terms* $p(s,t)$.

Now consider

$$F(t) = -\log_e Q[\tau > t]$$

The value $F(t)$ starts at $t = 0$ at $F(0) = 0$ and then increases monotonically until the value $F(T-)$, after which it stays at the fixed value $-\log_e Q[\tau = \infty]$, where $Q[\tau = \infty]$ is the probability that no default occurs.

Moreover, $F$ is continuous from the right.

It follows that there is a Borel measure $\lambda$ on $[0, \infty)$ such that

$$F(t) = \lambda([0,t])$$

Thus,

$$\textit{probability that by time } t \textit{ no default occurs } = e^{-\lambda([0,t])} \tag{8.8}$$

The probability that a default occurs in a time interval $(a, b]$ given that no default occurred by time $a$ turns out to be about $\lambda(a, b]$, if $\lambda\big((a, b]\big)$ is small enough:

$$
\begin{aligned}
Q[a < \tau \leq b|\tau > a] &= \frac{Q[\tau > a] - Q[\tau > b]}{Q[\tau > a]} \\
&= \frac{e^{-\lambda([0,a])} - e^{-\lambda([0,b])}}{e^{-\lambda([0,a])}} \\
&= 1 - e^{-\lambda((a,b])} \\
&\simeq \lambda(a, b] \qquad \text{if } \lambda(a, b] \text{ is small.}
\end{aligned}
$$

This gives an intuitive feel for the *default measure* $\lambda$: roughly speaking, $d\lambda(t)$ is the *default probability over the interval* $[t, t + dt]$, given survival till time $t$.

The probability that default occurs in an interval $(a, b]$ is

$$
\begin{aligned}
Q[\tau > a]\, Q[a < \tau \leq b \mid \tau > a] &= e^{-\lambda([0,a])}\left(1 - e^{-\lambda((a,b])}\right) \\
&\simeq e^{-\lambda([0,a])}\lambda(a, b] \qquad \text{if } (a, b] \text{ is small}
\end{aligned}
$$

Finally, we note also that

$$
-\log_e p_1(s, t) = -\log_e Q[\tau > t|\tau > s] = \lambda((s, t]) \tag{8.9}
$$

Compare this with the corresponding equation (8.2) connecting $p(s, t)$ and $\nu$.

Let $p(0, t)$ be the scenario-dependent random variable denoting the time-0 value of unit currency deliverable at time $t$. Then the present value (scenario dependent) of the asset is:

$$
p(0, \tau)R_\tau 1_{\tau \leq T} + p(0, T)S_T\, 1_{[\text{no default}]},
$$

where $R_\tau$ is the recovery amount at default time.

The expected value of this according to the measure $Q$ is (using a mild technical assumption)

$$E_Q\left[\int_0^T p(0,t)e^{-\lambda([0,t])}R_t\,d\lambda(t) + p(0,T)e^{-\lambda([0,T])}S_T\right]$$

A typical model would take the default measure $\lambda$ to be given through a *default density* function $h$:

$$\lambda([a,b]) = \int_a^b h(x)\,dx$$

With this setting, and writing $p(0,t)$ in terms of the interest rate process $r_s$, the expected present value is

$$E_Q\left[\int_0^T e^{-\int_0^t (r_s+h_s)\,ds}R_t h_t\,dt + e^{-\int_0^T (r_s+h_s)\,ds}S_T\right]$$

Let us consider the special situation where nothing is recovered in case of default, i.e. $R_t = 0$. Assume also that this asset is a bond that yields the amount 1 at maturity $T$ if there is no default. Then the time-0 price of this bond is

$$E_{Q_0}\left[e^{-\int_0^T (r_s+h_s)\,ds}\right] \tag{8.10}$$

Notice how the default density $h_t$ acts as an increment over the default-free rate $r_t$. Of course, common sense tells us that a bond with default risk must pay the owner a higher interest rate $r_t + h_t$ as compensation for the risk of default.

The analysis carried out above gives a quantitative formulation of this commonsense notion, and gives an additional understanding of how the *spread* $h_s$, the additional interest rate one pays above the default-free rate, is related to *default risk*.

## CREDIT DEFAULT SWAPS: CDS

There are myriad, complex credit derivative products. The investigation of these instruments is outside our scope. We shall only take a quick look at one standard credit product, the *credit default swap* (CDS), but will not go into its pricing. The reason for choosing the CDS is that this is often effectively used as a substitute for a defaultable bond. A CDS protection buyer creates a type of synthetic short position in a bond with a suitable maturity, even though no actual bond for the given entity with that maturity may be available. For the CDS protection seller, it is a way to leverage exposure to the credit without any up-front payment.

A CDS is an agreement between two parties, the *protection seller* and *protection buyer*, that requires the protection buyer to pay a certain premium to the seller over a period of time in return for a guarantee that a certain asset, the *reference entity*, will not default during the given period. The premium paid is usually called the *spread* (not to be confused with the same term used in the preceding section), and is quoted as a percentage of the notional value of the reference entity.

To get a more concrete sense, let us consider a hypothetical example: suppose that the 5-year CDS spread for General Electric credit is quoted at 80bps (basis points; 1 basis point = .01%). A bank that is looking for a 5-year protection on $20 million dollars worth of GE credit will enter into a CDS agreement with a seller, say an insurance company. The bank will make quarterly payments of

$$\frac{1}{4} \times \frac{.01}{100} \times 80 \times \$20,000,000 = \$40,000$$

to the protection seller over the 5-year duration of the swap. In case of default during this period, the insurer must pay the bank the difference between $20 million and the bonds' prevailing recovery value at the credit event.

CDS contracts are standardized by the International Swaps and Derivatives Association (ISDA). Typical credit events for the reference entity covered include bankruptcy, restructuring, and failure to pay.

CHAPTER 9

# Forward Prices

A *forward agreement* is an instrument that allows a buyer to assure delivery of a desired asset on a future date at an agreed-upon price. Thus, for the buyer, it is a way to guard against an unaffordable rise in price of the needed asset. In this chapter we study the *forward price* of an asset, the price agreed upon at a given time, to be paid on a future date when delivery of the asset will take place.

There are two fundamental numeraires that we will use often:

**(i)** 1 unit of currency at time 0;

**(ii)** 1 unit of currency at time $t$.

We denote by $Q_t$ the probability measure corresponding to the numeraire (ii).

The conversion factor between time $s$-money and time $t$-money, in market scenario $\omega$, will be denoted

$$p(s, t; \omega)$$

This amount, placed in a money market account at time $s$, will evolve into unit cash at time $t$. As we have seen in the previous chapter, the price at time $s$ of the $t$-maturity bond, determined by all information up till time $s$, is

$$P(s,t) = E_{Q_s}[p(s,t)|\mathcal{F}_s] \tag{9.1}$$

If $Y_t$ is the random variable describing the price of an asset at time $t$, then, without having any special knowledge about the market,

$$E_{Q_t}[Y_t]$$

is the fair price of the asset, cash to be paid at time $t$, for the asset.

The fair price, again as cash to be paid at time $t$, based on information available up till time $s$ is

$$E_{Q_t}[Y_t|\mathcal{F}_s],$$

where $\mathcal{F}_s$ is the collection of all market events up till time $s$. This is the *forward price*, agreed upon at time $s$ but to be paid at time $t$ (in the future) in exchange for the asset:

$$\boxed{\text{FORWARD PRICE } F_s Y_t = E_{Q_t}[Y_t|\mathcal{F}_s]} \tag{9.2}$$

It will be convenient to assume that the values of all market variables are known with certainty at time 0, and so we take $\mathcal{F}_0$ to be all the events that either certainly hold (have probability 1) or certainly do not hold (have probability 0), for all $Q_t$. Then

$$E_{Q_t}(X|\mathcal{F}_0) = E_{Q_t}(X)$$

for any random variable $X$ (for which either side exists).

So the forward price decided at time 0 is

$$\boxed{F_0 Y_t = E_{Q_t}(Y_t)} \tag{9.3}$$

For this reason the measure $Q_t$ may be called the *forward measure*.

Let $P(0,t)$ be the fair price at time 0 for a $t$-maturity bond. The fair price, paid cash at time 0, for the asset (which will be delivered at time $t$) is

$$P(0,t)F_0Y_t$$

where $P(0,t)$ is the fair price at time 0 of a $t$-maturity bond. Because of the multiplier role it plays, the bond price $P(0,t)$ is also called a *discount factor*. Thus

$$\boxed{\text{fair present value} = \text{discount factor} \times \text{forward price}} \tag{9.4}$$

This is a very useful observation and we will spend some time examining it in different ways. It is both an example of the change of numeraire process and the fact that discounted prices are martingales.

Let us first see how the relation (9.4) is an example of the change-of-numeraire process discussed in Chapter 4.

The fair price $P(0,t)$ of the $t$-maturity bond is

$$P(0,t) = E_{Q_0}[p(0,t)] \tag{9.5}$$

The fair price, in terms of cash paid at time 0, for the asset worth $Y_t$ at time $t$ is

$$E_{Q_0}[p(0,t)Y_t] \tag{9.6}$$

Thus, putting everything together (more specifically, equations (9.2), (9.4), (9.5) and (9.6)), we have

$$E_{Q_t}(Y) = F_0Y = \frac{E_{Q_0}[p(0,t)Y]}{E_{Q_0}[p(0,t)]} \tag{9.7}$$

which is another way of stating (9.4). We have dropped the subscript $t$ to indicate that we intend (9.7) to be valid for any random variable $Y$ (for which either side is meaningful).

Let us do this in slightly greater generality. Consider two time instants $s$ and $t$, with $s \leq t$. Let

$$p(s,t;\omega) = \text{price at time } s \text{ of unit cash to be paid at time } t\text{, in scenario } \omega \qquad (9.8)$$

Consider an instrument whose worth/payoff at time $t$ in scenario $\omega$ is $Y(\omega)$ units of cash at time $t$. This is equivalent to

$$p(s,t;\omega)Y(\omega)$$

units of time-$s$ cash in market scenario $\omega$. Therefore, with no knowledge of the market state, the fair price of the instrument in terms of time-$s$ cash would be

$$E_{Q_s}[p(s,t)Y]$$

However, given full knowledge about the market up till time $s$, the fair price of the instrument in terms of time-$s$ cash is given by the random variable

$$Y_s = E_{Q_s}[p(s,t)Y \,|\, \mathcal{F}_s] \qquad (9.9)$$

Indeed, this is a form of the martingale property of prices studied in Chapter 7.

On the other hand, the fair price of the instrument in terms of time-$t$ cash, given $\mathcal{F}_s$, is the *forward price*

$$E_{Q_t}[Y \,|\, \mathcal{F}_s]$$

and the fair price of time-$t$ cash in terms of time-$s$ cash, given $\mathcal{F}_s$, is

$$P(s,t) = E_{Q_s}[p(s,t) | \mathcal{F}_s]$$

So viewed this way, the fair price of the instrument in terms of time-$s$ cash should be

$$Y_s = P(s,t)E_{Q_t}[Y \,|\, \mathcal{F}_s] \qquad (9.10)$$

which is the (discount factor) $\times$ (forward price) formula again.

Comparing the two expressions (9.9) and (9.10) for $Y_s$ we conclude:

$$\text{Forward price } F_s Y = E_{Q_t}[Y|\mathcal{F}_s] = \frac{E_{Q_s}[p(s,t)Y|\mathcal{F}_s]}{E_{Q_s}[p(s,t)|\mathcal{F}_s]} = \frac{Y_s}{P(s,t)} \tag{9.11}$$

whenever either side is meaningful.

Applying (9.10) to a $T$-maturity bond, we obtain the forward price

$$FP(s;t,T) = \frac{P(s,T)}{P(s,t)} \tag{9.12}$$

This can be rewritten as

$$P(s,T) = P(s,t)F\,P(s,T,) \tag{9.13}$$

which is, of course, a special case of

fair present value = discount factor × forward price

The strategy of transfering cash flows occurring at different points in time to one particular *focal point* in time is a very convenient technique in actuarial calculations.

CHAPTER 10

# Futures Prices

In a forward agreement, the party with the long position agrees to buy an asset at a preset price on a future date. A *futures* agreement has, at least in principle, a similar goal but the mechanism is quite different. Futures agreements are standardized exchange–traded instruments in which a vast market exists.

Before proceeding to the details, let us state in brief the contrast in the formulas for the forward and futures prices. Let $S_T$ denote the price of an asset at delivery time $T$. Then, with usual notation, the forward price, at time $t$, for the asset to be delivered at time $T$ is

$$\text{forward price } F_t S_T = E_{Q_T}[S_T \,|\, \mathcal{F}_t] \tag{10.1}$$

The *futures* price, at time $t$, for the same asset with delivery date $T$ is

$$\text{futures price } X_t = E_{Q_t}[S_T \,|\, \mathcal{F}_t] \tag{10.2}$$

Here we have taken an idealized futures agreement with continuous resettlement and assumed that the model for the interest rate market being used has some broad regularity properties. The "futures price" is actually not the price of any instrument but simply a moving marker associated with the futures agreement.

## THE FUTURES AGREEMENT

We now describe an idealized version of a typical futures agreement. The description here is abstracted from the many detailed qualifications that accompany a real futures agreement.

Suppose trader $A$ takes the *long position* in a futures agreement with trader $B$, whereby an asset will be delivered to $A$ by $B$ at a date $T$ in the future. The agreement proceeds as follows. At the initial date $t_0$, the "futures price" $X_0$ of the asset is noted. On the next day, date $t_1$, the futures price $X_1$ is noted, and $A$ receives the amount $X_1 - X_0$ from $B$ (if $X_1 < X_0$, this means $A$ pays $B$ the amount $X_0 - X_1$).

On the following day, date $t_2$, $A$ receives amount $X_2 - X_1$ from $B$, where $X_2$ is the "futures price" on that day. This proceeds until the terminal date $t_N = T$ of the agreement, when $A$ receives amount $X_N - X_{N-1}$ from $B$, where now $X_N = S(T)$, the price of the asset underlying the agreement on the date $t_N = T$. Thus, by the terminal date $T$, $A$ has received a total amount of

$$X_N - X_{N-1} + X_{N-1} - X_{N-2} + \cdots + X_1 - X_0 = S(T) - X_0$$

from $B$. On this date, $A$ can, if he or she so wishes, buy the asset for the price $S(T)$; so, through this futures agreement, $A$ is able to buy the asset on date $T$ for a total outlay of $S(T) - (S(T) - X_0)$, i.e., for a total outlay of $X_0$.

Thus, in this simplistic sense, the futures agreement made by $A$ at the initial time for the initial futures price $X_0$ allows $A$ to buy the asset at time $T$ for the amount $X_0$.

## FUTURES PRICES IN THE DISCRETE CASE

For a more careful analysis of the futures agreement, we look first at the cashflows for $A$:

| $t_0$ | $t_1$ | $t_2$ | | $t_N = T$ |
|---|---|---|---|---|
| | $X_1 - X_0$ ↓ | $X_2 - X_0$ ↓ | …… | $X_N - X_{N-1}$ with $X_N = S(T)$ ↓ |

The futures agreement can be terminated on any of the dates $t_1, \ldots, t_N$. Thus, for the agreement to be fair, the following conditions must hold:

$$\begin{aligned} E_{Q_{t_1}}[X_1 - X_0|\mathcal{F}_{t_0}] &= 0 \\ E_{Q_{t_2}}[X_2 - X_1|\mathcal{F}_{t_1}] &= 0 \\ \vdots \quad & \quad \vdots \\ E_{Q_{t_N}}[X_N - X_{N-1}|\mathcal{F}_{t_{N-1}}] &= 0 \end{aligned}$$

Solving these equations one by one, we obtain:

$$\begin{aligned} X_0 = E_{Q_{t_1}}[X_1|\mathcal{F}_{t_0}] &= \frac{E_{Q_{t_0}}[p(t_0, t_1)X_2|\mathcal{F}_{t_0}]}{E_{Q_{t_0}}[p(t_0, t_1)|\mathcal{F}_{t_0}]} \\ X_1 = E_{Q_{t_2}}[X_2|\mathcal{F}_{t_1}] &= \frac{E_{Q_{t_1}}[p(t_1, t_2)X_1|\mathcal{F}_{t_1}]}{E_{Q_{t_1}}[p(t_1, t_2)|\mathcal{F}_{t_1}]} \\ \vdots \quad \vdots & \\ X_{N-1} = E_{Q_{t_N}}[X_N|\mathcal{F}_{t_{N-1}}] &= \frac{E_{Q_{t_{N-1}}}[p(t_{N-1}, t_N)X_N|\mathcal{F}_{t_{N-1}}]}{E_{Q_{t_{N-1}}}[p(t_{N-1}, t_N)|\mathcal{F}_{t_{N-1}}]} \end{aligned}$$

and

$$X_N = S(T)$$

Thus, $X_0$ can be obtained by working "backward" from the price $S(T)$, the price at each step being the forward price of the quantity in the preceding step. Thus the futures price is obtained as an iteration of forward prices.

Though not a single simple formula, the above equations form a clear recipe for determining the futures price $X_0$.

## FUTURES PRICES IN THE CONTINUOUS CASE

Let us now consider the case of a futures agreement where the cash flows take place in continuous time. The claim then is that the futures price process is given by

$$X_t = E_{Q_0}[S(T)|\mathcal{F}_t] = E_{Q_t}[S(T)|\mathcal{F}_t] \tag{10.3}$$

The second equality above follows from

$$E_{Q_t}[S(T)|\mathcal{F}_t] = \frac{E_{Q_0}[p(0,t)S(T)|\mathcal{F}_t]}{E_{Q_0}[p(0,t)|\mathcal{F}_t]}$$

$$= \frac{p(0,t)E_{Q_0}[S(T)|\mathcal{F}_t]}{p(0,t)} \quad \text{since } p(0,t) \text{ is } \mathcal{F}_t\text{-measurable}$$

Note that there is no cost in entering into a futures agreement (at least in the idealization we are working in). Thus, whatever the process $t \mapsto X_t$ is, the total cash flow it generates should have present value equal to zero. Instead of deducing (10.3), we shall verify that if we take $X_t$ to be given by (10.3), then the present value of the total future cash flows is zero. Of course, we do need to set $X_T = S(T)$, the time-$T$ spot price of the asset/commodity underlying the futures agreement.

So assume $X_t$ is given by (10.3) with $X_T = S(T)$. Then $t \mapsto X_t$ is a martingale, i.e.

$$E_{Q_0}(X_t|\mathcal{F}_s) = X_s$$

for all $0 \le s \le t \le T$. Indeed, $X_t$ is uniquely determined by the condition that the process $t \mapsto X_t$ is a martingale relative to the family $\{\mathcal{F}_t\}_{t\ge 0}$ and the terminal value $X_T = S(T)$.

To obtain the present value of all future cash flows, first select a discretization $0 < t_1 < \cdots < t_N = T$ of the time interval $[0, T]$. At each time $t_j$ the amount $X_{t_j} - X_{t_{j-1}}$ is received; the present value of this cash flow is

$$p(0,t_j)\left(X_{t_j} - X_{t_{j-1}}\right)$$

The present value of all future cash flows is thus the limit of

$$V_0 = E_{Q_0}\left[\sum_{j=1}^{N} p(0,t_j)\left(X_{t_j} - X_{t_{j-1}}\right)\right]$$

as $\max_j(t_j - t_{j-1}) \to 0$.

Let $V_0'$ be the value obtained by putting $p(0,t_{j-1})$ instead of $p(0,t_j)$ in the above expression for $V_0$. Then

$$V_0' = 0$$

because

$$\begin{aligned} &E_{Q_0}\left[p(0,t_{j-1})(X_{t_j} - X_{t_{j-1}})\right] \\ &\quad = E_{Q_0}\left[E_{Q_0}\left(p(0,t_{j-1})(X_{t_j} - X_{t_{j-1}})|\mathcal{F}_{t_{j-1}}\right)\right] \\ &\quad = E_{Q_0}\left[p(0,t_{j-1})E_{Q_0}(X_{t_j} - X_{t_{j-1}}|\mathcal{F}_{t_{j-1}})\right] \\ &\quad = 0 \qquad \text{because } E_{Q_0}(X_{t_j}|\mathcal{F}_{t_{j-1}}) = X_{t_{j-1}} \end{aligned}$$

In all models of interest rate theory, the discount factor $p(0,t)$ is taken to be of the form

$$p(0,t) = e^{-\int_0^t r_s\,ds}$$

where $r_s$ is the (random variable representing the) spot interest rate at time $s$. Then, writing $\Delta t$ for $t_j - t_{j-1}$ we have

$$\left[p(0,t_j) - p(0,t_{j-1})\right]\left(X_{t_j} - X_{t_{j-1}}\right) \simeq c_{t_j}(\Delta t)(\Delta t)^{1/2}$$

for standard models. Thus, under reasonable conditions and for a broad class of models,

$$V_0 - V_0' \text{ goes to } 0 \text{ as } \max_j\{t_j - t_{j-1}\} \to 0.$$

Thus

$$V_0 = 0$$

and this is exactly what we needed.

CHAPTER 11

# Calls and Puts

Options are the most basic derivative instruments. A *call option* gives the right to buy an asset at a predetermined price, while a *put option* gives the right to sell at a predetermined price. As with any derivative instrument, options are bought and sold by two basic types of agents: those who use options for security and those, such as speculators and arbitrageurs, who are in the market for trading profits. Those seeking security use options as instruments of insurance to hedge against adverse price movements of assets they own.

A European *call option* on an asset, with strike $K$ and expiration date $T$, is an agreement between two parties, the *holder*, or *owner*, and the *writer*, whereby the holder has the right to buy the asset from the writer for the price $K$ on the date $T$. The writer is obliged to sell the asset under these conditions if the owner *exercises* the option. The price of the option is also called the *premium*. It is the amount one must pay to acquire the right to buy the underlying asset at the given strike and exercise date.

A European *put option* on an asset, with strike $K$ and expiration date $T$, is an agreement between two parties, the *holder*, or *owner*, and the *writer*, whereby the holder has the right to sell the asset to the writer for the price $K$ on the date $T$. The writer is obliged to buy the asset if the owner decides to *exercise* the option.

An *American option* is an option that can be exercised at any time before the expiration date $T$. A *Bermuda option* is one that can be exercised at any one of a finite set of dates.

Virtually all options we shall study are European, and we shall drop the qualifier "European," and simply use the terms "option," "call option," and "put option."

Our discussion has the aim of understanding the essential points, and so we deal with an idealized situation. For instance, we shall not include any consideration of transaction costs or taxes. Furthermore, for convenience of analysis, we will also assume that the asset generates no cash flow (such as a stock producing dividends or an asset paying rent) in the relevant period.

Our goal in this chapter is to derive the general price formulas for call and put options. For a call option on an asset with strike $K$, expiration date $t$, we shall show that

$$\boxed{\text{Call Option Price} = X_0 q_2 - e^{-rt} K q_1} \tag{11.1}$$

where $X_0$ is the present price of the asset, $r$ is the interest rate on the $t$-maturity bond, and $q_1$ and $q_2$ are two probabilities; specifically,

$$q_2 = Q_t^*[X(t) > K] \qquad \text{and} \qquad q_1 = Q_t[X(t) > K] \tag{11.2}$$

where $X(t)$ is the asset price at time $t$, $Q_t$ is the pricing measure for the time-$t$ cash numeraire, and $Q_t^*$ is the pricing measure when the numeraire is the underlying asset deliverable at time $t$. A similar formula (11.18) holds for a put option.

After reading this chapter the reader may wish to read Chapter 17 for a model-specific computation of option prices.

## OPTIONS: A CLOSER LOOK

In this section we shall take a close look at option concepts by means of an example. Our example will focus on call options.

As mentioned earlier, an option of the type we are considering here is specified by:

- A strike price for the underlying asset;
- An expiration date.

Each option has a symbol, just as each traded company has a symbol. The option symbol is made up of the company symbol, along with suffixes indicating the month of expiration and the strike level. A table of prices of options on a company will list the company name and symbol, the price of the stock itself, along with a list of active options, given with their specifications. The price data will show, along with the price from the last trade, bid prices and ask prices.

Table 11-1 shows prices, on September 17, 2004, of call options on Google at various strikes, with expiration in December, 2004. The second column lists the last trading price for the option. The option symbol GOQLB consists of the *root* GOQ, which

**TABLE 11-1**

Google Call Options at 9:17am ET on September 17, 2004, with Expiration December 17, 2004.
Stock Price: $117.49.

| Symbols | Last Trade | Bid | Ask | Strike |
|---|---|---|---|---|
| GOQLT | 19.00 | 20.70 | 21.10 | 100.00 |
| GOQLA | 15.80 | 17.00 | 17.40 | 105.00 |
| GOQLB | 13.80 | 13.60 | 13.90 | 110.00 |
| GOQLC | 10.60 | 10.60 | 10.90 | 115.00 |
| GOQLD | 8.10 | 8.10 | 8.30 | 120.00 |
| GOQLE | 5.20 | 5.90 | 6.10 | 125.00 |

refers to Google, the letter L, which signifies a call option expiring in December, and the letter B indicating that the strike price is of the form $\times 10$.

Notice that only certain strike prices are available. The expiration date on the options shown in Table 11-1 is December 17, but expiration dates in each of the months September through January were available.

The last two rows of the table describe calls with strikes above the current share price of \$117.49. These options are *in the money*. Exercising such an option would yield an immediate positive cash flow (however, we will see below that it is not worth exercising). The top four rows are calls with strikes lower than the prevailing share price. These are *out of the money* options. They are worthless in terms of immediate exercise payoff, but still command good premiums because the prospective call buyers clearly expect the share price to rise.

The excess of the premium over the immediate cash payoff from exercising the option (or viewing it as worthless, if it is out of the money) is the *time value* of the option, reflecting how much the stock is expected to appreciate till the expiration date. Of course, an important factor in deciding the time value of the option is the volatility of the underlying stock.

A trader wishing to buy one option contract of 100 December calls with strike \$110.00 may agree to pay the asking premium of \$13.90 per call. Ignoring interest, this would correspond to buying the stock at \$123.90 on December 17. Because the September 17th price is only \$117.49, the option buyer clearly expects the stock to perform very well, at least till the December expiration date.

About a week later, on September 23, the same option has a bid price of \$16.10. Thus, the opinion on the stock's performance has gone up. The call holder could sell off the option, making a \$220 profit minus brokerage fees and taxes, or continue till an even better day.

Let us look at the price of the call options with strike \$110 on various expiration months. This is illustrated in Table 11-2.

**TABLE 11-2**

Google Call Options, with strike $110, at 9:17am ET on September 17, 2004.
Stock Price: $117.49.

| Symbol | Last Trade | Expiration |
|---|---|---|
| GOQIB | 7.40 | September 17 |
| GOQJB | 9.90 | October 15 |
| GOQLB | 13.80 | December 17 |

Notice that for these calls, all having the same strike:

*The call with later expiration has a higher premium.* (11.3)

We shall derive this later in (11.37) as a general feature of call prices.

These considerations show us that, ignoring the interest rate, it makes sense to

*compare "Premium + Strike Price" with*
*the Current Price of the Stock*

There is a slightly different way to look at this:

*compare Premium with*
*Current Price of the Stock − Strike Price*

Examination of Table 11-1 shows that the premium is always strictly greater than the excess of current share price over the strike:

$$\text{Call Price} > \text{Asset Price} - \text{Strike Price} \tag{11.4}$$

We shall go through a conceptual and mathematical derivation of this relationship later in (11.31).

The inequality (11.4) has an important operational significance: the call option is worth more than the proceeds of exercising the option. Thus, there is no sense in exercising the option:

**TABLE 11–3**

Google September Call Options on Expiration Date September 17, 2004.
Stock Price: \$117.49.

| Symbol | Last Trade | Bid | Ask | Strike |
|---|---|---|---|---|
| GOQIT | 15.90 | 17.10 | 17.40 | 100.00 |
| GOQIA | 12.40 | 12.10 | 12.30 | 105.00 |
| GOQIB | 7.40 | 7.20 | 7.30 | 110.00 |
| GOQIC | 2.30 | 2.30 | 2.35 | 115.00 |
| GOQID | 0.05 | N/A | 0.05 | 120.00 |
| GOQIE | 0.05 | N/A | 0.05 | 125.00 |

one should simply sell it, if one doesn't want to hold it till expiration. Thus, *the call option is not exercised prior to the expiration time*.

The preceding observation naturally raises the question of how prices look on the option expiration day. As an illustration, we look again at Google options on Friday, September 17, 2004, which expire on this day. See Table 11-3.

This being the last trading day of this option, it is no surprise that the premium is pretty much equal to the excess of the stock price over the strike. We also see that there are no buyers for the out-of-the-money calls GOQID and GOQIE.

## CALL PRICE

Consider a call option on a security $X$, with strike $K$ and expiration date $t$. We denote the price of the security at any time $s$ by $X(s)$.

If the price $X(t)$ at expiration is greater than the strike $K$, then it is worthwhile for the option holder to exercise the option, which would result in ownership of the asset worth $X(t)$ for a lower–than–market price of $K$. Thus, if $X(t) > K$ then the option is exercised resulting in receipt of the asset for a cash outflow amount $K$ (in practice, the option holder might simply receive the amount $X(t) - K$ from the option writer). If $X(t) \leq K$, then there is no point exercising the option and it is worth 0.

Thus the call option is a sum of two instruments (I) and (II):

**(I)** Receive one unit of the security at time $t$ if its price $X(t)$ exceeds $K$, and nothing otherwise;

**(II)** Pay amount $K$ at time $t$ if $X(t) > K$, and nothing otherwise.

Let $Q_t$ be the pricing probability measure when the numeraire is unit cash at time $t$, and let $Q_0$ be the pricing measure for time-0 cash numeraire. Let $Q_t^*$ be the probability measure when the numeraire is the asset itself at time $t$. As always, *pricing measure* means a probability measure used to determine prices; for example, it might be the market equilibrium measure in some model for the market.

By definition of the forward measure $Q_t^*$,

$$\text{forward value of (I)} = Q_t^*[X(t) > K] \text{ units of the asset at time } t$$

where $[X(t) > K]$ denotes the event that the price $X(t)$ exceeds $K$. The forward price of the asset at time $t$ is

$$FX_t = E_{Q_t}[X_t] = X_0/P(0,t) \tag{11.5}$$

units of time-$t$ cash, using the definition of forward price and also our old observation that present value equals discount factor $P(0,t)$ times forward price $FX_t$ (see equations (9.3) and (9.11). So:

$$\text{forward value of (I)} = (FX_t)Q_t^*[X(t) > K] \text{ in cash at time } t$$

On the other hand,

$$\text{forward value of instrument (II) is } -KQ_t[X(t) > K]$$
$$\text{units of time-}t\text{ cash.}$$

Thus the forward price of the call option in terms of the time-$t$ cash is

$$\text{forward price of the call option} = (FX_t)q_2 - Kq_1 \tag{11.6}$$

where

$$q_2 = Q_t^*[X(t) > K] \qquad \text{and} \qquad q_1 = Q_t[X(t) > K] \quad (11.7)$$

Converting to time-0 cash, we obtain the present value of the call option as

$$\boxed{\text{Call Price} = P(0,t)\,[(FX_t)q_2 - Kq_1]} \quad (11.8)$$

Because the forward price $FX_t$ equals $X_0/P(0,t)$ we can write this also as:

$$\boxed{\text{Call Price} = X_0 q_2 - P(0,t)Kq_1 = X_0 q_2 - e^{-rt}Kq_1} \quad (11.9)$$

where $r$ is the interest rate on the $t$-maturity bond specified by the relation

$$P(0,t) = e^{-rt} \quad (11.10)$$

Note that this simply specifies the $t$-period interest rate at time 0, and does not mean that we are assuming that the interest rate remains constant.

We could also have worked with $[X(t) \geq K]$, and this would give us a slightly different formula:

$$\text{Call Price} = P(0,t)\left[(FX_t)q_2' - Kq_1'\right] \quad (11.11)$$

where

$$q_2' = Q_t^*[X(t) \geq K] \qquad \text{and} \qquad q_1' = Q_t[X(t) \geq K] \quad (11.12)$$

It is a good exercise to verify that the right sides in (11.8) and (11.11) are in fact equal.

The probability $q_2$ can be expressed in terms of $Q_t$ using the numeraire conversion procedure studied in Chapter 4. Specifically, equation (4.4) allows us to obtain:

$$q_2 = \frac{E_{Q_t}\left(X_t 1_{[X_t > K]}\right)}{E_{Q_t}(X_t)} \quad (11.13)$$

Since the denominator here is the forward price $FX_t$, we have

$$\text{Call Price} = P(0,t)\left(E_{Q_t}\left(X_t 1_{[X_t>K]}\right) - Kq_1\right) \qquad (11.14)$$

Changing the numeraire to time-0 cash gives the expression

$$\text{Call Price} = E_{Q_0}\left(p(0,t)X_t 1_{[X_t>K]}\right) - KE_{Q_0}\left(p(0,t)1_{[X_t>K]}\right) \qquad (11.15)$$

## PUT PRICE

A *put option*, with exercise date $t$ and strike $K$, is exercised if the time-$t$ price $X(t)$ of the underlying is below the strike $K$ and is allowed to expire worthless if $X(t) \geq K$. Reasoning as we did for call options, we have:

$$\begin{aligned}\text{Forward price of the put option} &= KQ_t[X(t) < K] \\ &\quad -(FX_t)Q_t^*[X(t) < K] \qquad (11.16)\end{aligned}$$

Converting to time-0 cash:

$$\begin{aligned}\text{Put Price} &= P(0,t)(KQ_t[X(t) < K] \\ &\quad -(FX_t)Q_t^*[X(t) < K]) \qquad (11.17)\end{aligned}$$

As with the call option price, we can rewrite this as:

$$\boxed{\text{Put Price} = e^{-rt}KQ_t[X(t) < K] - X_0 Q_t^*[X(t) < K]} \qquad (11.18)$$

where $r$ is the interest rate on the $t$-maturity bond.

The strict inequality can be replaced by an inequality:

$$\text{Put Price} = P(0,t)(KQ_t[X(t) \leq K] - (FX_t)Q_t^*[X(t) \leq K]) \qquad (11.19)$$

Converting $Q_t^*$ to $Q_t$ gives:

$$\text{Put Price} = P(0,t)\left(KQ_t[X(t) < K] - E_{Q_t}\left[X(t)1_{[X(t)<K]}\right]\right) \qquad (11.20)$$

## PUT-CALL PARITY

Consider call and put options having the same strike $K$ and expiration date $t$. Intuitively, it is clear that if $K$ is less than the forward price $FX_t$ then the call is more likely to be exercised than the put and so should be worth more. On the other hand, if $K > FX_t$, then the put is more likely to yield a profit than a call. Using the formulas for the put and call prices, we see that this is indeed the case; in fact, we have the following relation between call and put prices for the same strike $K$ and expiration $t$:

$$\text{Call Price} - \text{Put Price} = P(0,t)[FX_t - K] \tag{11.21}$$

We can rewrite this relationship in words as:

$$\begin{aligned}\text{Put Price} = {} & \text{Call Price} - \text{Asset Price} \\ & + \text{Present Value of Strike Price}\end{aligned} \tag{11.22}$$

Consider now *at-the-money options*, i.e., options with strike equal to the forward price. This means that the current asset price equals the present value of the strike. Because the forward price $FX_t$ is the expected price at the relevant date $t$, surely the price of a call with strike $K = FX_t$ expiring $t$ should be the same as the price of a put with the same strike and expiration. Indeed, the formulas (11.21) and (11.22) yield the *put-call parity* relation:

$$\boxed{\text{Call Price} = \text{Put Price}, \qquad \text{for at-the-money options}} \tag{11.23}$$

## ANOTHER PROOF OF THE OPTION PRICE FORMULA

It will be useful to look at a more standard way to write down the prices of calls and puts.

Consider a call option with strike $K$ and expiration $t$ on an asset whose price at any time $s$ is $X_s$. If at time $t$, the price $X_t$

exceeds $K$, then the option is exercised and the owner receives the underlying worth $X_t$ for a price of only $K$. Thus, if $X_t > K$, then the call is exercised and, effectively, it results in a cash inflow of $X_t - K$. If $X_t$ is less than $K$, then the option is not exercised and the cash flow is 0. Thus the cash inflow resulting from the option at time $t$ is

$$\{X_t - K\}_+$$

where the notation $y_+$ is defined by

$$y_+ = \begin{cases} y & \text{if } y \geq 0 \\ 0 & \text{if } y \leq 0 \end{cases}$$

So the forward price of the call is

$$E_{Q_t}[\{X_t - K\}_+] \tag{11.24}$$

The price at time 0 should therefore be

$$\begin{aligned} \text{Call Price} &= P(0,t)E_{Q_t}[\{X_t - K\}_+] \\ &= E_{Q_0}[p(0,t)\{X_t - K\}_+] \end{aligned} \tag{11.25}$$

Similarly, the put price is

$$\begin{aligned} \text{Put Price} &= P(0,t)E_{Q_t}[\{K - X_t\}_+] \\ &= E_{Q_0}[p(0,t)\{K - X_t\}_+] \end{aligned} \tag{11.26}$$

## OPTION PRICE INEQUALITIES

Earlier in this chapter, we made several empirical observations concerning prices of call options. In this section we shall establish these and other inequalities between option prices on theoretical grounds, arguing both conceptually and mathematically. These inequalities originate in Merton's elegant classic [31], which we follow in some respects.

We are considering options on an underlying asset whose value is positive.

We work with call options, but a similar discussion can be carried out with puts.

The call price formula (11.25) shows that the forward price of a call with strike $K$ and expiration $T$ is given by

$$E_{Q_T}[\{X_T - K\}_+],$$

where $X_T$ is the time-$T$ price of the underlying asset.

Now, for fixed $X_T$, the function $g$ given by

$$g(K) = \{X_T - K\}_+ = \begin{cases} X_T - K & \text{if } K \leq X_T \\ 0 & \text{otherwise.} \end{cases}$$

has as graph a downward-sloping line that flattens out once it hits the zero level. Thus, $g$ is a *convex* function, in the sense that

$$g(\lambda K + (1-\lambda)K') \leq \lambda g(K) + (1-\lambda)g(K'),$$

for all $K, K'$ and $\lambda \in [0, 1]$. Taking the expectation, we get

$$E_{Q_T}[g(\lambda K + (1-\lambda)K')] \leq \lambda E_{Q_T}[g(K)] + (1-\lambda)E_{Q_T}[g(K')],$$

which shows that the forward call price, viewed as a function of $K$, is convex. Multiplying by the discount factor $P(0, T)$ proves then that, for a fixed maturity date,

| *The Call Price is a convex function of the strike.* | (11.27) |
|---|---|

Looking back again at the function $g$, observe that it is a monotone decreasing function:

$$\text{If } K_1 \leq K_2 \text{ then } g(K_1) \geq g(K_2)$$

Slapping on the expected values, we see then that

$$\boxed{C(K_1) \geq C(K_2) \textit{ if } K_1 \leq K_2} \qquad (11.28)$$

This fact is eminently clear from common sense: *the right to buy the asset at a lower price should require a higher premium.*

more difficult to analyze. However, as we shall verify in this section, it turns out that there is essentially no difference between American and European *call* options. The case of put options is quite different.

Consider then an American call option with strike $K$, expiration $T$. Let $X_t$ denote the time-$t$ price of the underlying asset. The holder may choose to exercise the option at some time $\tau(\omega)$, as determined by the market scenario $\omega$, to the extent it is visible until the time of exercise. The payoff upon exercise will be

$$X_{\tau(\omega)}(\omega) - K$$

We may as well take the positive part, since there will surely be no exercise if the above value is negative. Converting to time-0 cash we get

$$p(0, \tau(\omega))\left(X_{\tau(\omega)}(\omega) - K\right)_+$$

king the expectation value, we have

$$E_{Q_0}\left(p(0, \tau)(X_\tau - K)_+\right)$$

the exercise time $\tau$ has to be chosen so as to maximize this:

$$\text{merican Call Price} = \max_{\tau} E_{Q_0}\left[p(0, \tau)(X_\tau - K)_+\right] \quad (11.33)$$

ximum here runs over all *stopping times* $\tau$, i.e., a random
time such that whether $\tau(\omega)$ is $\leq t$ is determined entirely
edge of the market up till time $t$. See Chapter 25 for a
se formulation of the notion of stopping time.

is a similar price for a put option.

sider options on an underlying asset whose value is

l examination of the American call reveals a re-
ervation (from Merton [31]): *an American call is*
*prior to the expiration date, and is thus effectively*
*European call, and, in particular, has the same*
*pean call* with same strike and expiration date.



We can do a little better than the preceding inequality. Observe that the slope of the graph of $g$ lies between $-1$ and 0:

$$\frac{g(K_2) - g(K_1)}{K_2 - K_1} \in [-1, 0]$$

Thus, if $K_1 \leq K_2$ then:

$$g(K_1) - g(K_2) \leq K_2 - K_1$$

Taking expected values, and then multiplying by the discount factor $P(0, T)$ to transfer the cash flow focal point to time 0, we see that

$$\boxed{C(K_1) - C(K_2) \leq P(0, T)[K_2 - K_1], \ \textit{if } K_1 \leq K_2.} \quad (11.29)$$

Thus, if the strike of a call is lowered by amount $x$, keeping maturity constant, then the excess premium needed is at most the amount $x$, discounted to time-0.

Next, we examine the inequality

$$\boxed{C + P(0, T)K \geq X_0} \quad (11.30)$$

where $C$ is the time-0 price of a call option with strike $K$ and maturity $T$, $X_0$ is the time-0 price of the asset (which is assumed not to pay dividends), and $P(0, T)$ is the usual discount factor. We shall prove the inequality first by a commonsense argument, and then by mathematical reasoning.

Suppose at time 0 we buy the call option, along with a bond that will yield amount $K$ at maturity date $T$. The options costs $C$, while the bond requires a cash outflow at time 0 of

$$P(0, T)K,$$

because $P(0, T)$ is the discount factor. Thus, the total initial outlay for this will be:

$$C + P(0, T)K$$

With this portfolio we are assured we can purchase the asset on date $T$ with no additional funds needed. For, if on date $T$ the asset price is lower than the strike $K$, then we can simply use the proceeds from the bond to buy the asset; if, on the other hand, the asset price on date $T$ is at or above the strike $K$, then we exercise the option and call in the asset using the amount $K$ from the proceeds of our bond. Thus, the portfolio is definitely going to be worth at least the asset, and possibly more, on the date $T$. Hence, its worth at time 0 has to be at least the price $X_0$ of the asset. This establishes the inequality (11.30). The "commonsense" argument we have used here is really a case of the principle of no-arbitrage.

Next, we verify (11.30) again, this time using the call price formula. We have

$$\begin{aligned} C &= P(0,T)E_{Q_T}\left[(X_T - K)_+\right] \\ &\geq P(0,T)E_{Q_T}\left[X_T - K\right] \qquad \text{because } y_+ \geq y, \text{ for all } y \in \mathbf{R} \\ &= P(0,T)E_{Q_T}(X_T) - P(0,T)K \\ &= X_0 - P(0,T)K, \end{aligned}$$

where, in the last step, we used the fact that the present value $X_0$ is the discount factor $P(0,T)$ times the forward price $E_{Q_T}(X_T)$.

Let $T > 0$. Now suppose, as is eminently reasonable, that interest rates are positive. This implies, in particular, that the bond price $P(0,T)$ is strictly less than 1:

$$P(0,T) < 1 \text{ if the } T\text{-period interest rate is} > 0$$

The inequality (11.30) then implies the strict inequality

$$C + K > X_0, \text{ if the interest rate over } [0,T] \text{ is positive.} \tag{11.31}$$

We have seen an empirical illustration of this earlier in (11.4).

Let us now understand the inequality (11.31) in a conceptual way. Consider, at time 0, buying the call for amount $C$, along



with a $T$-maturity bond with initial deposit of amount $K$. Then, at time $T$, if the asset price is at or below the strike $K$, then the call expires worthless, and our portfolio is worth the bond's matured value, an amount strictly greater than the initial deposit $K$; in particular, *the portfolio is worth strictly more than the asset*. On the other hand, if at time $T$ the asset is worth more than $K$, then we can exercise the call, paying amount $K$ from the proceeds of the matured bond, and end up with both the asset and the remaining positive amount from the bond proceeds. Thus, *no matter what happens, at time $T$ our portfolio would b worth strictly more than the asset*. Therefore, of course, the pr folio should be worth strictly more than the asset at time well, and this is precisely the inequality (11.31). This is a "commonsense" argument, which is an application of th ple of no-arbitrage.

Observe that the strict inequality (11.31) requir strictly greater than 0 (this was the harmless-loo $T > 0$ we had put in earlier). Thus, *the inequality at any time prior to the expiration of the option*

Finally, we also have the inequality

$$X_0 \geq C$$

which just says that there is no point in to buy an asset than the worth of th asset itself isn't worth a negative a mathematically, observe first tha

$$y \geq (y - K)_+, i$$

and then put $X_T$ in place o

## THE AMERICAN C

Recall that an Amer been studying in t time prior to the ex

To see this, recall our *strict* inequality (11.31) about the European call price:

$$\text{European Call Price} + \text{Strike} > \text{Asset Price}, \qquad (11.34)$$

at any time *prior* to the option expiration date. This was derived assuming positive interest rates prevail.

Now consider a "live" American call at any time prior to the expiration date. Of course, it is worth at least as much as the corresponding European call. Then, using (11.34), we have:

$$\text{American Call Price} + \text{Strike} > \text{Asset Price}, \qquad (11.35)$$

at any time prior to the option expiration date.

Therefore,

$$\text{American Call Price} > \text{Asset Price} - \text{Strike}, \qquad (11.36)$$

at any time prior to the option expiration date.

Now observe that the right side in (11.36) is the amount that would be realized upon exercising the call. Thus, the preceding inequality says that *at any time prior to the expiration date, the American call itself is worth more than the value that would be realized on exercising it.*

In the words of Merton [31], the option is worth more "alive" than "dead." Thus, *an American call will not be exercised prior to the expiration date, and hence is equivalent to a European call.* In particular, the American call has the same price as the European call.

Note that we have used the assumption that interest rates are strictly positive over the life of the option, and that the underlying asset pays no dividends.

We have then, under the preceding hypotheses, another inequality to add to those we considered in the preceding section:

$$\boxed{C_{T_2} \geq C_{T_1} \text{ if } T_2 \geq T_1,} \qquad (11.37)$$

where $C_{T_j}$ is the price of a call expiring at time $T_j$, on a common underlying asset. We had seen a practical example of this earlier in (11.3). Viewed as an inequality for European call prices, the reason for the inequality is not apparent. Yet, viewed as an inequality between American call prices, this is eminently reasonable: the call with the later expiration "contains," as a "subinstrument," the call with the earlier expiration, and hence must cost at least as much.

# CHAPTER 12
# Forward Rate

We have discussed in earlier sections the notion of *forward price* for an asset: this is the price agreed upon today but to be paid at a future date in return for delivery of an asset. A company planning to purchase some asset at a known future date may lock in a price using a forward agreement. A typical situation involves purchase of an asset in a foreign currency, in which case the buyer may also want to enter into a currency forward agreement, to secure an acceptable exchange rate. Of course, if the spot price on the future date turns out to be actually lower than the originally agreed-upon forward price, then the buyer of the forward will have incurred a loss.

In this chapter we are concerned with forward agreements for bonds. When the underlying asset is a bond, the forward price essentially corresponds to delivery, at the future date, of an implied interest rate. This rate is the corresponding *forward rate*, and the transaction is called a *forward rate agreement*. Our task in the chapter is to determine formulas for fair forward rates in terms of bond prices.

Consider a bond to be purchased at time $t$, and maturing at a later date $t + \tau$. The cash flow structure, as seen by the owner of the bond, is:

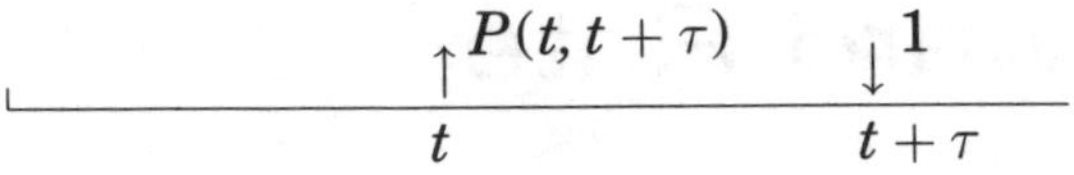

$$\underset{t}{\uparrow P(t,t+\tau)} \qquad\qquad \underset{t+\tau}{\downarrow 1}$$

By definition of $P(t, t+\tau)$, this is a fair cash flow at time $t$ and so has worth 0 at time $t$, and so of course also prior to time $t$.

Scaling the initial payment, we see that the following cash flow also has worth 0 at time $\leq t$:

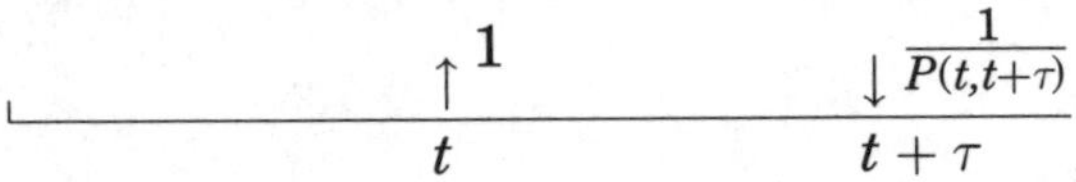

$$\underset{t}{\uparrow 1} \qquad\qquad \underset{t+\tau}{\downarrow \frac{1}{P(t,t+\tau)}}$$

It is useful to write the final cash inflow as a sum

$$\frac{1}{P(t,t+\tau)} = \text{principal} + \text{interest} = 1 + \frac{1-P(t,t+\tau)}{P(t,t+\tau)}$$

So we write the fair cash flow as:

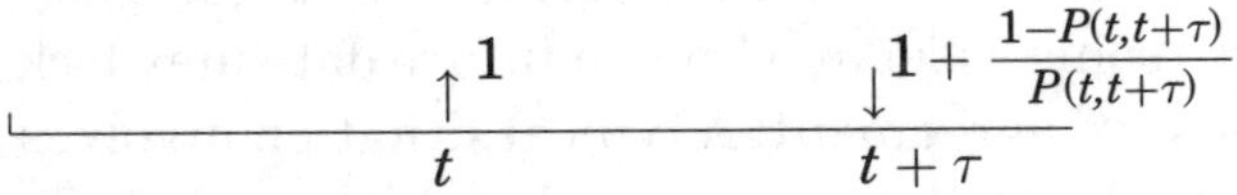

$$\underset{t}{\uparrow 1} \qquad\qquad \underset{t+\tau}{\downarrow 1 + \frac{1-P(t,t+\tau)}{P(t,t+\tau)}}$$

This has worth 0 at all times $\leq t$.

Thus, over the period $[t, t+\tau]$ the interest, as observed at time $t$, is

$$r = \frac{1}{P(t,t+\tau)} - 1, \tag{12.1}$$

on the nominal amount 1.

Written in terms of $r$, we have the fair cash flow

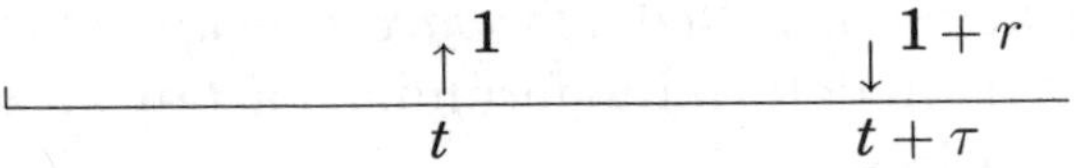

$$\underset{t}{\uparrow 1} \qquad\qquad \underset{t+\tau}{\downarrow 1+r}$$

This has worth 0 at times $\leq t$.

Consequently, by "diagram algebra," we have the following equality (in the sense that these cashflows have equal value at time $\leq t$):

$$\underset{t}{\uparrow^{0}} \qquad \underset{t+\tau}{\downarrow^{r}} \quad = \quad \underset{t}{\downarrow^{1}} \qquad \underset{t+\tau}{\uparrow^{1}}$$

Looking at the picture on the right and discounting to obtain present values, we see that the fair present value, at time 0, of this instrument is

$$P(0,t) - P(0,t+\tau) \tag{12.2}$$

We shall do this again in a more technical way. The fair present value, at time 0, of the instrument is

$$E_{Q_0}[p(0,t+\tau)r] = E_{Q_0}\left[p(0,t+\tau)\left\{\frac{1-P(t,t+\tau)}{P(t,t+\tau)}\right\}\right] \tag{12.3}$$

which is equal to

$$E_{Q_0}\left[p(0,t+\tau)\left\{\frac{1}{P(t,t+\tau)}\right\}\right] - P(0,t+\tau) \tag{12.4}$$

Working out the first term we have, on converting from $Q_0$ to $Q_t$ :

$$E_{Q_0}\left[p(0,t+\tau)\frac{1}{P(t,t+\tau)}\right] = E_{Q_0}\left[p(0,t)\frac{1}{P(t,t+\tau)}p(t,t+\tau)\right]$$

$$= P(0,t)E_{Q_t}\left[\frac{1}{P(t,t+\tau)}p(t,t+\tau)\right]$$

We can now use conditional expectation to the intermediate time $t$ to obtain

$$\begin{aligned} E_{Q_0}&\left[p(0,t+\tau)\frac{1}{P(t,t+\tau)}\right] \\ &= P(0,t)E_{Q_t}\left[\frac{1}{P(t,t+\tau)}E_{Q_t}[p(t,t+\tau)|\mathcal{F}_t]\right] \\ &= P(0,t)E_{Q_t}\left[\frac{1}{P(t,t+\tau)}P(t,t+\tau)\right] \\ &= P(0,t) \end{aligned} \tag{12.5}$$

Thus, going back to (12.4), the present value of the instrument is indeed

$$P(0,t) - P(0,t+\tau)$$

as seen earlier in (12.2).

Since the cash flow $r$ occurs at time $t+\tau$, dividing by the discount factor $P(0,t+\tau)$ gives the *forward price* of the instrument:

$$\frac{P(0,t) - P(0,t+\tau)}{P(0,t+\tau)}$$

Dividing numerator and denominator by $P(0,t)$ turns this into:

$$\frac{1 - FP(t,t+\tau)}{FP(t,t+\tau)},$$

where

$$FP(s,t) = \frac{P(0,t)}{P(0,s)}$$

is the forward price of a $t$-maturity bond at time $s$.

Recall that the instrument is designed to pay at time $t+\tau$ the $\tau$-period zero-coupon-bond yield/interest-rate (scaled to unit

We can now use conditional expectation to the intermediate time $t$ to obtain

$$
\begin{aligned}
E_{Q_0}&\left[p(0,t+\tau)\frac{1}{P(t,t+\tau)}\right] \\
&= P(0,t)E_{Q_t}\left[\frac{1}{P(t,t+\tau)}E_{Q_t}[p(t,t+\tau)|\mathcal{F}_t]\right] \\
&= P(0,t)E_{Q_t}\left[\frac{1}{P(t,t+\tau)}P(t,t+\tau)\right] \\
&= P(0,t) \qquad (12.5)
\end{aligned}
$$

Thus, going back to (12.4), the present value of the instrument is indeed

$$P(0,t) - P(0,t+\tau)$$

as seen earlier in (12.2).

Since the cash flow $r$ occurs at time $t+\tau$, dividing by the discount factor $P(0,t+\tau)$ gives the *forward price* of the instrument:

$$\frac{P(0,t) - P(0,t+\tau)}{P(0,t+\tau)}$$

Dividing numerator and denominator by $P(0,t)$ turns this into:

$$\frac{1 - FP(t,t+\tau)}{FP(t,t+\tau)},$$

where

$$FP(s,t) = \frac{P(0,t)}{P(0,s)}$$

is the forward price of a $t$-maturity bond at time $s$.

Recall that the instrument is designed to pay at time $t+\tau$ the $\tau$-period zero-coupon-bond yield/interest-rate (scaled to unit

Consequently, by "diagram algebra," we have the following equality (in the sense that these cashflows have equal value at time $\leq t$):

$$\underset{t}{\uparrow 0} \qquad \underset{t+\tau}{\downarrow r} \quad = \quad \underset{t}{\downarrow 1} \qquad \underset{t+\tau}{\uparrow 1}$$

Looking at the picture on the right and discounting to obtain present values, we see that the fair present value, at time 0, of this instrument is

$$P(0,t) - P(0,t+\tau) \tag{12.2}$$

We shall do this again in a more technical way. The fair present value, at time 0, of the instrument is

$$E_{Q_0}[p(0,t+\tau)r] = E_{Q_0}\left[p(0,t+\tau)\left\{\frac{1-P(t,t+\tau)}{P(t,t+\tau)}\right\}\right] \tag{12.3}$$

which is equal to

$$E_{Q_0}\left[p(0,t+\tau)\left\{\frac{1}{P(t,t+\tau)}\right\}\right] - P(0,t+\tau) \tag{12.4}$$

Working out the first term we have, on converting from $Q_0$ to $Q_t$ :

$$\begin{aligned} E_{Q_0}\left[p(0,t+\tau)\frac{1}{P(t,t+\tau)}\right] &= E_{Q_0}\left[p(0,t)\frac{1}{P(t,t+\tau)}p(t,t+\tau)\right] \\ &= P(0,t)E_{Q_t}\left[\frac{1}{P(t,t+\tau)}p(t,t+\tau)\right] \end{aligned}$$

of thc bond, is:

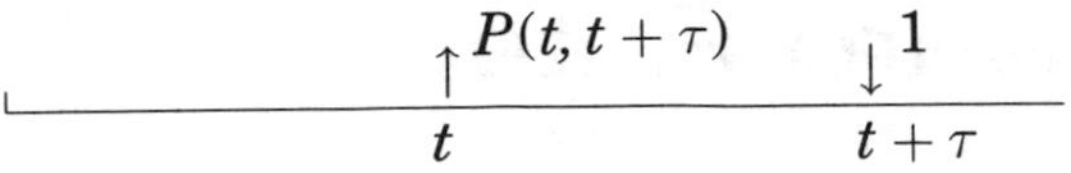

$$\begin{array}{c|c} \uparrow P(t,t+\tau) & \downarrow 1 \\ \hline t & t+\tau \end{array}$$

By definition of $P(t, t+\tau)$, this is a fair cash flow at time $t$ and so has worth 0 at time $t$, and so of course also prior to time $t$.

Scaling the initial payment, we see that the following cash flow also has worth 0 at time $\leq t$:

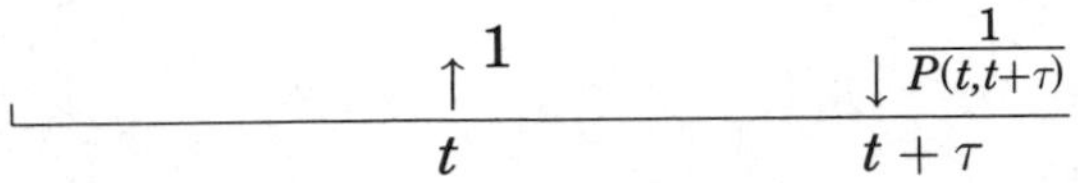

$$\begin{array}{c|c} \uparrow 1 & \downarrow \frac{1}{P(t,t+\tau)} \\ \hline t & t+\tau \end{array}$$

It is useful to write the final cash inflow as a sum

$$\frac{1}{P(t,t+\tau)} = \text{principal} + \text{interest} = 1 + \frac{1-P(t,t+\tau)}{P(t,t+\tau)}$$

So we write the fair cash flow as:

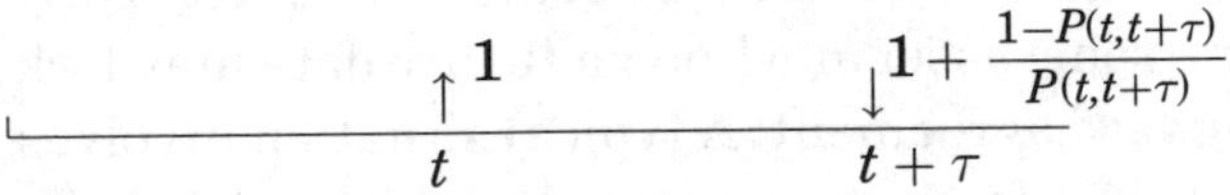

$$\begin{array}{c|c} \uparrow 1 & \downarrow 1 + \frac{1-P(t,t+\tau)}{P(t,t+\tau)} \\ \hline t & t+\tau \end{array}$$

This has worth 0 at all times $\leq t$.

Thus, over the period $[t, t+\tau]$ the interest, as observed at time $t$, is

$$r = \frac{1}{P(t,t+\tau)} - 1, \tag{12.1}$$

on the nominal amount 1.

Written in terms of $r$, we have the fair cash flow

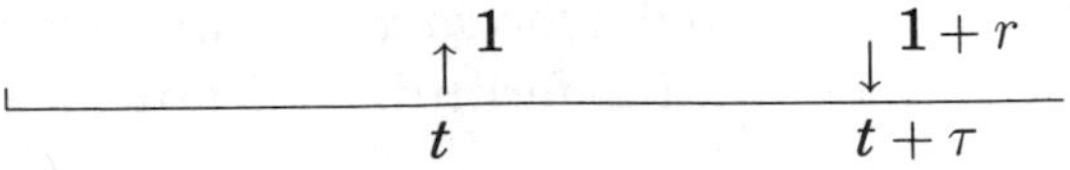

$$\begin{array}{c|c} \uparrow 1 & \downarrow 1+r \\ \hline t & t+\tau \end{array}$$

This has worth 0 at times $\leq t$.

CHAPTER 12

# Forward Rate

We have discussed in earlier sections the notion of *forward price* for an asset: this is the price agreed upon today but to be paid at a future date in return for delivery of an asset. A company planning to purchase some asset at a known future date may lock in a price using a forward agreement. A typical situation involves purchase of an asset in a foreign currency, in which case the buyer may also want to enter into a currency forward agreement, to secure an acceptable exchange rate. Of course, if the spot price on the future date turns out to be actually lower than the originally agreed-upon forward price, then the buyer of the forward will have incurred a loss.

In this chapter we are concerned with forward agreements for bonds. When the underlying asset is a bond, the forward price essentially corresponds to delivery, at the future date, of an implied interest rate. This rate is the corresponding *forward rate*, and the transaction is called a *forward rate agreement*. Our task in the chapter is to determine formulas for fair forward rates in terms of bond prices.

Consider a bond to be purchased at time $t$, and maturing at a later date $t + \tau$. The cash flow structure, as seen by the owner where $C_{T_j}$ is the price of a call expiring at time $T_j$, on a common underlying asset. We had seen a practical example of this earlier in (11.3). Viewed as an inequality for European call prices, the reason for the inequality is not apparent. Yet, viewed as an inequality between American call prices, this is eminently reasonable: the call with the later expiration "contains," as a "subinstrument," the call with the earlier expiration, and hence must cost at least as much.

To see this, recall our *strict* inequality (11.31) about the European call price:

$$\text{European Call Price} + \text{Strike} > \text{Asset Price}, \quad (11.34)$$

at any time *prior* to the option expiration date. This was derived assuming positive interest rates prevail.

Now consider a "live" American call at any time prior to the expiration date. Of course, it is worth at least as much as the corresponding European call. Then, using (11.34), we have:

$$\text{American Call Price} + \text{Strike} > \text{Asset Price}, \quad (11.35)$$

at any time prior to the option expiration date.

Therefore,

$$\text{American Call Price} > \text{Asset Price} - \text{Strike}, \quad (11.36)$$

at any time prior to the option expiration date.

Now observe that the right side in (11.36) is the amount that would be realized upon exercising the call. Thus, the preceding inequality says that *at any time prior to the expiration date, the American call itself is worth more than the value that would be realized on exercising it.*

In the words of Merton [31], the option is worth more "alive" than "dead." Thus, *an American call will not be exercised prior to the expiration date, and hence is equivalent to a European call*. In particular, the American call has the same price as the European call.

Note that we have used the assumption that interest rates are strictly positive over the life of the option, and that the underlying asset pays no dividends.

We have then, under the preceding hypotheses, another inequality to add to those we considered in the preceding section:

$$\boxed{C_{T_2} \geq C_{T_1} \text{ if } T_2 \geq T_1,} \quad (11.37)$$

We can do a little better than the preceding inequality. Observe that the slope of the graph of $g$ lies between $-1$ and 0:

$$\frac{g(K_2) - g(K_1)}{K_2 - K_1} \in [-1, 0]$$

Thus, if $K_1 \leq K_2$ then:

$$g(K_1) - g(K_2) \leq K_2 - K_1$$

Taking expected values, and then multiplying by the discount factor $P(0, T)$ to transfer the cash flow focal point to time 0, we see that

$$\boxed{C(K_1) - C(K_2) \leq P(0, T)[K_2 - K_1], \ \textit{if}\ K_1 \leq K_2.} \tag{11.29}$$

Thus, if the strike of a call is lowered by amount $x$, keeping maturity constant, then the excess premium needed is at most the amount $x$, discounted to time-0.

Next, we examine the inequality

$$\boxed{C + P(0, T)K \geq X_0} \tag{11.30}$$

where $C$ is the time-0 price of a call option with strike $K$ and maturity $T$, $X_0$ is the time-0 price of the asset (which is assumed not to pay dividends), and $P(0, T)$ is the usual discount factor. We shall prove the inequality first by a commonsense argument, and then by mathematical reasoning.

Suppose at time 0 we buy the call option, along with a bond that will yield amount $K$ at maturity date $T$. The options costs $C$, while the bond requires a cash outflow at time 0 of

$$P(0, T)K,$$

because $P(0, T)$ is the discount factor. Thus, the total initial outlay for this will be:

$$C + P(0, T)K$$

With this portfolio we are assured we can purchase the asset on date $T$ with no additional funds needed. For, if on date $T$ the asset price is lower than the strike $K$, then we can simply use the proceeds from the bond to buy the asset; if, on the other hand, the asset price on date $T$ is at or above the strike $K$, then we exercise the option and call in the asset using the amount $K$ from the proceeds of our bond. Thus, the portfolio is definitely going to be worth at least the asset, and possibly more, on the date $T$. Hence, its worth at time 0 has to be at least the price $X_0$ of the asset. This establishes the inequality (11.30). The "commonsense" argument we have used here is really a case of the principle of no-arbitrage.

Next, we verify (11.30) again, this time using the call price formula. We have

$$\begin{aligned} C &= P(0,T)E_{Q_T}[(X_T - K)_+] \\ &\geq P(0,T)E_{Q_T}[X_T - K] \qquad \text{because } y_+ \geq y, \text{ for all } y \in \mathbf{R} \\ &= P(0,T)E_{Q_T}(X_T) - P(0,T)K \\ &= X_0 - P(0,T)K, \end{aligned}$$

where, in the last step, we used the fact that the present value $X_0$ is the discount factor $P(0,T)$ times the forward price $E_{Q_T}(X_T)$.

Let $T > 0$. Now suppose, as is eminently reasonable, that interest rates are positive. This implies, in particular, that the bond price $P(0,T)$ is strictly less than 1:

$$P(0,T) < 1 \text{ if the } T\text{-period interest rate is} > 0$$

The inequality (11.30) then implies the strict inequality

$$\boxed{C + K > X_0, \text{ if the interest rate over } [0,T] \text{ is positive.}} \qquad (11.31)$$

We have seen an empirical illustration of this earlier in (11.4).

Let us now understand the inequality (11.31) in a conceptual way. Consider, at time 0, buying the call for amount $C$, along with a $T$-maturity bond with initial deposit of amount $K$. Then, at time $T$, if the asset price is at or below the strike $K$, then the call expires worthless, and our portfolio is worth the bond's matured value, an amount strictly greater than the initial deposit $K$; in particular, *the portfolio is worth strictly more than the asset*. On the other hand, if at time $T$ the asset is worth more than $K$, then we can exercise the call, paying amount $K$ from the proceeds of the matured bond, and end up with both the asset and the remaining positive amount from the bond proceeds. Thus, *no matter what happens, at time $T$ our portfolio would be worth strictly more than the asset*. Therefore, of course, the portfolio should be worth strictly more than the asset at time 0 as well, and this is precisely the inequality (11.31). This is again a "commonsense" argument, which is an application of the principle of no-arbitrage.

Observe that the strict inequality (11.31) requires that $T$ be strictly greater than 0 (this was the harmless-looking qualifier $T > 0$ we had put in earlier). Thus, *the inequality (11.31) is valid at any time prior to the expiration of the option*.

Finally, we also have the inequality

$$X_0 \geq C \tag{11.32}$$

which just says that there is no point in paying more for the right to buy an asset than the worth of the asset itself (assuming the asset itself isn't worth a negative amount). To see the inequality mathematically, observe first that

$$y \geq (y - K)_+, \text{ if } y \text{ and } K \text{ are} \geq 0,$$

and then put $X_T$ in place of $y$, after which take expectations.

## THE AMERICAN CALL OPTION

Recall that an American option differs from the options we have been studying in that it allows for exercise of the option at any time prior to the expiration date. This makes such options more difficult to analyze. However, as we shall verify in this section, it turns out that there is essentially no difference between American and European *call* options. The case of put options is quite different.

Consider then an American call option with strike $K$, expiration $T$. Let $X_t$ denote the time-$t$ price of the underlying asset. The holder may choose to exercise the option at some time $\tau(\omega)$, as determined by the market scenario $\omega$, to the extent it is visible until the time of exercise. The payoff upon exercise will be

$$X_{\tau(\omega)}(\omega) - K$$

We may as well take the positive part, since there will surely be no exercise if the above value is negative. Converting to time-0 cash we get

$$p\big(0, \tau(\omega)\big)\big(X_{\tau(\omega)}(\omega) - K\big)_+$$

Taking the expectation value, we have

$$E_{Q_0}\left(p(0, \tau)\,(X_\tau - K)_+\right)$$

Now the exercise time $\tau$ has to be chosen so as to maximize this:

$$\text{American Call Price} = \max_{\tau} E_{Q_0}\left[p(0, \tau)\,(X_\tau - K)_+\right] \quad (11.33)$$

The maximum here runs over all *stopping times* $\tau$, i.e., a random choice of time such that whether $\tau(\omega)$ is $\leq t$ is determined entirely by knowledge of the market up till time $t$. See Chapter 25 for a more precise formulation of the notion of stopping time.

There is a similar price for a put option.

We consider options on an underlying asset whose value is positive.

A careful examination of the American call reveals a remarkable observation (from Merton [31]): *an American call is never exercised prior to the expiration date, and is thus effectively equivalent to a European call, and, in particular, has the same price as the European call* with same strike and expiration date.

time if desired). Thus it is natural to take this as the *forward rate* between times $t$ and $t+\tau$:

$$\text{Forward rate} = E_{Q_{t+\tau}}\left[\frac{1-P(t,t+\tau)}{P(t,t+\tau)}\right] = \frac{1-FP(t,t+\tau)}{FP(t,t+\tau)} \tag{12.6}$$

It is interesting to rewrite the expression on the right in terms of $E_{Q_t}$:

$$\text{Forward rate} = \frac{1-E_{Q_t}[P(t,t+\tau)]}{E_{Q_t}[P(t,t+\tau)]} \tag{12.7}$$

# CHAPTER 13

# Swaps and the Swap Rate

A *swap* is an exchange of assets between two parties lasting over a certain time period. In this chapter we are concerned with the simplest *interest rate swaps*. These are agreements in which loans carrying fixed interest rates are swapped for loans carrying floating-rate interest.

The typical interest rate swap we will be concerned with is an agreement between two parties $A$ and $B$: $A$ pays $B$ a *fixed* rate of interest on a sum of money called the *nominal*, with payments made at regular intervals, while $B$ pays $A$ a *floating* rate—the prevailing market rate—on the same nominal. The dates on which the floating rates are observed are called *reset dates*.

The swap can thus be decomposed into two legs, the fixed leg and the floating leg. We shall show that the floating leg is a fair cash flow, i.e., has a worth of zero. This will let us determine the correct value of the fixed interest rate—called the *swap rate*—to be charged on the fixed leg.

The type of swap we deal with here involves observing the floating rate at the *beginning* of a period and making the interest payment at the *end* of the period.

## THE FLOATING LEG

A conceptual way to understand the floating leg of a swap is to break it down into the individual payment periods. The analysis of each such period was essentially done in the preceding chapter, but we will repeat the ideas here.

The cash flow structure of a bond maturing at time $t_1$, as seen by the person who buys the bond at time $t_0$, is:

$$\underset{t_0}{\uparrow P(t_0,t_1)} \qquad \underset{t_1}{\downarrow 1}$$

By definition of $P(t_0, t_1)$, this is a fair cash flow at time $t_0$ and so has worth 0 at time $t_0$, and so of course also prior to time $t_0$.

Scaling the initial outflow to amount 1, we see that the following cash flow also has worth 0 at time $\leq t_0$:

$$\underset{t_0}{\uparrow 1} \qquad \underset{t_1}{\downarrow \tfrac{1}{P(t_0,t_1)}}$$

The final cash inflow here is a sum

$$\frac{1}{P(t_0, t_1)} = \text{principal} + \text{interest} = 1 + \frac{1 - P(t_0, t_1)}{P(t_0, t_1)}$$

Diagramatically:

$$\underset{t_0}{\uparrow 1} \qquad \underset{t_1}{\downarrow 1 + \tfrac{1-P(t_0,t_1)}{P(t_0,t_1)}}$$

This has worth 0 at all times $\leq t_0$.

Once we have this, we can stick on a second such diagram next to it, covering the interval $[t_1, t_2]$:

$$\underset{t_0}{\uparrow 1} \qquad \underset{t_1}{\downarrow \tfrac{1-P(t_0,t_1)}{P(t_0,t_1)}} \qquad \underset{t_2}{\downarrow 1 + \tfrac{1-P(t_1,t_2)}{P(t_1,t_2)}}$$

*Notice how the inflowing* 1 *cancels the outflowing* 1 *at time* $t_1$.

Now we have the pattern and can see that the following cash flow is worth 0 at all times $\leq t_0$:

$$\begin{array}{cccccc} & \uparrow 1 & \downarrow r_1 & \downarrow r_2 & \cdots\cdots & \downarrow 1+r_N \\ \hline s & t_0 & t_1 & t_2 & & t_N \end{array}$$

where $r_i$ is the interest payment $\frac{1-P(t_{i-1},t_i)}{P(t_{i-1},t_i)}$:

$$r_i = \frac{1 - P(t_{i-1}, t_i)}{P(t_{i-1}, t_i)} \tag{13.1}$$

This cash flow describes the following agreement:

- Two parties $A$ and $B$ choose dates $t_0 < t_1 < \cdots < t_N$;
- At time $t_0$, party $A$ pays party $B$ the amount 1;
- At time $t_1$, $B$ pays $A$ the interest for the period $[t_0, t_1]$ as expected at time $t_0$;
- At time $t_2$, $B$ pays $A$ the interest observed at time $t_1$ for the period $[t_1, t_2]$;
- This proceeds till time $t_N$, when the transactions end with $B$ paying $A$ the interest plus the original principal 1.

Thus, the agreement to pay the *floating interest rate* at the *ends* of loan periods, applying the interest rate observed at the beginnings of these periods, has zero worth at the time of the initial loan and any time prior to that. We shall see later that the worth is not zero if the interest payments occur at the beginnings of the loan periods.

## THE SWAP RATE

First, a technical point about counting days. For any agreement that involves two dates $s$ and $t$, the actual time span $t - s$ is often not what is important; actual cash settlement may take place on business days or at some specified dates close to the dates $s$ and $t$.

For this reason, we denote by $d(s,t)$ the "day count" from $s$ to $t$, keeping in mind that it might not be equal to $t-s$.

In a swap agreement between two parties $A$ and $B$, party $A$ pays party $B$ a floating interest rate over a period of time and receives from $B$ a fixed interest rate $c$. The payments are made on a chosen set of dates $t_0, t_1, \ldots, t_N$. Since, as already observed, the floating leg has value zero, we drop it from the picture and then have the following cash flows from the point of view of $A$, who receives the fixed rate:

$$
\begin{array}{ccccccc}
 & \uparrow 1 & \downarrow cd_1 & \downarrow cd_2 & \cdots\cdots & \downarrow 1+cd_N \\
\hline
s & t_0 & t_1 & t_2 & & t_N
\end{array}
$$

where $d_j = d(t_{j-1}, t_j)$ is the day count between $t_{j-1}$ and $t_j$.

The principal amount 1 is called the "nominal" because in reality it is not actually exchanged. If we drew the full cash flow picture, with payments made to $B$ as well, the 1s at the beginning and at the end would cancel each other out.

The value of the agreement at time $s \leq t_0$ is obtained by using the appropriate discount factors $P(s,t_j)$:

$$
-P(s,t_0) + P(s,t_1)cd_1 + \cdots + P(s,t_N)cd_N + P(s,t_N) \tag{13.2}
$$

Thus if the agreement is made at time $s$, then the fixed rate $c$ should be such that the value of the agreement at time $s$ is zero.

So, the value of the *swap rate* at time $s$ should be:

$$
\boxed{c_s = \frac{P(s,t_0) - P(s,t_N)}{P(s,t_1)d_1 + \cdots + P(s,t_N)d_N}} \tag{13.3}
$$

The denominator here is the *level*:

$$
L_s = P(s,t_1)d_1 + \cdots + P(s,t_N)d_N \tag{13.4}
$$

Note from (13.2) that the net cash inflow for $A$ with fixed rate $c$ is:

$$\begin{aligned} &-P(s,t_0)+P(s,t_1)cd_1+\cdots+P(s,t_N)cd_N+P(s,t_N) \\ &=cL_s-(P(s,t_0)-P(s,t_N)) \end{aligned} \tag{13.5}$$

## SWAP RATES AND FORWARD PRICES

The swap rate $c_s$ can be expressed in terms of forward bond prices:

$$c_s=\frac{1-FP(s,t_0,t_N)}{FP(s,t_0,t_1)d_1+\cdots+FP(s,t_0,t_N)d_N} \tag{13.6}$$

where

$$FP(s,u,v)=\frac{P(s,v)}{P(s,u)}$$

is the forward price at time $s$ of a $v$-maturity bond to be delivered at time $u$.

Note that, in general, the swap rate $c_0$ is *not* equal to $E_{Q_s}(c_s)$.

There is another expression for the swap rate that is conceptually useful. The fact that the floating leg is worth zero corresponds to the algebraic identity

$$P(s,t_0)-P(s,t_N)=P(s,t_1)f_1d_1+\cdots P(s,t_N)f_Nd_N \tag{13.7}$$

where $f_i$ is the forward rate

$$f_i=\frac{1}{d_i}\left(\frac{1-FP(s,t_{i-1},t_i)}{FP(s,t_{i-1},t_i)}\right),$$

and, as always, $FP(s,t_{i-1},t_i)=P(s,t_i)/P(s,t_{i-1})$ is the forward bond price. The right side of (13.7) is the time-$t$ present value of the interest payments on the floating leg.

Thus we can write the swap rate at time $s$ as

$$\boxed{c_s=\sum_{i=1}^{n}w_i f_i} \tag{13.8}$$

where the weight $w_i$ is

$$w_i = \frac{P(s,t_i)d_i}{P(s,t_1)d_1 + \cdots P(s,t_N)d_N}$$

$$= \frac{FP(s,t_0,t_i)d_i}{FP(s,t_0,t_1)d_1 + \cdots FP(s,t_0,t_N)d_N}$$

Equation (13.8) expresses the swap rate as a weighted average of forward rates over the swap payment periods.

CHAPTER 14

# Natural Time Lag and the Convexity Adjustment

**A** forward rate agreement is an instrument that allows the owner to have a guaranteed interest rate $r_\tau$ for a future time period $[t, t+\tau]$, with the interest payment made *at the end* time $t+\tau$. Thus, even though the agreement or bond is delivered at time $t$, the additional cash flow will be received at the end of a natural time lag period $\tau$. In contrast, consider an instrument $J$ that delivers the interest $r_\tau$ for the time period $[t, t+\tau]$ at the *beginning* of the period, i.e. at date $t$.

The time $t$-forward price of the instrument $J$ is

$$E_{Q_t}(r_\tau) \tag{14.1}$$

where the interest $r_\tau$ is given by

$$r_\tau = \frac{1 - P(t, t+\tau)}{P(t, t+\tau)} \tag{14.2}$$

In contrast, the correct forward rate, based on the forward bond price $FP(t, T)$, is

$$\frac{1 - FP(t, T)}{FP(t, T)} = \frac{P(0, t) - P(0, T)}{P(0, T)},$$

where we have used from (9.12) the expression for the forward bond price $FP(t,T) = P(0,T)/P(0,t)$. The formal definition of the forward price $FP(t,T)$ is

$$FP(t,T) = E_{Q_t}[P(t,t+\tau)]$$

So we can write the forward rate as:

$$\text{forward rate} = \frac{1}{FP(t,T)} - 1 = \frac{1}{E_{Q_t}[P(t,t+\tau)]} - 1$$

The difference between (14.1) and the actual forward rate is therefore

$$E_{Q_t}\left[\frac{1}{P(t,t+\tau)}\right] - \frac{1}{E_{Q_t}[P(t,t+\tau)]}$$

The left side is the average of $1/Y$, while the right side is the reciprocal of the average of $Y$, where $Y$ is the random variable $P(t,t+\tau)$. Thus, the difference reflects the convexity of the function $y \mapsto \frac{1}{y}$, and so is called the *convexity adjustment* that must be made to the forward rate in order to obtain the rate for the instrument without the natural time lag.

Many instruments have payment schedules that violate the "natural time lag"—for example, a swap whose floating payments are made in *advance*, at the beginnings of the loan periods. Consider, for example, a *Libor set in arrears* swap: an investor, noticing an upward-sloping yield curve, enters into a 3-year swap *paying* floating rate Libor every 6 months and *receives* Libor set in arrears minus, say, 20 basis points (= 0.2%). If, over the period of such a swap, Libor rises, on average, 30 basis points per half year, then the swap will yield a 10-basis-point advantage. A *constant maturity swap*, where the floating rate is exchanged for the prevailing swap rate (on a fixed type of swap), is another standard instrument where the natural time lag (of the swap) is violated. For example, a company, seeking a stable duration for debts, may enter into a 5-year swap, receiving 6-month Libor and paying the 7-year swap rate (on each reset date) minus, say, 20 basis points.

CHAPTER 15

# Swaption Price

In Chapter 13 we examined the structure and pricing of an interest rate swap. Options on such swaps are called *swaptions* and are much-traded instruments. Now we shall consider the pricing of such options.

Consider a call option on a swap with strike swap rate $c^*$, with exercise date $t$. If at the time $t$ the prevailing swap rate $c_t$ exceeds the strike rate $c^*$, then it would be profitable for the owner of the call to exercise the option. When exercised, the swap would result in a net cash inflow whose value at time $t$ is (from (13.5)):

$$c^* L_t - (P(t, t_0) - P(t, t_N))$$

Now, as we have observed earlier, the prevailing swap rate $c_t$ is such that

$$c_t L_t - (P(t, t_0) - P(t, t_N)) = 0$$

Thus the exercise of the option results in a net gain of

$$c^* L_t - c_t L_t$$

This would be the value at time $t$ if the option is exercised. Of course, if $c^* < c_t$, then the option will not be exercised and the gain will be zero. Thus, the value at time $t$ of the option is

$$\{c^* L_t - c_t L_t\}_+$$

The forward price of this option is therefore:

$$E_{Q_t}[\{c^* L_t - c_t L_t\}_+]$$

Hence the present value of the option is:

$$\text{swaption call price} = P(0,t)E_{Q_t}[\{c_t L_t - c^* L_t\}_+] \quad (15.1)$$

We can also write this as

$$\text{swaption call price} = P(0,t)E_{Q_t}$$
$$\left[\left\{P(t,t_0) - P(t,t_N) - \left(\sum_{j=1}^{N} P(t,t_j)d_j\right)c^*\right\}_+\right] \quad (15.2)$$

# CHAPTER 16

# Volatility and Hedging

The price of a risky asset fluctuates at random. *Volatility* is a measure of this fluctuation. *Hedging* is any means of reducing risk to a portfolio of holdings. If we have a way of measuring the volatility of a portfolio, then we may consider adding various instruments, options for example, which would reduce the volatility of the overall portfolio. Of course, as the market evolves there will be need for continuous recalibration of the hedging positions to keep risk within acceptable bounds. In this chapter we take a very brief look at these notions.

## VOLATILITY

The purpose of this section is to define the volatility of the price process of an asset and to relate it to the variance of the price itself at any instant of time.

Consider an asset and denote by $Y_t(\omega)$ its price at time $t$ in market scenario $\omega$. The price is being measured with respect to a fixed numeraire, say time-0 cash. Let $Q$ be the corresponding pricing measure. Then $Y_t$ is a random variable whose fluctuations contain the risk to the person who owns the asset.

The volatility of the price $Y_t$ over the time period $[t, t+\delta t]$ is the variance

$$E_Q[(Y_{t+\delta t} - Y_t)^2 | \mathcal{F}_t]$$

Sometimes one takes the square-root, i.e., the standard deviation, as the volatility.

The limit

$$\mathrm{vol}_t(Y) = \lim_{\delta t \downarrow 0} \frac{1}{\delta t} E_Q[(Y_{t+\delta t} - Y_t)^2 | \mathcal{F}_t] \tag{16.1}$$

is the instantaneous volatility at time $t$.

Suppose now that the price process

$$t \mapsto Y_t$$

has the following nice properties :

- It is a continuous, square-integrable martingale with respect to $Q$, and so, in particular, $E_Q[Y_t | \mathcal{F}_s] = Y_s$ for $0 \le s \le t$ and $E_Q(Y_t) = Y_0$;
- The instantaneous volatility exists for all times $t \in [0, T]$ and is a continuous function of time;
- The increments $\delta Y_t = Y_{t+\delta t} - Y_t$ (with $\delta t > 0$) are independent of the past.

Then, working with a partition $0 = t_0 < t_1 < \cdots < t_m = t$ of $[0, t]$, we have

$$\begin{aligned}
\int_0^t \mathrm{vol}_s(Y)\, ds &= \lim_{\max_j |t_j - t_{j-1}| \to 0} \sum_{j=1}^{m} E_Q\left[\left(Y_{t_j} - Y_{t_{j-1}}\right)^2 | \mathcal{F}_{t_{j-1}}\right] \\
&= \lim_{\max_j |t_j - t_{j-1}| \to 0} \sum_{j=1}^{m} E_Q\left[\left(Y_{t_j} - Y_{t_{j-1}}\right)^2\right] \\
&\qquad \text{because } \delta Y_s \text{ is independent of } \mathcal{F}_s \\
&= E_Q[(Y_t - Y_0)^2]
\end{aligned}$$

where again in the last step we used the independence of increments to add up the individual variances to get the variance of the sum. Thus

$$\int_0^t \mathrm{vol}_s(Y)\,ds = \sigma^2_{Y_t} \tag{16.2}$$

## HEDGING

*Hedging* is any method of reducing risk for an existing portfolio of assets. One may, for example, wish to minimize, or even make zero, the volatility of a portfolio by adjoining to the portfolio certain new instruments such as options.

In simple situations a hedge is obtained by "betting against oneself." A person owning stock in a company could buy an option that would result in positive cash flow if the stock price goes down; as stock owner, the person is hurt if the stock price goes down, but if this does happen then the option—viewed as a bet that "wins" if the stock goes down—payoff cushions the loss.

The hedging strategy for a portfolio will change with time as the prices of the portfolio constituents evolve. The classic paper [7] of Black and Scholes used the idea of continuous time hedging to derive option prices.

In reality it may not be feasible or worthwhile to form a volatility-free portfolio. Estimation and reduction of volatility of the portfolio is generally the practical course of action.

Suppose a portfolio consists of $c_1$ units of asset $A_1, \ldots, c_N$ units of asset $A_N$. Suppose the discounted price at any time $t$ of $A_i$ is $X_{i,t}$. Then the instantaneous volatility of the portfolio at time $t$ is

$$\sum_{i,j=1}^{N} c_i c_j \, dX_{i,t}\, dX_{j,t}/dt$$

A specific model for the evolution of the asset prices $X_{i,t}$ will give a concrete expression for instantaneous volatility, and then this may be minimized subject to various portfolio restrictions that may exist.

## "THE GREEKS"

A popular set of notions relating to the task of hedging is called "the Greeks." These are quantities, usually denoted by Greek (or, in one case, "faux-Greek") letters, that specify sensitivity of the price of a product to various parameters and input variables.

The *Delta*, denoted $\Delta$, of a derivative instrument is the sensitivity of the price of the derivative to changes in the price of the underlying instrument:

$$\Delta = \frac{\partial C}{\partial X} \tag{16.3}$$

where $C$ is the price of the derivative instrument, and $X$ is the price of the underlying.

Recall the Call Price formula (11.1):

$$\text{Call Option Price} = X_0 q_2 - e^{-rt} K q_1 \tag{16.4}$$

where $X_0$ is the present price of the asset, $r$ is the interest rate on the $t$-maturity bond, $t$ is the expiration date of the option, and $K$ is the strike price. The probabilities $q_1$ and $q_2$ are given by

$$q_2 = Q_t^*[X(t) > K] \qquad \text{and} \qquad q_1 = Q_t[X(t) > K], \tag{16.5}$$

where $X(t)$ is the asset price at time $t$, $Q_t$ is the pricing measure for the time-$t$ cash numeraire, and $Q_t^*$ is the pricing measure when the numeraire is the underlying asset deliverable at time $t$.

Thus, the Delta for a Call is

$$\Delta_{\text{Call}} = Q_t^*[X(t) > K] \tag{16.6}$$

Thus, the Delta of the call option is actually the probability of the asset price rising above the strike, using the pricing measure $Q_t^*$.

Similarly, from the Put Price formula (11.18), we have

$$\Delta_{\text{Put}} = -Q_t^*[X(t) < K] = Q_t^*[X(t) > K] - 1 = \Delta_{\text{Call}} - 1 \tag{16.7}$$

Observe that the Delta of a Put is *negative*. This makes sense: a rise in price of the underlying makes a put option less attractive.

Note also the put-call Delta relation

$$\Delta_{\text{Call}} - \Delta_{\text{Put}} = 1$$

Consider an investor who has written 15 call option contracts (each contract being 100 options) on shares in a company, each call having a price of \$12 and a Delta of 0.4. Suppose the underlying stock price is at \$100. If the stock price goes up by \$1, then the option contracts value increases by

$$15 \times 100 \times 0.4 \times \$1 = \$600,$$

which is a loss for the investor who has written the options. To offset this risk, the investor could add 600 shares of the stock to the portfolio. The \$1 rise in stock price would raise the worth of the shares by

$$\$1 \times 600 = \$600,$$

balancing out the loss in writing the options contracts. A decline in the stock price also has opposite effects on the two holdings, thereby keeping the portfolio balanced.

More generally, a riskless portfolio is obtained by using

$$\Delta \text{ units of the underlying, and } -1 \text{ units of the derivative}$$

Needless to say, the Delta fluctuates with time and the portfolio needs to be continuously rebalanced.

The second derivative of the derivative price with respect to the underlying is called the *Gamma* of the derivative, and is also useful in fine-tuning investment strategies.

The *Theta* of a portfolio is simply the rate of change with time of the value of the portfolio.

The *Vega* of a derivative instrument is the sensitivity of the price with respect to the volatility of the underlying asset.

The *rho* if a portfolio is the sensitivity of the portfolio price to interest rates.

**TABLE 16–1**

Summary of General Price Formulas I

| Instrument | Details | Price |
|---|---|---|
| Zero-Coupon Bond with maturity $T$ | Pays out amount 1 at time $T$ | Price at time 0 is $P(0, T) = E_{Q_0}[p(0, T)]$. Time-$t$ price is $P(t, T) = E_{Q_t}[p(t, T) \mid \mathcal{F}_t]$ |
| Forward agreement | Agree at time 0 to buy, at a future date $t$, a security worth $S(t)$ | *Forward Price*, agreed upon at time 0, that should be paid at time $t$ is $FS(t) = E_{Q_t}(S(t)) = \frac{E_{Q_0}(p(0,t)S(t))}{P(0,t)}$, with $Q_t$ being pricing measure with time-$t$ cash numeraire. |
| Forward agreement for bond/forward rate agreement | Agree at time 0 to buy, at a future date $t$, a $T$-maturity bond | *Forward Price*, agreed upon at time 0, to be paid at time $t$ is $$FP(t, T) = \frac{P(0, T)}{P(0, t)}$$ |
| Call Option, with strike $K$ and expiration date $t$, on a security $S$ | An agreement between two parties, *holder* and *writer*, which gives the holder the right, but not obligation, to buy from the writer at time $t$ a security worth $S(t)$ for price $K$ | Present value of the option is $P(0, t)[FS(t)q_2 - Kq_1]$, where $q_2 = Q_t^*[S(t) > K] = \frac{E_{Q_t}[S(t)1_{\{S(t)>K\}}]}{E_{Q_t}[S(t)]}$ and $q_1 = Q_t[S(t) > K]$, where $Q_t^*$ is the pricing measure with the security $S$ as numeraire. |

|  |  |  |
|---|---|---|
|  |  | Black-Scholes case: if $S(t)$ has log-normal distribution under the measure $Q_t$ then<br>Call Price $= S_0 N(d_+) - e^{-rt} K N(d_-)$<br>where $r$ is the interest rate for the period $[0, t]$, $d_\pm = \frac{\log \frac{e^{rt} S_0}{K} \pm \frac{1}{2}\sigma^2_{\log S(t)}}{\sigma_{\log S(t)}}$<br>and $N(\cdot)$ is the cumulative distribution function of the standard normal variable. |
| Call Option, with strike $K$ and expiration date $t$, on a $T$-maturity bond | An agreement between two parties, *holder* and *writer*, which gives the holder the right, but not obligation, to buy from the writer at time $t$ a $T$-maturity bond for price $K$ | Present value of the option is $P(0, t)[FP(t, T)q_2 - Kq_1]$, where<br>$q_2 = Q_t^*[P(t, T) > K] = \frac{E_{Q_t}[P(t, T)1_{\{P(t,T)>K\}}]}{E_{Q_t}[P(t, T)]}$ and<br>$q_1 = Q_t[P(t, T)) > K] = E_{Q_t}[1_{\{P(t,T)>K\}}]$ |

**TABLE 16–2**

Summary of General Price Formulas II

| Instrument | Details | Price |
|---|---|---|
| Swap Rate | Consider an initial time $s$, and later dates $t_0 < t_1 < \cdots < t_N$. In a swap between two parties $A$ and $B$, one party, say $A$, receives from the other a constant interest rate $c_s$, decided at time $s$, which is paid at times $t_1, \ldots, t_N$; in exchange, $A$ pays $B$ the floating rates observed at times $t_0, t_1, \ldots, t_{N-1}$, and paid at the ends of the periods $[t_0, t_1], \ldots, [t_{N-1}, t_N]$. | The present value of the swap rate $c_s$ is $c_s = \frac{P(s, t_0) - P(s, t_N)}{P(s, t_1)d_1 + \cdots + P(s, t_N)d_N}$, where $d_j$ is the *day-count* between $t_{j-1}$ and $t_j$. |
| Swaption (Call) | An agreement between two parties, *holder* and *writer*, giving the holder the right, but not obligation, to enter into the swap agreement with the writer at a future date $s$, receiving a fixed strike rate $c^*$, decided upon at time 0. | The fair price for the swaption is given in equation (15.2). |
| Futures | A futures agreement, between parties $A$ and $B$, involves a security $S$ and a time horizon $T$. The initial futures price $X_0$ is noted, and the party, say $A$, which holds the long position receives from the other the increments $\Delta X_t$ in the futures price (if it is negative, $A$ pays $B$) until the terminal date $T$, when the futures price $X_T$ is defined to be the spot-price $S(T)$ of the underlying security | The futures price, assuming continuous payments, at time 0 is $E_{Q_0}(S(T))$, where $S(T)$ is the price at time $T$ of the security underlying the futures agreement with delivery date $T$. The price at any time $t < T$ is $E_{Q_0}(S(T)\mid\mathcal{F}_t)$. |

# PART THREE

# Model Prices

In Part Three we study the general framework of stochastic models in finance and then examine some specific models, mainly for interest rate products.

Each model starts with a *state space* whose points correspond to market states. The market state space is taken to be $\mathbf{R}^N$ when we have an *N-factor model*, each coordinate corresponding to an underlying *factor* specifying the state of the market. These factors need not have any direct meaning in terms of prices of instruments.

The market state evolves in time, the evolution being described by an *Itô stochastic differential equation*. The way the state evolves is also described through the transition density, or *Green's function*, which will be a key tool for evaluating instrument prices. The Green's function, as well as instrument prices, obey a second order partial differential equation. This differential equation and the probabilistic description are connected by the *Feynman–Kac formula*. Table 19-2 in Chapter 19 summarizes these ideas.

We shall use the general framework for evaluating prices in the particular cases of certain specific models—Gaussian (based on the model of Hull and White) and chi–squared (the model of Cox, Ingersoll, and Ross).

CHAPTER 17

# Option Prices in the Log-Normal Case

In this chapter we work out the option price formula in case the underlying asset price $X_t$ has a log-normal distribution with respect to the forward pricing measure $Q_t$. This is the situation in the famous Black-Scholes model, which is discussed in more detail in the next chapter.

## THE OPTION PRICE FORMULA

Consider an asset whose fair price at time $t$ is described by the random variable $X_t$. Assume that $X_t$ is *log-normal* with respect to the measure given by $Q_t$. Thus,

$$X_t = e^{Y_t}$$

with $Y_t = \log X_t$ being a Gaussian random variable with respect to the measure $Q_t$. At first the assumption of log-normality might appear to be strange. However, the idea behind such an assumption is not too difficult: price increases are best understood as ratios (for example, we usually say the price of a certain asset has gone up by a certain percentage), and so we may view $X_t$

as a product of a large number of such ratios (for time instants over the interval $[0, t]$), and so $\log X_t$ will be a sum of a large number of small fluctuating terms. Then, in view of the central limit theorem in probability theory, it is a reasonable first theory to assume that $\log X_t$ has a normal distribution. A more mathematical account of this will be given later in the context of the Black–Scholes model.

We shall prove that the price $C$, at time 0, of a call option on the asset with strike $K$ and expiration $t$ is given by

$$\boxed{C = X_0 N(d_+) - e^{-rt} K N(d_-)} \tag{17.1}$$

where $X_0$ is the present price (time 0) for the asset, $r$ is the interest rate on a $t$-maturity bond, $N$ is the standard Gaussian distribution function

$$N(s) = \int_{-\infty}^{s} \frac{e^{-x^2/2}\,dx}{\sqrt{2\pi}},$$

and the numbers $d_+$ and $d_-$ are given by

$$\begin{aligned} d_+ &= \frac{1}{\sigma_{\log X_t}} \log[e^{rt} X_0 / K] + \frac{1}{2}\sigma_{\log X_t} \qquad \text{and} \\ d_- &= \frac{1}{\sigma_{\log X_t}} \log[e^{rt} X_0 / K] - \frac{1}{2}\sigma_{\log X_t} \end{aligned} \tag{17.2}$$

In the same way, we have

$$\boxed{\text{Price of the put option} = e^{-rt} K N(d_+) - X_0 N(d_-)} \tag{17.3}$$

## DERIVATION OF THE FORMULA

Assume that the price $X_t$ at time $t$ of the asset underlying the option has a log-normal distribution with respect to the forward pricing measure $Q_t$ (recall that this is the pricing measure when the numeraire is time-$t$ cash). Thus, we assume that

$$X_t = e^{Y_t}$$

where $Y_t$ is a Gaussian random variable with respect to the measure $Q_t$.

For a random variable $S$ that is Gaussian with respect to a measure $P$, there is a very useful formula for the expected value of $e^S$:

$$\boxed{E_P(e^S) = e^{E_P(S)+\frac{1}{2}\sigma_S^2}} \tag{17.4}$$

where

$$\sigma_S^2 = E_P[(S - E_P(S)]^2 \tag{17.5}$$

is the variance of $S$ with respect to $P$. We apply this to the price $X_t$, to obtain:

$$E_{Q_t}(X_t) = e^{E_{Q_t}(Y_t)+\frac{1}{2}\sigma_{\log X_t}^2}$$

Because $E_{Q_t}(X_t)$ is the forward price $FX_t$, this shows that

$$E_{Q_t}(Y_t) = \log(FX_t) - \frac{1}{2}\sigma_{\log X_t}^2 \tag{17.6}$$

Observe that the forward price $FX_t$ is given by:

$$FX_t = E_{Q_t}[X_t] = X_0/P(0,t) = e^{rt}X_0 \tag{17.7}$$

Let $Q_t^*$ be the measure corresponding to the numeraire $X_t$. We have seen in Chapter 5 that $X_t$ is log-normal also with respect to $Q_t^*$, and the variable $Y_t = \log X_t$ has the same variance $\sigma_{\log X_t}^2$ with respect to $Q_t^*$, but has expectation

$$E_{Q_t^*}(Y_t) = E_{Q_t}(Y_t) + \sigma_{\log X_t}^2$$

Let $C$ be the price, at time 0, for a call on the asset with strike $K$ and expiration $t$. We have seen in (11.1) that

$$C = X_0 q_2 - P(0,t)Kq_1 \tag{17.8}$$

where $P(0,t)=e^{-rt}$ is the $t$-maturity bond price, and

$$q_2 = Q_t^*[X_t > K] \qquad \text{and} \qquad q_1 = Q_t[X_t > K] \qquad (17.9)$$

We shall work out two standard expressions for $q_2$ and $q_1$, using the following little calculation:

**Lemma 17.2.1** *If X is a Gaussian random variable, then*

$$P[X > t] = N(d)$$

*where* $d = (m-t)/\sigma$, *where* $m = E(X)$, $\sigma$ *is the standard deviation of* $X$, *and* $N$ *is the standard Gaussian distribution function*

$$N(s) = \int_{-\infty}^{s} \frac{e^{-x^2/2}\,dx}{\sqrt{2\pi}}$$

***Proof.*** The variable $Z = (X-m)/\sigma$ is standard normal, i.e. Gaussian with mean 0 and variance 1, and so

$$P[X > t] = P\left[Z > \frac{t-m}{\sigma}\right]$$

Because $-Z$ has the same distrubution as $Z$ we have then

$$P[X > t] = P\left[Z < \frac{m-t}{\sigma}\right] = N(d)$$

which is the desired formula. QED

Recall that $X_t = e^{\log Y_t}$. The variable $Y_t = \log X_t$ has the following distributions:

- With respect to $Q_t$, the variable $Y_t$ is Gaussian with mean $m_t = E_{Q_t}[Y_t]$ and variance $\sigma^2_{\log X_t}$;
- With respect to $Q_t^*$, the variable $Y_t$ is Gaussian with mean $m_t + \sigma^2_{\log X_t}$ and variance $\sigma^2_{\log X_t}$.

Using this we see, for example, that

$$Q_t[X_t > K] = Q_t[Y_t > \log K] = N(d_-)$$

where

$$d_- = \frac{E_{Q_t}(Y_t) - \log K}{\sigma_{Y_t}}$$

Using (17.6) we have then

$$d_- = \frac{\log(F X_t) - \frac{1}{2}\sigma_{Y_t}^2 - \log K}{\sigma_{Y_t}} = \frac{1}{\sigma_{Y_t}} \log(F X_t/K) - \frac{1}{2}\sigma_{Y_t}$$

Similarly,

$$Q_t^*[X_t > K] = Q_t^*[Y_t > \log K] = N(d_+)$$

where

$$d_+ = \frac{1}{\sigma_{Y_t}} \log(F X_t/K) + \frac{1}{2}\sigma_{Y_t}$$

the + sign arising from the shift in the mean

$$E_{Q_t^*}(Y_t) = E_{Q_t}(Y_t) + \sigma_{Y_t}^2$$

Substituting the values for $Q_t[X_t > K]$ and $Q_t^*[X_t > K]$ just obtained into the general call price formula (17.8) gives the desired formula (17.1).

## ANOTHER PROOF OF THE FORMULA

Recall that the time-$t$ forward price for the call option of strike $K$ and expiration $t$ on an asset whose price at time $t$ is described by $X_t$ is

$$E_{Q_t}[\{X_t - K\}_+] \tag{17.10}$$

Now for any Gaussian random variable $Y$, and any $K > 0$, a straightforward calculation produces the following useful expectation-value formula

$$E[(e^Y - K)_+] = E(e^Y)N(d_+) - KN(d_-) \tag{17.11}$$

where

$$d_{\pm} = \left[ \log(E[e^{Y}]/K) \pm \frac{1}{2}\sigma_Y^2 \right] / \sigma_Y ,$$

and $\sigma_Y$ is the standard deviation of $Y$.

Applying (17.11) to (17.10) leads again to the call price formula.

## CHAPTER 18

# The Black-Scholes Model

The Black-Scholes model was first described by Fischer Black and Myron Scholes in their classic paper [7], where they determined convenient formulas used widely for pricing stock options. The model provides explicit formulas for call and put prices for an asset whose price evolution is described by a particular stochastic differential equation.

We shall assume that the underlying asset, such as a stock, pays no dividends and there are no splits during the time interval being considered. The Black-Scholes model was extended by Robert Merton [29] to the case of assets that pay dividends. The interest rate is assumed to be deterministic (a somewhat less restrictive assumption would also work).

In our approach, the Black-Scholes formula will come out very easily from the general option price formulas we have already derived. In fact, we shall first obtain the formula without any use of stochastic differential equations (SDE) and then discuss the SDE formulation. Under the Black-Scholes model, the asset price $S_t$ at time $t$ turns out to have log-normal distribution relative to the pricing measure $Q_t$ and $\log S_t$ has variance given by $\sigma\sqrt{t}$, for some positive constant $\sigma$. So all we have to do is substitute this into the call price formula (17.1) to obtain the call price $C$ with strike $K$ and expiration $t$:

$$\boxed{C = S_0 N(d_+) - e^{-rt} K N(d_-)} \tag{18.1}$$

where $S_0$ is the present price (time 0) for the asset, $r$ is the interest rate on a $t$-maturity bond, $N$ is the standard Gaussian distribution function, and $d_+$ and $d_-$ are given by

$$\begin{aligned} d_+ &= \frac{1}{\sigma\sqrt{t}} \log[e^{rt} S_0/K] + \frac{1}{2}\sigma\sqrt{t} \quad \text{and} \\ d_- &= \frac{1}{\sigma\sqrt{t}} \log[e^{rt} S_0/K] - \frac{1}{2}\sigma\sqrt{t} \end{aligned} \tag{18.2}$$

## DERIVATION OF THE BLACK-SCHOLES FORMULA

Let $S_t(\omega)$ be the price, at time $t \geq 0$ in scenario $\omega$, of the asset under consideration. Its price in time-0 money is obtained by discounting:

$$\tilde{S}_t = p(0,t) S_t \tag{18.3}$$

Here $p(0,t)$ is the random variable describing the conversion of time-$t$ cash into time-0 cash:

$$p(0,t;\omega) = e^{-\int_0^t r_u(\omega)\,du}, \tag{18.4}$$

where $r_u(\omega)$ is the instantaneous interest rate at time $u$ in scenario $\omega$. We shall assume that $p(0,t)$ is deterministic. Consequently, the pricing measure $Q_t$ for the time-$t$ cash numeraire coincides with the pricing measure $Q_0$. This has been proven in section 5.1.

We start with assumptions on the behavior of the fractional increase in the discounted prices $\tilde{S}_t$ relative to the pricing measure $Q_0$:

- the fractional increase $\tilde{S}_{t'}/\tilde{S}_t$ over a time interval $[t, t']$ is independent of the corresponding fractional increase over any other disjoint time interval;
- the distribution of the fractional $\tilde{S}_{t'}/\tilde{S}_t$ over a time interval $[t, t']$ is determined entirely by the length $t' - t$ of the time interval $[t, t']$, and depends continuously on $t' - t$.

A bit more is needed to get to the log-normality of the asset price, and here is a more technically detailed statement of the hypotheses:

- For each $t$, the random variable $Y_t = \log \tilde{S}_t$ has finite variance, i.e., $E_{Q_0}(Y_t^2) < \infty$;
- The differences $Y_t - Y_s$ for disjoint intervals $[s, t]$ are independent, and, for intervals of equal length, identically distributed;
- For any $0 \leq s < t$, the variance of $Y_t - Y_s$ is a continuous function of $t - s$.

Note that $Y_0 = \log \tilde{S}_0$ is deterministic since $\tilde{S}_0$ is simply the time-0 price of the asset, which is known with certainty.

We shall prove the following result below:

**Proposition 18.1.1** *With the hypotheses stated above, the random variable* $\log \tilde{S}_t$ *has normal distribution with respect to the pricing measure* $Q_0$ *and there is a constant* $\sigma \geq 0$ *such that the variance of* $\log \tilde{S}_t$ *is* $\sigma^2 t$ *for all* $t \geq 0$.

We know that

$$\tilde{S}_t = p(0, t)S_t = e^{-rt} S_t,$$

where $r$ is the interest on the $t$-maturity bond. Then

$$\log \tilde{S}_t = -rt + \log S_t$$

and so it follows from the Proposition that $\log S_t$ is also a Gaussian variable with the same variance

$$\sigma^2_{\log S_t} = \sigma^2_{\log \tilde{S}_t} = \sigma^2 t.$$

Needless to say, we are concerned with the case $\sigma_{S_t} > 0$ (otherwise the asset price is deterministic).

For a call on the asset with strike $K$ and expiration $t$, the price is now read off from (17.1):

$$\boxed{C = S_0 N(d_+) - e^{-rt} K N(d_-)} \tag{18.5}$$

where $S_0$ is the present price (time 0) of the asset, $N$ is the standard Gaussian distribution function, and $d_+$ and $d_-$ are given by

$$\begin{aligned} d_+ &= \frac{1}{\sigma\sqrt{t}} \log[e^{rt} S_0/K] + \frac{1}{2}\sigma\sqrt{t} \qquad \text{and} \\ d_- &= \frac{1}{\sigma\sqrt{t}} \log[e^{rt} S_0/K] - \frac{1}{2}\sigma\sqrt{t} \end{aligned} \tag{18.6}$$

The put price is obtained similarly from (17.3).

**Proof of proposition 18.1.1** The random variable $Y_t$ is infinitely divisible; more precisely, for any $M \geq 1$, $Y_t$ is the sum of the independent and identically distributed random variables $Y_{jt/M} - Y_{(j-1)t/M}$ for $j = 1, \ldots, M$, and the variances of the random variables add up to $\sigma^2_{Y_t}$.

The argument for the Central Limit Theorem then implies that $Y_t$ has normal distribution. Let $f(t) = \sigma^2_{Y_t} = \sigma^2_{Y_t - Y_0}$, bearing in mind that $Y_0$ is deterministic. For any $t, s \geq 0$ we have

$$Y_{t+s} - Y_0 = Y_s - Y_0 + \{Y_{t+s} - Y_s\}$$

and on the right here we have two independent random variables, the second one having the same distribution as $Y_t - Y_0$. Taking the variance we have:

$$f(t+s) = f(t) + f(s)$$

We have also assumed that $f$ is continuous. Then by a standard argument it follows that there is a constant $k$ such that $f(t) = kt$ for every $t \geq 0$. Because $f(t)$ is a variance, we necessarily have $f(t) \geq 0$ and so may write $k$ as $\sigma^2$ for some $\sigma \geq 0$. QED

## THE BLACK-SCHOLES STOCHASTIC DIFFERENTIAL EQUATION

In the preceding section we were able to derive the call price without a detailed description of how the price $S_t$ evolves. A closer examination of this price process involves the stochastic differential equation that governs the evolution of $S_t$. The Black-Scholes model posits that the fractional increase in the discounted price $\tilde{S}_t$ is distributed normally around a mean value of 0, and the fluctuation around zero is described by some scaled version of standard Brownian motion $t \mapsto B_t$. More precisely, the model equation is

$$\frac{d\tilde{S}_t}{\tilde{S}_t} = \sigma dB_t \qquad (18.7)$$

where $\sigma > 0$ is a parameter.

The stochastic differential equation (18.7) has the unique solution

$$\tilde{S}_t = \tilde{S}_0 e^{\sigma B_t - \frac{1}{2}\sigma^2 t} \qquad (18.8)$$

which is readily checked using the Itô formula.

The main point to observe is that, with repect to the measure $Q_0$,

$\log \tilde{S}_t$ is Gaussian with variance $\sigma^2 t$

Now let us

*assume that $p(0, t)$ is deterministic,*

i.e., has the same value in all market scenarios. Let $r$ denote the corresponding interest rate, specified by

$$p(0,t) = e^{-rt}$$

Because the conversion of time-$t$ cash to time-0 cash is deterministic, the pricing measures $Q_t$ and $Q_0$ coincide:

$$Q_t = Q_0$$

Moreover,

$$\tilde{S}_t = e^{-rt} S_t$$

So equation (18.8) implies that, with respect $Q_t = Q_0$,

$$\log S_t \text{ is Gaussian with variance } \sigma^2_{\log S_t} = \sigma^2 t$$

Once we have this, the method used in the preceding section gives the option prices.

## BLACK-SCHOLES PARAMETERS

The Black-Scholes option prices are completely determined from:

- The initial asset price $S_0$,
- The interest rate $r$,
- The strike $K$,
- The expiration date $t$,
- The volatility $\sigma$.

The volatility of the asset can be calculated from any standard call/put option traded on the market, and then this value can be used to price other options.

In reality, options expiring on the same date but with different strikes imply different values of the volatility. Because of the shape of the volatility-strike curve, this is often called the "smile" effect. The existence of the smile effect implies that Black-Scholes is not a completely accurate model. Of course, the very starting assumption, that there is a market-equilibrium measure is itself only an idealized hypothesis. But we have to retain this hypothesis in order to have any theory. It is possible to explain the smile-effect by making the volatility $\sigma$ time-dependent. One also has to bear in mind all the other simplifying assumptions made, such as deterministic interest-rate and absence of transaction costs and taxes.

CHAPTER 19

# The State Space and Evolution

We shall discuss the general framework for financial models. There are two basic elements:

**(i)** The *state space* whose points describe market configurations, and

**(ii)** The *transition probabilities* or *Green's functions* describing the stochastic evolution of the market.

## THE STATE SPACE

The market scenario $\omega$ we have been working with describes one possible evolution of the market for *all* relevant time. It is also useful to introduce the notion of the *state* or *configuration* of the market at any particular time. Let us assume that there is a set

$$\mathcal{S}$$

whose points $y$ describe the various states the market might be in at any time.

Let $\Omega$ be the set of all market scenarios. Denote by $y(t;\omega)$ the configuration/state of the market at time $t$ in scenario $\omega$. Thus, time evolution of the market is described by an $\mathcal{S}$-valued function

$$[0,\infty)\times\Omega\to\mathcal{S}:(\omega,t)\mapsto y(t;\omega)$$

A particular time evolution (starting at an initial time 0) of the market, corresponding to scenario $\omega$, is described by a path

$$[0,\infty)\to\mathcal{S}:t\mapsto y(t;\omega)$$

So we may actually take $\Omega$ to be the set of all such paths. The market models we shall work with specify *stochastic differential equations* satisfied by the process $t\mapsto y_t$, under the pricing measure $Q_0$.

Coordinates on $\mathcal{S}$ are called *state variables*. If we take $\mathcal{S}$ to be an $N$-dimensional space, we have an $N$-factor model. In fact we shall often take

$$\mathcal{S}=\mathbf{R}^N$$

For example, if we are concerned basically with $N$ assets that evolve in an essentially self-contained manner, we can take $\mathcal{S}=\mathbf{R}^N$. However, in many situations, the coordinates in $\mathcal{S}$ will correspond to "hidden" market *factors*, which might not have any simple interpretation in terms of asset prices. For example, interest-rate instruments, which we shall study later, have prices determined through dynamics in an $N$-dimensional space whose natural coordinates have, in general, no direct interpretation as prices.

The set of market events up till time $t$ is described by a $\sigma$-algebra $\mathcal{F}_t$ of subsets of $\Omega$.

## MARKOV EVOLUTION OF MARKET STATES

We denote by $Q$ a fixed pricing measure, for instance the market equilibrium measure for the time-0 cash numeraire.

The evolution of the market state $y_t$ is, in most (but not all) models, taken to be a *Markov process*. Thus, it is assumed that the distribution of the state $y_t$ depends on market events at all times prior to an instant $s < t$ only through the market state $y_s$. More precisely, the conditional probability

$$Q\,[y_t \in B \,|\, \sigma\{y_u : u \leq s\}]$$

is a function of the state $y_s$. Thus, in this case, one has a *transition probability* function

$$G_Q(s, y; t, B)$$

for any $0 \leq s \leq t$, $B$ any measurable subset of $\mathcal{S}$, and $y$ any point in state space $\mathcal{S}$, specified by

$$Q[y_t \in B \,|\, \sigma\{y_u : u \leq s\}] = G_Q(s, y_s; t, B) \tag{19.1}$$

Because $Q$ is the pricing measure, the transition probability $G_Q(s, y_s; t, B)$ is the price of an instrument that yields a unit of the numeraire at time $t$ if event $B$ happens and nothing otherwise, given that at time $s$ the market state is $y_s$.

In all models, the configuration space $\mathcal{S}$ comes equipped with a $\sigma$-algebra $\mathcal{F}$ and a reference measure $m$. For example, $\mathcal{S}$ may be a finite set, in which case $m$ is counting measure on the $\sigma$-algebra of all subsets of $\mathcal{S}$. In other examples, $\mathcal{S}$ is $\mathbf{R}^N$, with $m$ being Lebesgue measure on the $\sigma$-algebra $\mathcal{F}$ of Lebesgue-measurable sets. The transition probability $G_Q(s, y_s; t, B)$ is then assumed to be expressed in terms of a *transition density* function $G_Q(s, y; t, z)$ through:

$$G_Q(s, y; t, B) = \int_B G_Q(s, y_s; t, z)\, dm(z) \tag{19.2}$$

The type of processes usually considered in the continuum case are *diffusion* processes on $\mathbf{R}^N$. A diffusion process $t \mapsto y_t$ has a *drift* component, together with a *fluctuation* part. The transition density function satisfies a second-order partial differential equation due to *Kolmogorov*. The transition density then appears as the "fundamental solution" or *Green's function* for this differential equation.

At a "microscopic" level, the process $t \mapsto y_t$ can be pieced together from the drift process and a fluctuating *Brownian motion* or *Wiener process*. The technical method by which the original diffusion $t \mapsto y_t$ is reconstructed from a Brownian motion and drift is the theory of *stochastic differential equations* due to *Itô*.

Suppose now that for any $s \leq t$ and state $y$, the transition probability $p_A(s, y; t, B)$ equals 1 for some countable set $B$. This is the setting for *discrete* models for market evolution. Such a model may have the form of a *random walk* on a lattice $\mathcal{S} \subset \mathbf{R}^N$. There are also *tree models*, so called because of the way one may start out at a particular value $y_s$ and branch out at each time step, the branches increasing in number as one moves forward in time. Tree models often appear as approximations to limiting continuum models.

## GREEN'S FUNCTIONS FOR MARKOV MODELS

Consider a market model, with state space $\mathbf{R}^N$, which is Markov in the sense discussed in the preceding section.

Recall that for most derivative pricing there are three types of numeraires that appear: (i) time-$t$ cash for an asset delivered at future date $T$; (ii) time-$T$ cash for an asset delivered at the future date $T$; (iii) an underlying asset at time-$t$. We will assume that our model is a Markov model for all these pricing measures.

The Green's function $G_Q(s, x; t, y)$, as a function of $y$, is the probability density of $y_t$, relative to a pricing measure $Q$, given that $y_s = x$. The notation for the pricing measures and Green's functions for three numeraires are summarized in Table 19.1, where $0 \leq t \leq T$:

The superscripts on the Green's functions $G^{\text{for}}_{Q_T}$ and $G^{\text{nd}}_{Q_t}$ are a reminder that they are used to determine forward and "nondiscounted" future prices. The superscript $G^{\text{shifted}}_{Q^*_t}$ is put in because in the two most basic models—Gaussian and chi-squared—this distribution differs from the forward measure only in that the parameters of the distribution are shifted.

**TABLE 19–1**

Green's Functions and Numeraires

| Green's Function $G_Q$ | Numeraire for the Pricing Measure $Q$ | Specification |
|---|---|---|
| $G^{\text{for}}_{Q_T}(t, x; T, y)$ | Time-$T$ cash | $E_{Q_T}(f(y_T)\|\mathcal{F}_t) = \int_{R^N} G^{\text{for}}_{Q_T}(t, y_t; T, y)\, f(y)\, dy$ |
| $G^{\text{nd}}_{Q_t}(t, x; T, y)$ | Time-$t$ cash | $E_{Q_t}(f(y_T)\|\mathcal{F}_t) = \int_{R^N} G^{\text{nd}}_{Q_t}(t, y_t; T, y)\, f(y)\, dy$ |
| $G^{\text{shifted}}_{Q_t^*}(s, x; t, y)$ | Asset delivered at time $t$ | $E_{Q_t^*}(F(y_t)\|\mathcal{F}_s) = \int_{R^N} G^{\text{shifted}}_{Q_t^*}(s, y_s; t, y)\, F(y)\, dy$ |

## GREEN'S FUNCTIONS AND FEYNMAN-KAC

In this section we shall show how the Green's function as well as certain instrument prices can be obtained by solving certain partial differential equations. This remarkable relation between solutions of certain partial differential equations and quantities that can be expressed as expectation values of stochastic functionals is summarized in the *Feynman-Kac formula*, which was discovered in the context of the Schrödinger equation in quantum mechanics.

The mathematical discussion in this section will be formal in the sense that we shall work out formulas and calculations without spelling out or worrying about the technical conditions under which they hold.

For the sake of notational simplicity we shall work with 1–factor models; the discussion extends in a straightforward way to $N$-factor models.

Let us begin with the framework of a probability space $(\Omega, \mathcal{F}, Q)$ and $\sigma$-algebras $\mathcal{F}_t$, for all $t \geq 0$, with

$$\mathcal{F}_s \subset \mathcal{F}_t \subset \mathcal{F} \text{ for all } 0 \leq s \leq t$$

As usual, elements $\omega$ in $\Omega$ describe scenarios of the market. The $\sigma$-algebra $\mathcal{F}_t$ is the collection of all market events up till time $t$.

Let

$$W : [0, \infty) \times \Omega \to \mathbf{R} : (t, \omega) \mapsto W_t(\omega)$$

be Brownian motion, with $W_t$ being $\mathcal{F}_t$-measurable for each $t \in [0, \infty)$, and the increment $W_t - W_s$ independent of $\mathcal{F}_s$ for all $0 \leq s < t$.

Now suppose

$$Y : [0, \infty) \times \Omega \to \mathbf{R} : (t, \omega) \mapsto Y_t(\omega)$$

is a stochastic process, again with $Y_t$ being $\mathcal{F}_t$-measurable for each $t \geq 0$, satisfying the Itô stochastic differential equation:

$$dY_t = -a(t, Y_t)dt + b(t, Y_t)dW_t \tag{19.3}$$

where $a$ and $b$ are well-behaved functions. For more on what such an equation means, see Chapter 25.

Now let

$$r : [0, \infty) \times \mathbf{R} \to \mathbf{R} : y \mapsto r(t, y)$$

be a function that we interpret as giving the interest rate $r(t, y)$ at time $t$ when the state is $y$. In our models, $r$ will be of the form

$$r(t, y) = \alpha_0(t) + a_1 y(t)$$

where $\alpha_0$ is a function and $a_1$ a constant.

The transition density or *Green's function* for the process $t \mapsto Y_t$ is a well-behaved function $G_Q(s, x; t, y)$ satisfying

$$Q([Y_t \in A] | \mathcal{F}_s) = \int_A G_Q(s, Y_s; t, y)\, dy$$

for any Borel set $A \subset \mathbf{R}$ and $0 \leq s < t$.

A typical derivative is an asset which at a date $T$ yields an amount $F(y)$ in market state $y$. For pricing such derivatives and related instruments, we are interested in quantities of the type

$$E_Q[F(Y_T) | \mathcal{F}_s] \tag{19.4}$$

and

$$f_F(s, Y_s) = E_Q\left[e^{-\int_s^T r(u)du} F(Y_T)\middle|\mathcal{F}_s\right] \tag{19.5}$$

The *Markov* nature of the process $s \mapsto Y_s$ guarantees that the expectations above are indeed functions of $(s, Y_s)$.

From Theorem 24.5.2, which we shall prove in Chapter 24, it follows that

$$\frac{f_F(s, Y_s)}{f_1(s, Y_s)} = E_{Q'}\left[F(Y_T)\middle|\mathcal{F}_s\right] \tag{19.6}$$

where $Q'$ is the measure given by

$$dQ' = \frac{e^{-\int_s^T r(u)du} dQ}{E_Q\left[e^{-\int_s^T r(u)du}\right]}$$

If we take, at a formal level, $F(y)$ to be the delta–function $\delta(y - y_0)$ then $f_F(s, Y_s)$ would be the Green's function $G_{Q'}(s, Y_s; T, y_0)$. However, it is easier to take a somewhat indirect route and set $F(y) = e^{-\lambda y}$. This yields the *Laplace transform* of the Green's function, and the latter can be recovered by Laplace inversion.

From the financial point of view, $f_F(s, Y_s)$ is the time-$s$ price of an asset and so, adjusted appropriately for numeraire, is a martingale. Thus, the process

$$s \mapsto e^{-\int_0^s r(u,Y_u)du} f_F(s, Y_s) = E_Q\left[e^{-\int_0^T r(u,Y_u)du} F(Y_T)|\mathcal{F}_s\right]$$

is a *martingale* for $s \in [0, T]$. We shall verify this in a formal way, working with $0 \leq s \leq t \leq T$. For notational simplicity we drop the subscript $F$ from $f_F$ and proceed:

$$\begin{aligned}
&E_Q\left[e^{-\int_0^t r(u,Y_u)du} f(t, Y_t)|\mathcal{F}_s\right] \\
&\quad = E_Q\left[e^{-\int_0^t r(u,Y_u)du} E_Q\left[e^{-\int_t^T r(u,Y_u)du} F(Y_T)\middle|\mathcal{F}_t\right]\middle|\mathcal{F}_s\right] \\
&\quad = E_Q\left[E_Q\left[e^{-\int_0^T r(u,Y_u)du} F(Y_T)\middle|\mathcal{F}_t\right]\middle|\mathcal{F}_s\right] \\
&\quad = E_Q\left[e^{-\int_0^T r(u,Y_u)du} F(Y_T)\middle|\mathcal{F}_s\right] \\
&\quad = e^{-\int_0^s r(u,Y_u)du} f(s, Y_s).
\end{aligned}$$

The Itô stochastic differential of $e^{-\int_0^t r(u,Y_u)\,du} f(t,Y_t)$ is

$$d\left[e^{-\int_0^t r(u,Y_u)\,du} f(t,Y_t)\right]$$
$$= e^{-\int_0^t r(u,Y_u)\,du}\left[\frac{\partial f}{\partial t} + \frac{1}{2}\frac{\partial^2 f}{\partial y^2} b^2 - a\frac{\partial f}{\partial y} - rf\right] dt + \star d W_t$$

where the last term collects together multiples of $dW_t$. Because the process

$$t \mapsto e^{-\int_0^t r(u,Y_u)\,du} f(t,Y_t)$$

is a martingale, it has no drift, and so the coefficient of $dt$ should be zero. This gives the partial differential equation obeyed by $f$:

$$\frac{\partial f}{\partial t} + \frac{b^2}{2}\frac{\partial^2 f}{\partial y^2} - a\frac{\partial f}{\partial y} - rf = 0 \tag{19.7}$$

The boundary condition is obtained from the value of $f(t,Y_t)$ at $t = T$:

$$f(T,y) = F(y)$$

As noted before, the solution of (19.7) with $F(y) = e^{-\lambda y}$ leads to the Laplace transforms of the Green's functions.

**TABLE 19–2**

Summary of Modeling Concepts

- Specification of a state space $\mathcal{S}$. Each state of the market corresponds to a point $y \in \mathcal{S}$. Usually $\mathbf{R}^N$, $N$ being the number of *factors* that determine the state of the market.
- A *stochastic differential equation* specifying a process $t \mapsto Y_t \in \mathcal{S}$, relative to some fixed pricing measure $Q$. Typically, the equation has the form

$$dY_t = a dt + b dW_t$$

where $a$, $b$ are functions of $t$ and $Y_t$, and $t \mapsto W_t$ is a Wiener process.
- An equation specifying the interest rate $r$ at each time in terms of the factors $y \in \mathcal{S}$; usually it is an affine equation such as $r(t, y) = \alpha_0(t) + a_1 y_1(t) + \cdots + a_N y_N(t)$ with $\alpha_0$ a function and $a_1, \ldots, a_N$ constants.
- The *task* then is to determine prices of assets in the interest–rate market. Mathematically this requires evaluation of integrals over $\Omega$. Typical integrals are conditioned versions of $\int_\Omega \phi(Y_t)\, dQ$ and $\int_\Omega \phi(Y_t)\, dQ'$, where $\phi$ is a function specified by the asset and $Q'$ is the measure given by

$$dQ' = \frac{e^{-\int_t^T r(s, Y_s)\, ds} dQ}{\int_\Omega e^{-\int_t^T r(s, Y_s)\, ds} dQ}$$

- Evaluation of the integrals over $\Omega$ can be transformed into the task of solving certain second order partial differential equations: the link between integrals over $\Omega$ and partial differential equations is the *Feynman–Kac formula* which expresses expectation values of Brownian/Wiener functionals as solutions of certain partial differential equations.
- The evolution of the process $t \mapsto Y_t$ is also described by the transition density or *Green's function* $G(s, x; t, y)$ which, as a function of $y$, is the density of $Y_t$ with respect to the relevant measure $Q$ or $Q^*$ conditional on $Y_s = x$. The Green's function $G(s, x; t, y)$ satisfies the Kolmogorov equation, a partial differential equation. A convenient method of determining the Green's function is to determine its *Laplace transform* $f_{t,\lambda}(s, x) = \int e^{-\lambda \cdot y} G(s, x; t, y)\, dy$. This transform also satisfies the partial differential equation with the final condition that $f_{t,\lambda}(t, y) = e^{-\lambda \cdot y}$.

CHAPTER 20

# Gaussian Models

In this chapter we study an $N$-factor model of the interest rate based on the two-factor model of Hull and White [23]. The Green's function is a fundamental entity associated with any model, and for the $N$-factor model we develop in this chapter, it will be Gaussian. For this reason we call this a *Gaussian model*.

A central object for the interest-rate market is the *yield curve*. This curve displays the interest rates/yields on zero-coupon bonds maturing at all times in the future. As time goes on, bond prices move and the yield curve changes. The basic interest-rate model must describe the dynamics of the yield curve.

In this chapter we state the stochastic differential equations that specify the Gaussian models. We then simply state the Green's functions for these models. The actual determination of the Green's functions is carried out in Chapter 22.

## THE MODEL FUNDAMENTALS

The market state space for our model is $\mathbf{R}^N$. This means that the state of the market at any time is coordinatized by $N$ *factors* $y_1, \ldots, y_N$, and the evolution of the market is described by a process

$$t \mapsto (y_1(t), \ldots, y_N(t))$$

The instrument that determines the interest rate is the zero-coupon bond. The price of such a $T$-maturity bond at time $t \le T$ is given by

$$P(t, T) = E_{Q_t}[p(t, T)|\mathcal{F}_t] \tag{20.1}$$

where $Q_t$ is the pricing measure for the time-$t$ cash numeraire, $\mathcal{F}_t$ is the $\sigma$-algebra of market events up till time $t$, and $p(t, T)$ is the random variable describing the scenario-dependent discount factor. For any market scenario $\omega \in \Omega$, the discount factor $p(t, T; \omega)$ can be expressed as

$$p(t, T; \omega) = e^{-\int_t^T r(u;\omega)\,du} \tag{20.2}$$

where $r(u; \omega)$ is the "spot rate" at time $u$ if market scenario $\omega$ is realized.

Our $N$-factor model assumes that the spot rate $r(t)$ is the sum of a deterministic factor $\alpha_0(t)$ together with certain fluctuating *factors* $y_1, \ldots, y_N$. Thus, according to our model, the process $t \mapsto r(t)$ is expressed as a sum:

$$r(t) = \alpha_0(t) + \sum_{j=1}^{N} y_j(t) \tag{20.3}$$

where $\alpha_0(\cdot)$ is a deterministic term (i.e., independent of the state of the system). A stochastic differential equation describing the dynamics of the $y_j$'s will be specified in later sections below.

Using the stochastic differential equation for the $y_j$'s, we determine the forward *Green's function* $G^{\text{for}}_{Q_t}(s, x; t, y)$ for $E_{Q_t}[\cdots|\mathcal{F}_s]$, where $Q_t$ is the pricing measure with time-$t$ cash as numeraire. The forward Green's function is the key to computing forward prices as expectation values. For example, the time-$T$ forward price, as seen at time $t < T$, of an asset which will yield cash $F(y)$

in market scenario $y$ is given by

$$E_{Q_T}[F(y(T))|\mathcal{F}_t] = \int_{\mathbf{R}^N} G^{\text{for}}_{Q_T}(t, y(t); T, x)F(x)\,dx \quad (20.4)$$

Recall that

$$E_{Q_T}[S(T)|\mathcal{F}_t] = \begin{array}{l}\text{Forward Price, as decided at}\\ \text{time } t\text{, for the security } S\\ \text{deliverable at time } T\end{array} \quad (20.5)$$

and

$$\begin{aligned}\begin{array}{l}\text{Present Value of secu-}\\ \text{rity } S \text{ to be purchased}\\ \text{at time } T\end{array} &= \text{Discount Factor} \times \text{Forward Price}\\ &= P(0, T)E_{Q_T}[S(T)]\end{aligned}$$

where $S(T)$ denotes the price of the security at time $T$, and $P(0, T)$ is the time-0 price of the $T$-maturity bond.

## ONE-FACTOR GAUSSIAN MODEL

The 1-factor Hull-White model was introduced in [23]. This model has the nice feature that it yields closed-form formulas for prices of all the basic instruments (in essence, even of swaptions).

A 1-factor model is not realistic. The state of the interest-rate market at any time $t$ is specified by the yield curve, i.e., the funcion $T \mapsto P(t, T)$. As time $t$ changes, so does the yield curve. If there were just one underlying factor, then the change in the entire curve would be determined by this one factor. This contradicts the observation that the yield curve changes in complicated ways. Nevertheless, the 1-factor model provides a good qualitative understanding of yield-curve dynamics. Secondly, it is a good warm-up for more complex $N$-factor models.

The short rate $r(t)$ is assumed to be the sum of a deterministic part $\alpha_0(t)$ and a stochastic factor $y(t)$. The stochastic factor

$y(t)$ evolves in a *mean-reverting* manner. This mean-reversion property is central to the Hull-White model and is also a useful general idea.

In detail, the short-rate $r$ is assumed to be given by

$$r(t) = \alpha_0(t) + y(t) \tag{20.6}$$

where $\alpha_0$ is a deterministic function and the process $t \mapsto y(t)$ satisfies the stochastic differential equation

$$dy(t) = -ay(t)dt + \sigma dw_t \tag{20.7}$$

where $t \mapsto w_t$ is standard Brownian motion with respect to the pricing measure $Q_0$ (with time-0 cash as numeraire), and $a, \sigma > 0$ are parameters.

The parameter $a$ governs the tendency for *mean reversion* for the interest rate process. From (20.7) we see that when $y(t)$ is large positive, the first term $-ay(t)dt$ on the right tends to bring it back to a lower value, while if $y(t)$ is a large negative then the term forces $y(t)$ to increase. Thus, either way, the first term tends to keep $y(t)$ from getting too far positive or negative.

The second term $\sigma dw(t)$ is a market fluctuation term, which, in this model, is taken simply as Gaussian.

A drawback of this model is that $r(t)$ could become negative. However, if the parameters are appropriate, the probability of this happening could be very small.

Once prices of some standard instruments have been determined in closed form, these price formulas can be compared with market prices of the instruments to *calibrate* the model, i.e. to estimate best values for the parameters $a$ and $\sigma$.

The price at time $t$ of the $T$-maturity bond is the discount factor

$$P(t,T) = E_{Q_t}\left[e^{-\int_t^T r(s)ds} \middle| \mathcal{F}_t\right] \tag{20.8}$$

In Chapter 22 we will see that $P(t,T)$ works out to be:

$$P(t,T) = e^{A(t,T)-B(t,T)y(t)} \tag{20.9}$$

where

$$A(t,T) = -\int_t^T \alpha_0(s)\,ds + \frac{\sigma^2}{2a^2} \times \left[\tau - \frac{2}{a}(1 - E_a(\tau)) + \frac{1}{2a}(1 - E_a(2\tau))\right] \quad (20.10)$$

and

$$B(t,T) = \frac{1 - E_a(\tau)}{a} \quad (20.11)$$

where

$$\tau = T - t \text{ and } E_a(x) \stackrel{\text{def}}{=} e^{-ax} \quad (20.12)$$

The expressions for the bond prices $P(0,s)$ yield the forward bond prices

$$FP(t,T) = \frac{P(0,T)}{P(0,t)} \quad (20.13)$$

for a $T$-maturity bond deliverable at time $t \leq T$.

The Green's function for $E_{Q_T}[\cdot|\mathcal{F}_t]$ works out to be the Gaussian kernel

$$G_{Q_T}^{\text{for}}\left(t, y(t);\, T, x\right) = \frac{1}{\sqrt{2\pi\Sigma^2}} e^{-\frac{(x-m)^2}{2\Sigma^2}} \quad (20.14)$$

with mean

$$m = E_a(\tau)y(t) - \frac{\sigma^2}{2a^2}(1 - E_a(\tau))^2 \quad (20.15)$$

and variance

$$\Sigma^2 = \frac{\sigma^2}{2a}(1 - E_a(2\tau)) \quad (20.16)$$

Note that this means, in particular, that the random variable $y(T)$ is Gaussian under the measure $Q_T$, conditional on any given value for $y(t)$.

For calculating futures prices, it is necessary to have the "nondiscounted" Green's function $G^{\mathrm{nd}}_{Q_t}(t, y(t); T, x)$ for which

$$E_{Q_t}[F(y(T))|\mathcal{F}_t] = \int_{\mathbf{R}} G^{\mathrm{nd}}_{Q_t}(t, y(t); T, x) F(x)\, dx$$

This Green's function turns out to be also Gaussian:

$$G^{\mathrm{nd}}_{Q_t}(t, y(t); T, x) = \frac{1}{\sqrt{2\pi\, \Sigma^2_{\mathrm{nd}}}} e^{-\frac{(x-m_{\mathrm{nd}})^2}{2\Sigma^2_{\mathrm{nd}}}} \tag{20.17}$$

where

$$m_{\mathrm{nd}} = E_{Q_t}(y(T)|\mathcal{F}_t) = E_a(\tau) y(t) \tag{20.18}$$

and

$$\Sigma^2_{\mathrm{nd}} = \mathrm{var}(y(T)|\mathcal{F}_t) = \frac{\sigma^2}{2a}(1 - E_a(2\tau)) \tag{20.19}$$

In particular, the random variable $y(T)$ is Gaussian under the measure $Q_0$.

From the expression for $P(t, T)$ given in (20.9), and the fact that $y(t)$ is Gaussian under $Q_0$ and $Q_T$, we see that $P(t, T)$ is *log-normal* under the measures $Q_0$ and $Q_T$. So the price of a call or put option on the $T$-maturity bond can be computed as in Chapter 17.

The price of a call option, with strike $K$ and expiration $t$, on a $T$-maturity bond works out to

$$\begin{aligned} &\text{Price of Call Option} \\ &\quad = P(0,t)\left[F P(t,T) N\left(d_+^{\text{Gauss 1-factor}}\right) - K N\left(d_-^{\text{Gauss 1-factor}}\right)\right] \end{aligned} \tag{20.20}$$

where $N(x)$ denotes the Gaussian cumulative probability

$$N(x) = \int_{-\infty}^{x} \frac{e^{-y^2/2}}{\sqrt{2\pi}}\, dy,$$

and

$$d_{+}^{\text{Gauss 1-factor}} = \frac{\log \frac{FP(t,T)}{K} + \frac{s^2}{2}}{s} \tag{20.21}$$

and

$$d_{-}^{\text{Gauss 1-factor}} = \frac{\log \frac{FP(t,T)}{K} - \frac{s^2}{2}}{s} \tag{20.22}$$

with

$$s^2 = \sigma^2(1 - e^{-a\tau})^2 \frac{(1 - e^{-2a\tau})}{2a^3} \tag{20.23}$$

This is a special case of the call price for multifactor Gaussian models discussed below.

## MULTIFACTOR GAUSSIAN MODEL

As mentioned earlier, the 1-factor model is not rich enough to explain the full complexity of yield curve dynamics. Thus a multifactor version is called for. Rebonato [34, Table 3.2] explains the utility and significance of having several factors.

The spot interest rate $r(t)$ is specified by

$$r(t) = \alpha_0(t) + \sum_{j=1}^{N} y_j(t) \tag{20.24}$$

where $\alpha_0$ is deterministic and the $y_j$ satisfy the stochastic differential equations

$$dy_j(t) = -a_j y_j(t)dt + \sigma_j dw_j(t) \tag{20.25}$$

where $a_j, \sigma_j > 0$, and the $w_j$ are Brownian motions with respect to the pricing measure $Q_0$ and satisfy

$$dw_j(t)dw_k(t) = \rho_{jk}dt \tag{20.26}$$

We may assume that each $\rho_{jj} = 1$. Note again the mean-reverting feature of the equation for $y_j$.

As in the one-factor case, this model has the drawback that there is positive probability for $r(t)$ to be negative.

The time-$t$ price of the $T$-maturity bond is given by

$$P(t, T) = e^{A(t,T) - B(t,T)\cdot y(t)} \tag{20.27}$$

where, as we show in Chapter 22,

$$A(t, T) = -\int_t^T \alpha_0(s)\,ds + \frac{1}{2}\sum_{j,k=1}^{N} \sigma_j \sigma_k \rho_{jk} \times \left[\frac{\left(1 - e^{-(a_j+a_k)\tau}\right)}{a_j a_k (a_j + a_k)} - \frac{2}{a_j a_k}\frac{1 - e^{-a_j \tau}}{a_j} + \frac{1}{a_j a_k}\tau\right] \tag{20.28}$$

and

$$B_j(t, T) = \frac{1 - e^{-a_j \tau}}{a_j} \tag{20.29}$$

with

$$\tau = T - t$$

Let $0 \le u < t$. The distribution of $y(t)$ with respect to the measure $Q_t$, conditional on all information up to time $u$ (i.e. conditioned to $\mathcal{F}_u$) has the $N$-dimensional Gaussian density function:

$$G^{\text{for}}_{Q_t}(u, y; t, x) = (2\pi \det C)^{-N/2} e^{-\frac{(x-m)\cdot C^{-1}(x-m)}{2}} \tag{20.30}$$

with mean $m = (m_1, \ldots, m_N)$ and variance-covariance matrix $[C_{jk}]$, where

$$m_j = \frac{1}{2}\sum_{k=1}^{N} \sigma_j \sigma_k \rho_{jk} \frac{1}{a_k} \times \left[\frac{1 - e^{-(a_j+a_k)(t-u)}}{a_j + a_k} - \frac{1 - e^{-a_j(t-u)}}{a_j}\right] + e^{-a_j(t-u)} y_j(u)$$

and $C_{jk}$, a function of $t - u$, is given by

$$C_{jk} = \rho_{jk}\sigma_j\sigma_k \frac{\left[1 - e^{-(a_j+a_k)(t-u)}\right]}{a_j + a_k} \tag{20.31}$$

The distribution of $y(t)$ with respect to the measure $Q_u$, conditional on all information up to time $u$ (i.e. conditioned to $\mathcal{F}_u$) has $N$-dimensional Gaussian density function with mean $m^{\text{nd}} = (m_1^{\text{nd}}, \ldots, m_N^{\text{nd}})$, where

$$m_j^{\text{nd}} = e^{-a_j(t-u)} y_j(u) \tag{20.32}$$

and the variance-covariance matrix $[C_{jk}]$ is as before.

Because $\log P(t,T)$ is Gaussian with respect to $Q_t$ (we work now with $u = 0$, for notational simplicity), we can apply the Black-Scholes formula to determine the price of a call option. The formula involves the variance of $\log P(t,T)$, which is (with $\tau = T - t$)

$$\begin{aligned}\operatorname{var}(\log P(t,T)) &= \sum_{j,k=1}^{N} C_{jk}(t) B_j(t,T) B_k(t,T) \\ &= \sum_{j,k=1}^{N} \rho_{jk}\sigma_j\sigma_k(1-e^{-a_j\tau})(1-e^{-a_k\tau})\frac{(1-e^{-(a_j+a_k)t})}{a_j a_k(a_j+a_k)}\end{aligned} \tag{20.33}$$

So the price of a call option, with strike $K$ and expiration $t$, on a $T$–maturity bond works out to

$$\text{Price of Call Option} = P(0,t)[FP(t,T)N(d_+) - KN(d_-)] \tag{20.34}$$

where $N(x)$ denotes the Gaussian cumulative probability

$$N(x) = \int_{-\infty}^{x} \frac{e^{-y^2/2}}{\sqrt{2\pi}}\, dy,$$

and

$$d_+ = \frac{\log \frac{FP(t,T)}{K} + \frac{s^2}{2}}{s} \tag{20.35}$$

and

$$d_- = \frac{\log \frac{FP(t,T)}{K} - \frac{s^2}{2}}{s} \tag{20.36}$$

with

$$s^2 = \sum_{j,k=1}^{N} \rho_{jk}\sigma_j\sigma_k(1 - e^{-a_j\tau})(1 - e^{-a_k\tau})\frac{\left(1 - e^{-(a_j+a_k)t}\right)}{a_j a_k(a_j + a_k)} \quad (20.37)$$

## VOLATILITY AND CORRELATIONS

A mathematical model for a market should provide a good qualitative understanding as well as computability of the relationship between model parameters and volatility/correlations of market variables such as prices or rates. In this section we examine volatility and correlations between various interest rates predicted by the Gaussian models considered above.

The *forward rate*, as seen at time $t$, over a future period from $T$ to $T'$ is the quantity $f(t, T, T')$ specified through the forward bond price

$$FP(t, T, T') = \frac{P(t, T')}{P(t, T)} = e^{-f(t,T,T')(T'-T)} \quad (20.38)$$

Solving for the forward rate, we have:

$$f(t, T, T') = -\frac{\log P(t, T') - \log P(t, T)}{T' - T} \quad (20.39)$$

The *forward spot rate* is the expected spot rate at a future time $T$ as seen at a time $t \leq T$. It is obtained by letting $T' \to T$ in the forward rate $f(t, T, T')$:

$$f(t, T) = -\partial_T \log P(t, T) = -\partial_T A(t, T) + \partial_T B(t, T) \cdot y(t) \quad (20.40)$$

To see how the forward spot rate behaves, we consider the stochastic differential $d_t f(t, T)$:

$$d_t f(t, T) = \star dt + \partial_T B(t, T) \cdot dy(t) \quad (20.41)$$

Assume that $a_2 > a_1$. Then, letting $T \to \infty$, we get the limiting correlation

$$R_{0\infty} = \frac{\sigma_1 + \rho\sigma_2}{\sqrt{\sigma_1^2 + \sigma_2^2 + 2\rho\sigma_1\sigma_2}} \tag{20.45}$$

If $\sigma_2 > \sigma_1$ and $\rho = -1$ then there is perfect negative $-1$ correlation between the short- and long-term volatilities. If, on the other hand, $\sigma_1 > \sigma_2$ and $\rho = -1$, then there is perfect positive $+1$ correlation between the two volatilities.

Solving for $\rho$ in terms of $R_{0\infty}$ we have

$$\rho = -\frac{\sigma_1}{\sigma_2}\left(1 - R_{0\infty}^2\right) \pm |R_{0\infty}|\sqrt{1 - \frac{\sigma_1^2}{\sigma_2^2}\left(1 - R_{0\infty}^2\right)} \tag{20.46}$$

For this to be real, $|R_{0\infty}|$ must be greater or equal to $\sqrt{\max\left\{0, 1 - \frac{\sigma_2^2}{\sigma_1^2}\right\}}$.

Returning now to the expression for the per-unit-time covariance of the forward rates given by (20.42), we have, upon setting $T_1 = T_2 = T$,

$$\frac{\operatorname{var}(d_t f(0,T))}{dt} = \sum_{j,k=1}^{N} \rho_{jk}\sigma_j\sigma_k e^{-(a_j + a_k)T} \tag{20.47}$$

which, for the 2-factor model, reads

$$\frac{\operatorname{var}(d_t f(0,T))}{dt} = \sigma_1^2 e^{-2a_1T} + \sigma_2^2 e^{-2a_2T} + 2\rho\sigma_1\sigma_2 e^{-(a_1+a_2)T} \tag{20.48}$$

This is positive at $T = 0$ and goes to 0 as $T \to \infty$.

If $\rho$ were $\geq 0$ then the function would be monotone decreasing.

The curve for the forward short–rate volatility usually shows a hump (see, for example, Rebonato [34, Figure 4.12]). The formula (20.48) shows that to have a hump it is necessary for $\rho$

and thus

$$\begin{aligned}\text{cov}(d_t f(t,T_1), d_t f(t,T_2)) &= E[d_t f(t,T_1) d_t f(t,T_2)] \\ &= \sum_{j,k=1}^{N} \partial_T B_j(t,T_1)\partial_T B_k(t,T_2)\sigma_j\sigma_k\rho_{jk} dt\end{aligned}$$

Using the expression for $B_j(t,T)$:

$$B_j(t,T) = \frac{1-e^{-a_j(T-t)}}{a_j}$$

this gives the per-unit-time covariance, as (setting $t=0$ for convenience):

$$\frac{\text{cov}\big(d_t f(0,T_1), d_t f(0,T_2)\big)}{dt} = \sum_{j,k=1}^{N} \rho_{jk}\sigma_j\sigma_k e^{-(a_j T_1 + a_k T_2)} \qquad (20.42)$$

For the 2-factor model this is:

$$\begin{aligned}\frac{\text{cov}(d_t f(0,T_1), d_t f(0,T_2))}{dt} &= \sigma_1^2 e^{-a_1(T_1+T_2)} + \sigma_2^2 e^{-a_2(T_1+T_2)} + \rho\sigma_1\sigma_2 \\ &\quad \times \left[e^{-(a_1T_1+a_2T_2)} + e^{-(a_2T_1+a_1T_2)}\right]\end{aligned} \qquad (20.43)$$

So the correlation, with $T_1=0$ and $T_2=T$, is:

$$\frac{\sigma_1^2 e^{-a_1T} + \sigma_2^2 e^{-a_2T} + \rho\sigma_1\sigma_2[e^{-a_1T} + e^{-a_2T}]}{\sqrt{\left(\sigma_1^2+\sigma_2^2+2\rho\sigma_1\sigma_2\right)\left(\sigma_1^2 e^{-2a_1T} + \sigma_2^2 e^{-2a_2T} + 2\rho\sigma_1\sigma_2 e^{-(a_1+a_2)T}\right)}}$$

Multiplying numerator and denominator by $e^{a_1T}$ we write this as

$$R_{0T} = \frac{\sigma_1^2 + \rho\sigma_1\sigma_2 + \left(\sigma_2^2+\rho\sigma_1\sigma_2\right)e^{-(a_2-a_1)T}}{\sqrt{\left(\sigma_1^2+\sigma_2^2+2\rho\sigma_1\sigma_2\right)\left(\sigma_1^2 + 2\rho\sigma_1\sigma_2 e^{-(a_2-a_1)T} + \sigma_2^2 e^{-2(a_2-a_1)T}\right)}} \qquad (20.44)$$

to be negative. Assuming that $\rho < 0$, then a sufficient condition for there to be a hump would be that the function is initially increasing in $T$ (i.e., its derivative at $T = 0$ is positive). This is the requirement that

$$a_1\sigma_1^2 + a_2\sigma_2^2 - |\rho|\sigma_1\sigma_2(a_1 + a_2) < 0$$

which is equivalent to

$$|\rho| > \frac{a_1}{a_1 + a_2}\left(\frac{\sigma_1}{\sigma_2}\right) + \frac{a_2}{a_1 + a_2}\left(\frac{\sigma_2}{\sigma_1}\right) \tag{20.49}$$

This, together with $\rho < 0$, is sufficient to ensure a hump in the forward rate volatility curve. Because $|\rho| \leq 1$, it places restrictions on $a_1, a_2, \sigma_1, \sigma_2$.

Quantities of the type $\frac{\mathrm{var}(d_t f(0,T))}{dt}$ are "volatilities in time," as opposed to the volatilities-at-any-given-time (such as the $\sigma_i$) that we have been working with. The following considerations (essentially discussed earlier in Chapter 16) may throw some light on the relationship between the two types of volatilities. By definition, $\int_0^t dX_s^2$ is the limit in probability of $\sum_{j=1}^N [X_{s_j} - X_{s_{j-1}}]^2$, where $0 < s_1 < \cdots < s_N$, as $\max_j |s_j - s_{j-1}| \to 0$. On the other hand, $X_t = X_0 + \int_0^t dX_s$, which, by definition, is the limit in probability $X_0 + \lim \sum_j (X_j - X_{j-1})$. Taking $X_0$ to be known (i.e. deterministic), it follows that $\mathrm{var}[X_t] = \int_0^t \mathrm{var}[dX_s]$, with the integral interpreted in the obvious way. Under reasonable conditions we then have

$$\mathrm{var}[X_t] = \int_0^t \frac{\mathrm{var}[dX_s]}{ds}\, ds.$$

Thus the derivative of the absolute volatility $\mathrm{var}[X_t]$ is in fact equal to the volatility-per-unit-time $\frac{\mathrm{var}[dX_s]}{ds}$:

$$\frac{d\,\mathrm{var}[X_t]}{dt} = \frac{\mathrm{var}[dX_t]}{dt} \tag{20.50}$$

Now set $X_s = \log F P(s, t, T) = \log \frac{P(s,T)}{P(s,t)}$, which equals log $P(t, T)$ when $s = t$. Therefore,

$$\text{var}[\log P(t, T)] = \int_0^t \frac{\text{var}\big[d_s \log F P(s, t, T)\big]}{ds} ds \quad (20.51)$$

Compare this with [34, Equation (13.55)], where the argument relies on a complex expression obtained by Hull and White [23] by carrying out the integration on the right. From our perspective, the left side is calculated directly because we know that $\log P(t, T) = A(t, T) - B(t, T) \cdot y(t)$ and have the covariances of the $y_j(t)$.

## CONVEXITY ADJUSTMENT

Consider two instruments:

**(A)** The payoff, made at time $t$, is the nominal \$1 times the rate $R_{t,\tau}$ over the period $[t, t + \tau]$.

**(B)** The payoff, made at time $t + \tau$, is \$1 times the rate $R_{t,\tau}$.

As we have seen before, the present value $F R_{t,\tau}$ of instrument B is the *forward rate* for the time period $[t, t + \tau]$ as observed now:

$$F R_{t,\tau} = \frac{1}{F P(t, t + \tau)} - 1$$

The present value $f R_{t,\tau}$ of instrument $A$ is, in general, different, since, for one thing, the payoff is received sooner. As we have seen, the difference,

$$c = f R_{t,\tau} - F R_{t,\tau}$$

is the *convexity adjustment*.

Assume we are working in a theory where $\log P(t, t + \tau)$ is normal with variance $\sigma^2$. Recall the formula

$$E_Q\left[e^X\right] = e^{E_Q(X) + \frac{1}{2}\sigma_X^2}$$

valid for a random variable $X$ whose distribution under a measure $Q$ is Gaussian. Then

$$E_Q\left[e^{-X}\right]=\frac{e^{\frac{1}{2}\sigma X^2}}{E_Q(e^X)}$$

So the convexity adjustment works out to

$$c=\frac{1}{FP(t,t+\tau)}\left[e^{\sigma^2}-1\right]$$

Some essential facts about Gaussian models are summarized in Table 20-1.

**TABLE 20–1**

Summary of Gaussian Models

**1–factor Gauss**

$$r(t) = \alpha_0(t) + y(t)$$

and

$$dy(t) = -y(t)dt + \sigma\, dw_t$$

where $t \mapsto w_t$ is standard Brownian motion, satisfying $dw_t^2 = dt$.
The discount factor is $P(t, T) = e^{A(t,T) - B(t,T)y(t)}$ where

$$A(t, T) = -\int_t^T \alpha_0(s)\, ds + \frac{\sigma^2}{2a^2}\left[\tau - \frac{2}{a}(1 - E_a(\tau)) + \frac{1}{2a}(1 - E_a(2\tau))\right]$$

and

$$B(t, T) = \frac{1 - E_a(\tau)}{a}$$

where

$$\tau = T - t \text{ and } E_a(x) = e^{-ax}$$

The Green's function for $E_{Q_T}[\cdot|\mathcal{F}_t]$ is

$$G^{\text{for}}_{Q_T}(t, y(t)[; T, x) = \frac{1}{\sqrt{2\pi\Sigma^2}} e^{-\frac{(x-m)^2}{2\Sigma^2}}$$

with mean

$$m = E_a(\tau)y(t) - \frac{\sigma^2}{2a^2}(1 - E_a(\tau))^2$$

and variance

$$\Sigma^2 = \frac{\sigma^2}{2a}(1 - E_a(2\tau))$$

---

***N*–factor Gauss model**

$$r(t) = \alpha_0(t) + \sum_{j=1}^{N} y_j(t)$$

where $dy_j = -a_j y_j dt + \sigma_j dz_j$ and $dz_j dz_k = \rho_{jk} dt$
The discount factor is $P(t, T) = e^{A(t,T) - \sum_{j=1}^{N} B_j(t,T) y_j(t)}$ where $A(t, T)$ is given in (20.28) and $B_j(t, T)$ in (20.29).
The Green's function $G^{\text{for}}_{Q_t}(0, y_0; t, y)$, giving the density at point $y$ of the random variable $y_t$ relative to the pricing measure $Q_t$ given the initial state $y_0$, is Gaussian with mean vector $m = (m_1, \ldots, m_N)$ and covariance matrix $[C_{jk}]$, where

$$\begin{aligned} m_j &= -\frac{1}{a_j}\left(\sum_k \rho_{jk}\frac{\sigma_k\sigma_j}{a_k}\right)(1 - e^{-a_j t}) \\ &\quad + \textstyle\sum_k \rho_{jk}\dfrac{\sigma_k\sigma_j}{a_k(a_j + a_k)}\left\{1 - e^{-(a_j+a_k)t}\right\} \quad \text{and} \\ &\quad + e^{-a_j t} y_j(0) \\ C_{jk} &= \frac{\rho_{jk}\sigma_j\sigma_k}{a_j + a_k}\left\{1 - e^{-(a_j+a_k)t}\right\} \end{aligned}$$

CHAPTER 21

# The $\chi^2$ Model

As we have noted before, the Gaussian model has the drawback that the interest rate can be negative. The $\chi^2$ (chi-squared) model, introduced by Cox, Ingersoll, and Ross [10, 11], does not have this defect. In this chapter we discuss the 1-factor model, leaving technical derivations of formulas for later.

## MODEL FUNDAMENTALS

In the 1–factor Cox-Ingersoll-Ross (CIR) model, the state of the market at any time is assumed to be specified by one coordinate value $y$, which is nonnegative. Thus the market state space is $[0, \infty)$.

As usual, let $\Omega$ denote the full space of all market scenarios over all time. Let $\mathcal{F}$ be the collection of all market events.

For each time $t \geq 0$, we have a probability measure $Q_t$ on $\mathcal{F}$, which is the pricing measure for the time-$t$ cash numeraire.

For each time $t \geq 0$, we also have a $\sigma$-algebra $\mathcal{F}_t$ of subsets of $\Omega$, describing all market events up till time $t$.

Denote the state of the market at time $t$ by $y_t(\omega)$. The random variable $y_t$ is, of course, assumed to be $\mathcal{F}_t$-measurable, i.e., determined by all market events up till time $t$.

Thus market evolution is described by a process

$$[0, \infty) \times \Omega \mapsto [0, \infty) : (t, \omega) \mapsto y(t; \omega) = y_t(\omega)$$

The factor $y$ is an implicit market variable. The interest rate $r(t)$ at any instant of time $t$ is assumed in this model to be a sum

$$\boxed{r_t = \alpha_0(t) + y_t} \tag{21.1}$$

where $\alpha_0(t)$ is a deterministic quantity. Note that $y_t$ is a random variable measurable with respect to $\mathcal{F}_t$, and hence so is $r_t$. We will sometimes write $r(t)$ for $r_t$, and $y(t)$ for $y_t$.

The evolution of the factor $y_t$ is assumed to be described by the stochastic differential equation

$$\boxed{dy_t = a(\theta - y_t)dt + \sigma\sqrt{y_t}\,dw_t} \tag{21.2}$$

where $a, \theta$, and $\sigma$ are constant, and $t \mapsto w_t$ is a standard Brownian motion process (with $w_t$ being $\mathcal{F}_t$–measurable) with respect to the initial pricing measure $Q_0$.

It can be proven that in order for the square-root to be meaningful for all time $t$, it is necessary that $a\theta > \sigma^2/2$. Roughly speaking, this ensures that the deterministic part of the right side of (21.2) gives a strong enough upward kick to $y_t$ to prevent the stochastic term $\sigma\sqrt{y_t}\,dw_t$ from pushing $y_t$ into negative territory.

As usual, the scenario–dependent discount factor for a time interval $[t, T]$ is the random variable

$$p(t, T) = e^{-\int_t^T r_s\,ds}$$

and the price of a $T$-maturity bond at time $t \leq T$ is

$$P(t, T) = E_{Q_t}[p(t, T)|\mathcal{F}_t] \tag{21.3}$$

which is determined by knowledge of the market scenario up till time $t$.

## GREEN'S FUNCTIONS

We are typically interested in three Green's functions:

(i) The *forward Green's function* $G^{\text{for}}_{Q_t}$ for computing forward prices;

(ii) The "nondiscounted" Green's function $G^{\text{nd}}_{Q_s}$, which describes the expected value, at time $s$, of a future payoff but *without* discounting;

(iii) The "shifted" Green's function $G^{\text{shifted}}_{Q_t^*}$, which uses the time-$t$ asset as numeraire.

We shall describe these Green's functions for the $\chi^2$–model. Derivation of the formulas will be presented in the next chapter.

The distribution of any random variable $Y$ is completely specified through its *characteristic function* $\chi^Y$, which is defined by

$$\chi^Y(t) = E(e^{itY}) \text{ for all } t \in \mathbf{R}.$$

For our purposes, a more convenient object is the *Laplace transform* $E[e^{-\lambda Y}]$, viewed as a function of complex $\lambda$; for a general $Y$, the Laplace transform will be meaningful only for $\lambda$ in some subset of the complex plane. A random variable $Y$ is said to have a $\chi^2_{\delta,\eta}$ distribution if its Laplace transform is

$$E(e^{-\lambda \chi^2_{\delta,\eta}}) = (1+2\lambda)^{-\frac{\delta}{2}} \exp\left[-\frac{\lambda\eta}{1+2\lambda}\right] \tag{21.4}$$

where $\delta > 0$ and $\eta$ are parameters related to the mean and variance of the distribution. The Laplace transform (21.4) is defined for complex $\lambda$ with real part greater than $-1/2$. The parameter $\delta$ is called the *degree of freedom* of the distribution. It is known that if $X_1, \ldots, X_n$ are independent standard Gaussians, then the sum squared $\sum_{j=1}^n X_j^2$ has $\chi^2_{n,0}$ distribution with $n$ degrees of freedom.

## The Forward Green's Function

The forward Green's function $G^{\text{for}}_{Q_t}$ is specified through the formula

$$E_{Q_T}[F(y(T))|\mathcal{F}_t] = \int_{\mathbf{R}^N} G^{\text{for}}_{Q_T}(t, y(t); T, x)F(x)\,dx \qquad (21.5)$$

which gives the time-$T$ forward price $E_{Q_T}[F(y(T))|\mathcal{F}_t]$, as seen at time $t < T$, of an asset which will yield cash $F(y)$ in market state $y$.

The stochastic differential equation (21.2) for $y_t$ can be used to determine the distribution of the random variable $y_T$ relative to the measure $Q_T$, subject to all information up till any given time $t < T$. As noted above, the density of this distribution is the Green's function $G^{\text{for}}_{Q_T}(t, x; T, y)$.

In Chapter 22 we will work with Laplace transforms, and find that, with respect to the measure $Q_T$ and for a given value of $y(t)$,

$$\text{the random variable } 2(\phi + \psi)y(T) \text{ has distribution } \sim\chi^2_{\delta,\eta} \qquad (21.6)$$

The parameters $\delta$ and $\eta$ are determined by the model parameters $a, \theta, \sigma$, and the time $\tau = T - t$ to maturity. The degree of freedom $\delta$ is given by

$$\delta = \frac{4a\theta}{\sigma^2} \qquad (21.7)$$

The other parameter $\eta$ is given by

$$\eta = \frac{2\phi(\tau)^2 e^{\gamma\tau}}{\psi(\tau) + \phi(\tau)} y(t) \qquad (21.8)$$

where $\tau = T - t$, and the functions $\phi$ and $\psi$ are

$$\phi(\tau) = \frac{2\gamma/\sigma^2}{e^{\gamma\tau} - 1}, \qquad (21.9)$$

$$\psi(\tau) = \frac{\gamma + a}{\sigma^2}, \qquad (21.10)$$

and

$$\gamma = \sqrt{a^2 + 2\sigma^2} \tag{21.11}$$

The distribution of $y(T)$ is equally expressed through the Green's function $G^{\text{for}}_{Q_T}$:

$$E_{Q_T}[F(y(T))|\mathcal{F}_t] = \int_{\mathbf{R}} F(y) G^{\text{for}}_{Q_T}(t, y(t); T, y)\, dy \tag{21.12}$$

where the Green's function $G^{\text{for}}_{Q_T}(t, x; T, y)$ is given by

$$G^{\text{for}}_{Q_T}(t, x; T, y) = 2(\phi + \psi)\chi^2_{\delta,\eta}(2(\phi + \psi)y) \tag{21.13}$$

## The Nondiscounted Green's Function

For the futures price at time $t$ on an asset with delivery date $T$, we need the "futures" expectation $E_{Q_t}[F(y(T))|\mathcal{F}_t]$. The "nondiscounted" Green's function for this is the density of $y(T)$ relative to the measure $Q_t$, conditional on $\mathcal{F}_t$.

In the next chapter we shall work out this distribution for $y(T)$, and find that it is again a $\chi^2$:

$$2(\phi_{\text{nd}} + \psi_{\text{nd}})y(T) \sim \chi^2_{\delta_{\text{nd}}, \eta_{\text{nd}}} \tag{21.14}$$

where the parameters in this case are obtained by setting $\gamma$ equal to $a$ in the expressions mentioned earlier, i.e.

$$\delta_{\text{nd}} = \frac{4a\theta}{\sigma^2} \tag{21.15}$$

and, with $\tau = T - t$,

$$\eta_{\text{nd}} = \frac{2\phi^2_{\text{nd}} e^{a\tau}}{\psi_{\text{nd}} + \phi_{\text{nd}}} y(t) \tag{21.16}$$

with

$$\phi_{\text{nd}} = \frac{2a/\sigma^2}{e^{a\tau} - 1} \tag{21.17}$$

$$\psi_{\text{nd}} = \frac{2a}{\sigma^2} \tag{21.18}$$

Thus

$$E_{Q_t}\left[F(y(T))|\mathcal{F}_t\right] = \int_{\mathbf{R}} F(y) G^{\mathrm{nd}}_{Q_t}(t, y(t); T, y)\, dy \quad (21.19)$$

where the Green's function $G^{\mathrm{nd}}_{Q_t}(t, x; T, y)$ is given by

$$G^{\mathrm{nd}}(t, x; T, y) = 2(\phi_{\mathrm{nd}} + \psi_{\mathrm{nd}})\chi^2_{\delta^{\mathrm{nd}}, \eta^{\mathrm{nd}}}(2(\phi_{\mathrm{nd}} + \psi_{\mathrm{nd}})y) \quad (21.20)$$

## The Shifted Green's Function

Recall the general formula (11.8) for the price of a call option on an asset:

$$\text{Call Price} = P(0, t)\left[ F S(t) \frac{E_{Q_t}[S(t) 1_{\{S(t)>K\}}]}{E_{Q_t}[S(t)]} - K E_{Q_t}[1_{\{S(t)>K\}}] \right]$$

where $S(t)$ is the asset price at time $t$, $K$ is the strike, and $t$ the expiration.

To compute the bond call-option price, we use this formula with

$$S(t) = P(t, T) = e^{A(t,T) - B(t,T)y(t)},$$

the time-$t$ price of a $T$-maturity bond.

Thus, it is useful to bring in the "shifted" Green's function $G^{\mathrm{shifted}}_{Q^*_t}$ specified by

$$\frac{E_{Q_t}[P(t, T) F(y_t)|\mathcal{F}_s]}{E_{Q_t}[P(t, T)|\mathcal{F}_s]} = E_{Q^*_t}[F(y_t)|\mathcal{F}_s]$$

$$= \int_{\mathbf{R}} F(y) G^{\mathrm{shifted}}_{Q^*_t}(s, y_s; t, y)\, dy \quad (21.21)$$

where, $0 \le s \le t \le T$, and $Q^*_t$ is the pricing measure with the $T$-maturity bond at time $t$ as numeraire.

The Green's function $G^{\mathrm{shifted}}_{Q^*_t}(s, x; t, y)$, as a function of $y$, is the probability density of the random variable $y_t$, with respect to the pricing measure $Q^*_t$, given the state $y_s = x$ at time $s$. For notational convenience, we will work mainly with $s = 0$.

This Green's function $G^{\text{shifted}}_{Q_t^*}(0, x; t, y)$ is again $\chi^2$, with all parameters unchanged except that $\phi + \psi$ is replaced by $\phi(t) + \psi(t) + B(t, T)$:

$$2(\phi(t) + \psi(t) + B(t, T))y(t) \sim \chi^2_{\delta, \eta^{\text{shifted}}} \quad (21.22)$$

where, with $\tau = T - t$,

$$\eta^{\text{shifted}} = \frac{2\phi(t)^2 e^{\gamma\tau}}{\psi(t) + \phi(t) + B(t, T)} y(t) \quad (21.23)$$

Thus

$$E_{Q_t^*}[F(y(T))|\mathcal{F}_s] = \int_{\mathbf{R}} F(y) G^{\text{shifted}}_{Q_t^*}(s, y(s); t, y)\, dy \quad (21.24)$$

where the Green's function $G^{\text{shifted}}_{Q_t^*}(s, x; t, y)$ is given by

$$G^{\text{shifted}}_{Q_t^*}(s, x; t, y) = k\chi^2_{\delta, \eta_{\text{shifted}}}(ky) \quad (21.25)$$

where

$$k = 2(\phi(t - s) + \psi(t - s) + B(t, T))$$

Thus the time-0 price of a call option, with strike $K$ and expiration $t$, on a $T$-maturity bond is

$$\text{Price of Call Option} = P(0, T)\chi^2_{\delta, \eta^{\text{shifted}}}\left(d_+^{\text{CIR}}\right) - KP(0, t)\chi^2_{\delta, \eta}\left(d_-^{\text{CIR}}\right) \quad (21.26)$$

where

$$d_+^{\text{CIR}} = 2(B(t, T) + \phi(t) + \psi(t)) \frac{A(t, T) - \log K}{B(t, T)} \quad (21.27)$$

and

$$d_-^{\text{CIR}} = 2(\phi(t) + \psi(t)) \frac{A(t, T) - \log K}{B(t, T)} \quad (21.28)$$

CHAPTER 22

# Derivation of Green's Functions

In this chapter we derive the explicit formulas for the Green's functions for the Gaussian and chi-squared models. This chapter may be viewed as a technical appendix and contains rather heavy-duty calculations offered with little pause or apology.

The general methodology has been discussed earlier in Chapter 19 and here again we follow the same formal approach. However, we will state the arguments here in a self-contained way without using anything directly from Chapter 19.

Let $\Omega$ be a set, which we think of as constituting the space of all market scenarios. The structure of this set will be assumed to be rich enough to accommodate the stochastic structures discussed below; for instance, we may assume $\Omega$ is the space of continuous paths in $\mathbf{R}^N$.

For each time $t \geq 0$ we have a $\sigma$-algebra $\mathcal{F}_t$ of subsets of $\Omega$ representing all market events up till time $t$. Naturally, we assume that $\mathcal{F}_s \subset \mathcal{F}_t$ for $s \leq t$. Let $\mathcal{F} = \sigma(\{\mathcal{F}_t\}_{t\geq 0})$, the $\sigma$-algebra of all the market events. As always, we assume given probability measures $Q_t$ on $\mathcal{F}$, for each time $t \geq 0$; the probability $Q_t(A)$ of an event $A$ is the price of an instrument which pays off 1 unit of time-$t$ cash if event $A$ occurs and nothing otherwise. Note that $Q_t$ should *not* be thought of as being a measure only on the $\sigma$-algebra $\mathcal{F}_t$.

We will work with certain processes

$$[0, \infty) \times \Omega \to \mathbf{R}^N : (t, \omega) \mapsto y(t, \omega) = y_t(\omega),$$

with $y_t$ being $\mathcal{F}_t$-measurable. Each model we deal with specifies a stochastic differential equation governing the process $t \mapsto y_t$. These equations will involve Brownian motion relative to the measure $Q_0$. Our procedure will require determination of the distribution of $y_t$ under various measures. For example, we will determine the distribution of $y_t$ under the measure $Q_0$. We will also determine the distribution of $y_T$ under the measures $Q_T$ and $Q_t$, given $\mathcal{F}_t$, for $t \leq T$. Here, of course, we will need to use the relationship between the measures $Q_t$. This relationship, as we have seen before, involves the interest rate $r_t$, which itself will be assumed in each model to be determined by $y_t$.

The general strategy for finding the Green's function is as follows. For any $\lambda = (\lambda_1, \ldots, \lambda_N) \in \mathbf{R}^N$, consider the function

$$f_\lambda(t, y) \stackrel{\text{def}}{=} f_\lambda(t, y; T) = E_{Q_t}\left[e^{-\int_t^T r(u)\,du - \sum_{j=1}^N \lambda_j y_j(T)} \middle| \mathcal{F}_t\right] \tag{22.1}$$

where $t \leq T$ and $y = y(t) \in \mathbf{R}^N$. The function $f_\lambda$ depends on $T$, but we generally suppress this to keep things readable. We assume that the process $t \mapsto y(t)$ has the Markov property that the conditional expectation on the right in (22.1) is indeed a function of $y = y(t)$.

**Proposition 22.0.1** *With notation as above and appropriate regularity hypotheses on the process $t \mapsto y(t)$, we have the equalities*

$$f_\lambda(t, y(t)) = E_{Q_s}\left[e^{-\int_t^T r(u)\,du} e^{-\lambda \cdot y(T)} \middle| \mathcal{F}_t\right], \tag{22.2}$$

*for all $0 \leq s \leq t \leq T$, and*

$$E_{Q_T}\left[e^{-\lambda \cdot y(T)} \middle| \mathcal{F}_t\right] = \frac{f_\lambda(t, y(t))}{f_0(t, y(t))} \tag{22.3}$$

*Moreover, the process*

$$t \mapsto e^{-\int_0^t r(u)\,du} f_\lambda(t, y(t)) \tag{22.4}$$

*is a martingale with respect to the family of* $\sigma$*-algebras* $\{\mathcal{F}_t\}_{t\geq 0}$ *and the measure* $Q_0$.

***Proof.*** We know the conversion of numeraires formula:

$$dQ_t = \frac{1}{E_{Q_s}(p(s,t))} p(s,t)\, d\, Q_s$$

So, by using Theorem 7.4.1 of Chapter 7 we obtain:

$$\begin{aligned} f_\lambda(t, y(t)) &= E_{Q_t}\left[e^{-\int_t^T r(u)\,du} e^{-\lambda\cdot y(T)} \middle| \mathcal{F}_t\right] \\ &= \frac{E_{Q_s}\left[p(s,t)p(t,T)e^{-\lambda\cdot y(T)} \middle| \mathcal{F}_t\right]}{E_{Q_s}[p(s,t)|\mathcal{F}_t]} \\ &= \frac{p(s,t)E_{Q_s}\left[p(t,T)e^{-\lambda\cdot y(T)} \middle| \mathcal{F}_t\right]}{p(s,t)} \quad \text{because } p(s,t) \text{ is } \mathcal{F}_t\text{-measurable} \\ &= E_{Q_s}\left[p(t,T)e^{-\lambda\cdot y(T)} \middle| \mathcal{F}_t\right] \quad \text{which is the right side of (22.2)} \end{aligned}$$

Proceeding again in a similar way, we have

$$\begin{aligned} E_{Q_T}\left[e^{-\lambda\cdot y(T)} \middle| \mathcal{F}_t\right] &= \frac{E_{Q_0}\left[p(0,T)e^{-\lambda\cdot y(T)} \middle| \mathcal{F}_t\right]}{E_{Q_0}[p(0,T)|\mathcal{F}_t]} \\ &= \frac{p(0,t)E_{Q_0}\left[e^{-\int_t^T r(s)\,ds} e^{-\lambda\cdot y(T)} \middle| \mathcal{F}_t\right]}{p(0,t)E_{Q_0}[p(t,T)|\mathcal{F}_t]} \\ &= \frac{f_\lambda(t, y(t))}{f_0(t, y(t))}, \end{aligned}$$

as claimed. QED

What we have here is the Laplace transform of the Green's function $G^{\text{for}}_{Q_T}(t, y; T, x)$:

$$E_{Q_T}\left[e^{-\lambda\cdot y_T}\middle|\mathcal{F}_t\right] = \int_{\mathbf{R}^N} e^{-\lambda\cdot x} G^{\text{for}}_{Q_T}(t, y; T, x)\, dx \qquad (22.5)$$

So

$$\frac{f_\lambda(t, y)}{f_0(t, y)} = \int_{\mathbf{R}^N} e^{-\lambda\cdot x} G^{\text{for}}_{Q_T}(t, y; T, x)\, dx \qquad (22.6)$$

Thus, knowing $f_\lambda$, we can determine the Green's function by Laplace inversion.

Now $f_\lambda(t, y(t))$ is the price at time $t$ of the security whose payoff at time $T$ is $e^{-\lambda\cdot y(T)}$. Then,

$$e^{-\int_0^t r(s)\,ds} f_\lambda(t, y(t)) \text{ is a martingale, with respect to } Q_0.$$

This can be used, along the lines of Chapter 19 to prove that $f_\lambda$ satisfies a partial differential equation:

$$\frac{\partial f_\lambda}{\partial t} + \left(\mathcal{L}_t - \left(\alpha_0(t) + \sum_{j=1}^{N} y_j\right)\right) f_\lambda = 0 \qquad (22.7)$$

where $\mathcal{L}_t$ is a second order partial differential operator in the $y$-variables, and $f_\lambda$ satisfies the boundary (final-)condition:

$$f_\lambda(T, y) = e^{-\sum_{j=1}^{N} \lambda_j y_j} \qquad (22.8)$$

The partial differential equation (22.7) in itself is a purely analytic object, with no probability involved. It is thus remarkable that its solution can be expressed by means of the stochastic formula (22.1). The solution (22.1) is the Feynman-Kac formula for the partial differential equation (22.7).

A solution is obtained in the form

$$f_\lambda(t, y) = e^{A^\lambda(t,T) - \sum_{j=1}^{N} B_j^\lambda(t,T) y_j} \qquad (22.9)$$

Viewing this as a function if $\lambda$, we determine the function $G^{\text{for}}_{Q}(t, y; T, x)$ satisfying equation (22.6).

## THE ONE-FACTOR GAUSSIAN MODEL

The model is

$$r(t) = \alpha_0(t) + y(t) \tag{22.10}$$

where $\alpha_0$ is deterministic and $y(t)$ satisfies the stochastic differential equation

$$dy(t) = -ay(t)dt + \sigma dw(t) \tag{22.11}$$

where $w(t)$ is standard Brownian motion with respect to $Q_0$. Thus, we have:

$$dw(t)^2 = dt$$

The equation (22.11) is called an *Ornstein-Uhlenbeck* type equation.

### The Forward Green's Function

We implement the strategy outlined at the beginning of this chapter, but repeat some of the ideas for convenience.

The conditional expectation

$$E_{Q_t}\left[e^{-\int_t^T r(s)\,ds-\lambda y(T)}\middle|\mathcal{F}_t\right]$$

is a function of $y_t$, as the process $s \mapsto y_s$ is a Markov process. So we may write this conditional expectation as

$$E_{Q_t}\left[e^{-\int_t^T r(s)\,ds-\lambda y(T)}\middle|y(t)=y\right]$$

Let $f_\lambda$ then be the function specified by

$$f_\lambda(t,y) = E_{Q_t}\left[e^{-\int_t^T r(s)\,ds-\lambda y(T)}\middle|y(t)=y\right] \tag{22.12}$$

Note the boundary condition:

$$f_\lambda(T,y) = e^{-\lambda y} \tag{22.13}$$

Let

$$g(t) \stackrel{\text{def}}{=} e^{-\int_0^t r(s)\,ds} f_\lambda(t, y(t)), \tag{22.14}$$

Using Itô's formula, we have

$$\begin{aligned} dg(t) &= \left\{ \frac{\partial f_\lambda}{\partial t} dt + \frac{\partial f_\lambda}{\partial y} dy(t) + \frac{1}{2} \frac{\partial^2 f_\lambda}{\partial y^2} dy(t)^2 \right\} e^{-\int_0^t r(s)\,ds} - r(t) g(t) \\ &= \left[ \frac{\partial f_\lambda}{\partial t} - ay \frac{\partial f_\lambda}{\partial y} + \frac{1}{2} \sigma^2 \frac{\partial^2 f_\lambda}{\partial y^2} - r(t) f_\lambda(t, y(t)) \right] e^{-\int_0^t r(s)\,ds} dt + \star dw(t) \end{aligned}$$

We have seen in Proposition 22.0.1 that the process $t \mapsto g(t)$ is a martingale. Thus, the coefficient of $dt$ in the preceding differential must be zero:

$$\frac{\partial f_\lambda}{\partial t} - ay \frac{\partial f_\lambda}{\partial y} + \frac{\sigma^2}{2} \frac{\partial^2 f_\lambda}{\partial y^2} - (\alpha_0(t) + y) f_\lambda = 0 \tag{22.15}$$

We try a solution of the form

$$f_\lambda(t, y) = e^{A_\lambda(t,T) - B_\lambda(t,T) y} \tag{22.16}$$

Substituting this into the partial differential equation, we get:

$$\frac{\partial A_\lambda}{\partial t} - \frac{\partial B_\lambda}{\partial t} y + ay B_\lambda + \frac{1}{2} \sigma^2 B_\lambda^2 - (\alpha_0(t) + y) = 0 \tag{22.17}$$

The boundary conditions are:

$$A_\lambda(T, T) = 0 \text{ and } B_\lambda(T, T) = \lambda \tag{22.18}$$

So, separating the terms dependent on $y$ and those independent of $y$, we obtain the equations

$$\frac{\partial A_\lambda}{\partial t} = \alpha_0(t) - \frac{1}{2} \sigma^2 B_\lambda, \text{ and } A_\lambda(T, T) = 0 \tag{22.19}$$

and

$$\frac{\partial B_\lambda}{\partial t} - a B_\lambda = -1, \text{ and } B_\lambda(T, T) = \lambda \tag{22.20}$$

Solving for $B_\lambda$ we get

$$B_\lambda(t,T) = \lambda e^{-\int_t^T a\,ds} + \int_t^T e^{-\int_t^u a\,ds}\,du \tag{22.21}$$

Because we have assumed that $a$ is constant, we get

$$B_\lambda(t,T) = \lambda E_a(\tau) + \frac{1-E_a(\tau)}{a} \tag{22.22}$$

where

$$E_a(x) \stackrel{\text{def}}{=} e^{-ax} \tag{22.23}$$

and

$$\tau \stackrel{\text{def}}{=} T-t \tag{22.24}$$

Solving for $A_\lambda$ we get:

$$A_\lambda(t,T) = -\int_t^T \alpha_0(s)\,ds + \frac{1}{2}\sigma^2\int_t^T B_\lambda(s,T)^2\,ds \tag{22.25}$$

Using the expression for $B_\lambda(t,T)$ we get

$$\begin{aligned}A_\lambda(t,T) = &-\int_t^T \alpha_0(s)\,ds\\ &+\frac{1}{2}\sigma^2\left[\frac{\lambda^2}{2a}\{1-E_a(2\tau)\} + \frac{\lambda}{a^2}(1-E_a(\tau))^2\right]\\ &+\frac{\sigma^2}{2a^2}\left[\tau - \frac{2}{a}(1-E_a(\tau)) + \frac{1}{2a}(1-E_a(2\tau))\right]\end{aligned} \tag{22.26}$$

Using all this, we have

$$\frac{f_\lambda(t,y;T)}{f_0(t,y;T)} = e^{\lambda^2\frac{\sigma^2}{4a}(1-E_a(2\tau)) - \lambda\left[E_a(\tau)y - \frac{\sigma^2}{2a^2}(1-E_a(\tau))^2\right]} \tag{22.27}$$

Now recall from (22.6) that the ratio $\frac{f_\lambda(t,y)}{f_0(t,y)}$ is the Laplace transform of the forward Green's function. Thus, we have to determine a function $G(x)$ for which $\int e^{-\lambda x}G(x)\,dx$ equals $\frac{f_\lambda(t,y)}{f_0(t,y)}$. Now we use the Gaussian integration formula

$$E(e^{-\lambda X}) = e^{-\lambda E(X) + \frac{\lambda^2}{2}\text{var}(X)} \tag{22.28}$$

where $X$ is any Gaussian random variable, $E(X)$ its mean and var($X$) the variance. Thus, comparing (22.27) and (22.28), we can guess that the Green's function $G(t, y(t); T, x)$ is the Gaussian density function

$$G\big(t, y(t); T, x\big) = \frac{1}{\sqrt{2\pi\,\Sigma^2}} e^{-\frac{(x-m)^2}{2\Sigma^2}} \tag{22.29}$$

with mean

$$m = E_a(\tau)y(t) - \frac{\sigma^2}{2a^2}(1 - E_a(\tau))^2 \tag{22.30}$$

and variance

$$\Sigma^2 = \frac{\sigma^2}{2a}(1 - E_a(2\tau)) \tag{22.31}$$

The discount factor $P(t, T)$ is obtained by putting $\lambda = 0$ in $f_\lambda(t, y)$:

$$P(t, T) = e^{A(t,T) - B(t,T)y(t)} \tag{22.32}$$

where

$$\begin{aligned} A(t, T) = &- \int_t^T \alpha_0(s)\,ds \\ &+ \frac{\sigma^2}{2a^2}\left[\tau - \frac{2}{a}(1 - E_a(\tau)) + \frac{1}{2a}(1 - E_a(2\tau))\right] \end{aligned} \tag{22.33}$$

and

$$B(t, T) = \frac{1 - E_a(\tau)}{a} \tag{22.34}$$

## The Nondiscounted Green's Function

To find the nondiscounted Green's function, we solve the stochastic differential equation (22.11). First we note that

$$\begin{aligned} d\left(e^{a(u-t)}y(u)\right) &= ae^{a(u-t)}y(u)du + e^{a(u-t)}\left[-ay\,du + \sigma\,dw_u\right] \\ &= \sigma e^{a(u-t)}\,dw_u \end{aligned}$$

This leads to the solution:

$$y(T) = e^{-a(T-t)}y(t) + \sigma \int_t^T e^{-a(T-u)}\,dw(u) \qquad (22.35)$$

This shows that, given the value $y(t)$, the random variable $y(T)$ is Gaussian, with respect to the measure $Q_0$, with mean $e^{-a(T-t)}y(t)$ and variance $\sigma^2 \int_t^T e^{-2a(T-u)}du$.

Thus, the Green's function for the nondiscounted measure is Gaussian:

$$G_Q^{\mathrm{nd}}(t, y(t); T, x) = \frac{1}{\sqrt{2\pi\,\Sigma_{\mathrm{nd}}^2}} e^{-\frac{(x-m_{\mathrm{nd}})^2}{2\Sigma_{\mathrm{nd}}^2}} \qquad (22.36)$$

where

$$m_{\mathrm{nd}} = E\left(y(T)|\mathcal{F}_t\right) = E_a(\tau)y(t) \qquad (22.37)$$

and

$$\Sigma_{\mathrm{nd}}^2 = \mathrm{var}\left(y(T)|\mathcal{F}_t\right) = \frac{\sigma^2}{2a}(1 - E_a(2\tau)) \qquad (22.38)$$

Note that the variance is the same for the discounted case and the nondiscounted case.

## The Green's Function $G^{\mathrm{shifted}}$

Finally, we determine the Green's function when the pricing measure has as numeraire the $T$-maturity bond at time $t$.

This Green's function $G^{\text{shifted}}$ is specified through

$$E_{Q_t^*}(F(y_t)|\mathcal{F}_s) = \int_{\mathbf{R}} G^{\text{shifted}}_{Q_t^*}(s, y_s; t, y)F(y)\,dy \tag{22.39}$$

We are working with time instants

$$0 \leq s \leq t \leq T$$

Now the left side in (22.39) can be rewritten in terms of the measure $Q_t$:

$$\begin{aligned} E_{Q_t^*}(F(y_t)|\mathcal{F}_s) &= \frac{E_{Q_t}(p(t,T)F(y_t)|\mathcal{F}_s)}{E_{Q_t}(p(t,T)|\mathcal{F}_s)} \\ &= \frac{E_{Q_t}(E_{Q_t}[p(t,T)F(y_t)|\mathcal{F}_t]|\mathcal{F}_s)}{E_{Q_t}(E\,[p(t,T)|\mathcal{F}_t]\,|\mathcal{F}_s)} \\ &= \frac{E_{Q_t}(P(t,T)F(y_t)|\mathcal{F}_s)}{E_{Q_t}(P(t,T)|\mathcal{F}_s)} \end{aligned}$$

Let us take

$$F(y) = e^{-\lambda y}$$

Recalling the expression (22.32) for $P(t,T)$ we then have

$$\begin{aligned} E_{Q_t^*}\left(e^{-\lambda y_t}\middle|\mathcal{F}_s\right) &= \frac{E_{Q_t}\left(e^{-(\lambda+B(t,T))y_t}\middle|\mathcal{F}_s\right)}{E_{Q_t}\left(e^{-B(t,T)y_t}\middle|\mathcal{F}_s\right)} \\ &= \frac{f_{\lambda+B(t,T)}(s,y_s;t)}{f_0(s,y_s;t)} \Big/ \frac{f_{B(t,T)}(s,y_s;t)}{f_0(s,y_s;t)} \\ &= \frac{f_{\lambda+B(t,T)}(s,y_s;t)}{f_{B(t,T)}(s,y_s;t)} \end{aligned}$$

Looking back at the expression (22.27) for the ratio $f_\lambda/f_0$, we see then that

$$E_{Q_t^*}\left(e^{-\lambda y_t}\middle|\mathcal{F}_s\right) = e^{-(m-B(t,T)\Sigma^2)\lambda+\lambda^2\frac{\Sigma^2}{2}} \tag{22.40}$$

Here $m$ and $\Sigma^2$ are from (22.30) and (22.31), except with $t$ replaced by $s$, and $T$ replaced by $t$.

Recognizing the right side of (22.40) as the Laplace transform of a Gaussian with mean $m - B(t,T)\Sigma^2$ and variance $\Sigma^2$, we have the *shifted Green's function*:

$$G^{\text{shifted}}_{Q_t^*}(t, y(t); T, x) = \frac{1}{\sqrt{2\pi\,\Sigma^2_{\text{shifted}}}} e^{-\frac{(x - m_{\text{shifted}})^2}{2\Sigma^2_{\text{shifted}}}} \tag{22.41}$$

where

$$m_{\text{shifted}} = m - B(t,T)\Sigma^2 \tag{22.42}$$

and

$$\Sigma^2_{\text{shifted}} = \Sigma^2,$$

and $m$ and $\Sigma^2$ are as in (22.30) and (22.31).

## ONE-FACTOR CHI-SQUARED COX-INGERSOLL-ROSS MODEL

The model is given by the equations:

$$r(t) = \alpha_0(t) + y(t) \tag{22.43}$$

with $\alpha_0$ deterministic, and $y(t)$ satisfying the stochastic differential equation

$$dy(t) = a(\theta - y(t))dt + \sigma\sqrt{y(t)}\,dw(t) \tag{22.44}$$

where $a$, $\theta$, and $\sigma$ are constant. Here again $t \mapsto w(t)$ is Brownian motion with respect to the measure $Q_0$.

As usual, let

$$f(t, y) = E_{Q_0}\left[e^{-\mu \int_t^T y(s)\,ds - \lambda y(T)} \middle| \mathcal{F}_t\right], \tag{22.45}$$

where $Q_0$ may be replaced by $Q_s$ for any $s \le t$ without changing the value of $f(t,y)$. Let

$$g(t) = e^{-\mu \int_0^t y(s)\,ds} f(t, y(t)) = E_{Q_0}\left[e^{-\mu \int_0^T y(s)\,ds - \lambda y(T)} \middle| \mathcal{F}_t\right]$$

Then $t \mapsto g(t)$ is a martingale. By Itô, we have

$$dg(t) = \left[\frac{1}{2}\sigma^2 y \partial_2^2 f + a(\theta - y)\partial_2 f + \partial_1 f - \mu y f\right] \times e^{-\mu \int_0^t y(s)\,ds} dt + \star dw(t)$$

Because $t \mapsto g(t)$ is a martingale, the drift term must be zero;

$$\frac{1}{2}\sigma^2 y \partial_2^2 f + a(\theta - y)\partial_2 f + \partial_1 f - \mu y f = 0 \tag{22.46}$$

The boundary condition is

$$f(T, y) = e^{-\lambda y} \tag{22.47}$$

We try, as usual,

$$f(t, y) = e^{\tilde{A}_{\lambda,\mu}(t,T) - B_{\lambda,\mu}(t,T) y}$$

Substituting this into the pde (22.46), we get

$$\frac{\sigma^2}{2} y B_{\lambda,\mu}^2 - a(\theta - y) B_{\lambda,\mu} + \left(\frac{\partial \tilde{A}_{\lambda,\mu}}{\partial t} - \frac{\partial B_{\lambda,\mu}}{\partial t} y\right) - \mu y = 0$$

Because this must be valid for all $y$, we have

$$\frac{\partial B_{\lambda,\mu}}{\partial t} = \frac{1}{2}\sigma^2 B_{\lambda,\mu}^2 + a B_{\lambda,\mu} - \mu \tag{22.48}$$

and

$$\frac{\partial \tilde{A}_{\lambda,\mu}}{\partial t} = a\theta B_{\lambda,\mu} \tag{22.49}$$

The boundary condition (22.47) gives the conditions

$$\tilde{A}_{\lambda,\mu}(T, T) = 0 \qquad B_{\lambda,\mu}(T, T) = \lambda \tag{22.50}$$

Factorizing the right side in the equation for $B_{\lambda,\mu}$, we have

$$\frac{\partial B_{\lambda,\mu}}{\partial t} = \frac{\sigma^2}{2}\left(B_{\lambda,\mu} + \frac{a+\gamma_\mu}{\sigma^2}\right)\left(B_{\lambda,\mu} + \frac{a-\gamma_\mu}{\sigma^2}\right)$$

where

$$\gamma_\mu \stackrel{\text{def}}{=} \sqrt{a^2 + 2\sigma^2\mu} \tag{22.51}$$

So

$$-\frac{\sigma^2}{2\gamma_\mu}\int_{B(t,T)}^{\lambda}\left[\frac{dB}{B + \dfrac{a+\gamma_\mu}{\sigma^2}} - \frac{dB}{B + \dfrac{a-\gamma_\mu}{\sigma^2}}\right] = \frac{\sigma^2}{2}\int_t^T dt$$

This gives

$$-\frac{1}{\gamma_\mu}\left[\log\frac{\lambda + \dfrac{a+\gamma_\mu}{\sigma^2}}{B_{\lambda,\mu}(t, T) + \dfrac{a+\gamma_\mu}{\sigma^2}} - \log\frac{\lambda + \dfrac{a-\gamma_\mu}{\sigma^2}}{B_{\lambda,\mu}(t, T) + \dfrac{a-\gamma_\mu}{\sigma^2}}\right] = \tau$$

where

$$\tau = T - t \tag{22.52}$$

Taking exponentials, we obtain:

$$\left\{\frac{\lambda + \dfrac{a+\gamma_\mu}{\sigma^2}}{\lambda + \dfrac{a-\gamma_\mu}{\sigma^2}}\right\}\left\{\frac{B_{\lambda,\mu} + \dfrac{a-\gamma_\mu}{\sigma^2}}{B_{\lambda,\mu} + \dfrac{a+\gamma_\mu}{\sigma^2}}\right\} = e^{-\gamma_\mu\tau}$$

which gives

$$1 - \frac{2\gamma_\mu/\sigma^2}{B_{\lambda,\mu}(t, T) + \dfrac{a+\gamma_\mu}{\sigma^2}} = \left\{\frac{\lambda + \dfrac{a-\gamma_\mu}{\sigma^2}}{\lambda + \dfrac{a+\gamma_\mu}{\sigma^2}}\right\} e^{-\gamma_\mu\tau}$$

and so

$$
\begin{aligned}
B_{\lambda,\mu}(t,T) &= \frac{2\gamma_\mu/\sigma^2}{1-\left\{\dfrac{\lambda+\dfrac{a-\gamma_\mu}{\sigma^2}}{\lambda+\dfrac{a+\gamma_\mu}{\sigma^2}}\right\}e^{-\gamma_\mu\tau}} - \frac{a+\gamma_\mu}{\sigma^2} \\
&= \frac{e^{\tau\gamma_\mu}\left[\lambda+\dfrac{\gamma_\mu+a}{\sigma^2}\right]\dfrac{(\gamma_\mu-a)}{\sigma^2}+\left[\lambda-\dfrac{\gamma_\mu-a}{\sigma^2}\right]\dfrac{(\gamma_\mu+a)}{\sigma^2}}{\left[\lambda+\dfrac{\gamma_\mu+a}{\sigma^2}\right]e^{\tau\gamma_\mu}-\left[\lambda-\dfrac{\gamma_\mu-a}{\sigma^2}\right]} \\
&= \frac{WNe^{\gamma_\mu\tau}+ZP}{We^{\gamma_\mu\tau}-Z} = \frac{WNe^{\gamma_\mu\tau}}{We^{\gamma_\mu\tau}-Z} + \frac{ZPe^{-\gamma_\mu\tau}}{W-Ze^{-\gamma_\mu\tau}}
\end{aligned} \tag{22.53}
$$

where

$$
P=\frac{\gamma_\mu}{\sigma^2}+\frac{a}{\sigma^2}, \quad N=\frac{\gamma_\mu}{\sigma^2}-\frac{a}{\sigma^2}, \quad W=\lambda+P, \quad Z=\lambda-N
$$

From (22.49) and using the boundary condition $A(T,T)=0$, we have

$$
\tilde{A}_{\lambda,\mu}(t,T) = -a\theta\int_t^T B_{\lambda,\mu}(s,T)\,ds
$$

The integration is best done using the expression (22.53) for $B_{\lambda,\mu}$, and we get

$$
\tilde{A}_{\lambda,\mu}(t,T) = -a\theta\left[\frac{N}{\gamma_\mu}\int_0^{\gamma_\mu\tau}\frac{We^s}{We^s-Z}\,ds+\frac{P}{\gamma_\mu}\int_0^{\gamma_\mu\tau}\frac{Ze^{-s}}{W-Ze^{-s}}\,ds\right]
$$

and so

$$
\begin{aligned}
\tilde{A}_{\lambda,\mu}(t,T) &= -\frac{a\theta}{\gamma_\mu}\left[N\log\frac{We^{\gamma_\mu\tau}-Z}{W-Z}+P\log\frac{W-Ze^{-\gamma_\mu\tau}}{W-Z}\right] \\
&= -\frac{a\theta}{\gamma_\mu}\left[\frac{2\gamma_\mu}{\sigma^2}\log\frac{\left(\lambda+\dfrac{\gamma_\mu}{\sigma^2}+\dfrac{a}{\sigma^2}\right)e^{\gamma_\mu\tau}-\left(\lambda-\left(\dfrac{\gamma_\mu}{\sigma^2}-\dfrac{a}{\sigma^2}\right)\right)}{2\gamma_\mu/\sigma^2}\right. \\
&\qquad \left. -\left(\frac{\gamma_\mu}{\sigma^2}+\frac{a}{\sigma^2}\right)\gamma_\mu\tau\right]
\end{aligned}
$$

$$= \frac{2a\theta}{\sigma^2}\log\left[\frac{2\gamma_\mu/\sigma^2}{\left(\frac{\gamma_\mu}{\sigma^2}+\frac{a}{\sigma^2}+\lambda\right)+\left(\frac{\gamma_\mu}{\sigma^2}-\frac{a}{\sigma^2}-\lambda\right)e^{-\gamma_\mu\tau}}\right]$$

$$-(\gamma_\mu - a)\frac{a\theta}{\sigma^2}\tau$$

Now that we have $\tilde{A}_{\lambda,\mu}$ and $B_{\lambda,\mu}$ we can work out the discount factor $P(t,T)$. First, observe that

$$P(t,T) = E_{Q_t}\left[e^{-\int_t^T r(s)\,ds}\middle|\mathcal{F}_t\right]$$

$$= e^{-\int_t^T \alpha_0(s)\,ds} f(t, y(t)) = e^{-\int_t^T \alpha_0(s)\,ds + \tilde{A}_{0,1}(t,T) - B_{0,1}(t,T)y(t)}$$

Writing $B$ for $B_{0,1}$, we have then

$$P(t,T) = e^{A(t,T) - B(t,T)y(t)}$$

where

$$A(t,T) = -\int_t^T \alpha_0(s)\,ds + \frac{2a\theta}{\sigma^2}\log\left[\frac{2\gamma e^{(\gamma+a)\tau/2}}{(\gamma+a)e^{\gamma\tau}+\gamma-a}\right] \tag{22.54}$$

where

$$\gamma \stackrel{\text{def}}{=} \sqrt{a^2+2\sigma^2} \tag{22.55}$$

For $B(t,T)$, we have

$$B(t,T) = \frac{(e^{\gamma\tau}-1)(\gamma^2-a^2)/\sigma^4}{[(\gamma+a)e^{\gamma\tau}+\gamma-a]/\sigma^2}$$

which simplifies to

$$B(t,T) = \frac{2(e^{\gamma\tau}-1)}{(\gamma+a)e^{\gamma\tau}+\gamma-a} \tag{22.56}$$

In order to compute the Green's functions, we need to look at

$f_{\lambda,\mu}/f_{0,\mu}$. To this end, we determine

$$\tilde{A}_{\lambda,\mu}(t,T) - \tilde{A}_{0,\mu}(t,T)$$
$$= \frac{2a\theta}{\sigma^2}\log\left[\frac{(\gamma_\mu + a) + (\gamma_\mu - a)e^{-\gamma_\mu\tau}}{(\lambda\sigma^2 + \gamma_\mu + a) + (\gamma_\mu - a - \lambda\sigma^2)e^{-\gamma_\mu\tau}}\right]$$

which can also be written as

$$\tilde{A}_{\lambda,\mu}(t,T) - \tilde{A}_{0,\mu}(t,T) = \log\left[1 + 2\lambda\frac{1 - e^{-\gamma_\mu\tau}}{2(P + Ne^{-\gamma_\mu\tau})}\right]^{-\frac{2a\theta}{\sigma^2}}$$

For $B$, we have

$$B_{\lambda,\mu}(t,T) - B_{0,\mu}(t,T) = \frac{(\lambda + P)Ne^{\gamma_\mu\tau} + (\lambda - N)P}{(\lambda + P)e^{\gamma_\mu\tau} - (\lambda - N)} - \frac{PNe^{\gamma_\mu\tau} - NP}{Pe^{\gamma_\mu\tau} + N}$$

which simplifies to

$$B_{\lambda,\mu}(t,T) - B_{0,\mu}(t,T) = \frac{\lambda e^{-\gamma_\mu\tau}\frac{4\gamma_\mu{}^2}{\sigma^4}/[P + Ne^{-\gamma_\mu\tau}]^2}{1 + 2\lambda\frac{1 - e^{-\gamma_\mu\tau}}{2(P + Ne^{-\gamma_\mu\tau})}}$$

So

$$\frac{E_{Q_t}\left(e^{-\mu\int_t^T y(s)\,ds - \lambda y(T)}\middle|\mathcal{F}_t\right)}{E_{Q_t}\left(e^{-\mu\int_t^T y(s)\,ds}\middle|\mathcal{F}_t\right)}$$
$$= \left[1 + 2\lambda\frac{1 - e^{-\gamma_\mu\tau}}{2(P + Ne^{-\gamma_\mu\tau})}\right]^{-\frac{2a\theta}{\sigma^2}} e^{-y(t)\frac{\lambda e^{-\gamma_\mu\tau}\frac{4\gamma_\mu{}^2}{\sigma^4}/[P + Ne^{-\gamma_\mu\tau}]^2}{1 + 2\lambda\frac{1 - e^{-\gamma_\mu\tau}}{2(P + Ne^{-\gamma_\mu\tau})}}}$$

Now the Laplace transform of the $\chi^2_{\delta,\eta}$ random variable is given by

$$E\left(e^{-k\chi^2_{\delta,\eta}}\right) = (1 + 2k)^{-\frac{\delta}{2}}e^{-\frac{k\eta}{1+2k}}$$

So we conclude that, under the probability measure $\frac{e^{-\mu\int_t^T r(s)\,ds}}{E(e^{-\mu\int_t^T r(s)\,ds})}$

$dQ$, conditional on $\mathcal{F}_t$,

$$\frac{2(P+Ne^{-\gamma_\mu\tau})}{1-e^{-\gamma_\mu\tau}}y(T) \text{ is a } \chi^2_{\delta,\eta} \text{ random variable,}$$

where

$$\delta = \frac{4a\theta}{\sigma^2}$$

and

$$\begin{aligned}\eta &= 2e^{-\gamma_\mu\tau}\frac{\dfrac{4\gamma_\mu{}^2}{\sigma^4}}{(P+Ne^{-\gamma_\mu\tau})(1-e^{-\gamma_\mu\tau})}y(t) \\ &= 2e^{\gamma_\mu\tau}\frac{[(2\gamma_\mu/\sigma^2)/(e^{\gamma_\mu\tau}-1)^2]}{P+\dfrac{P+N}{e^{\gamma_\mu\tau}-1}}y(t)\end{aligned}$$

This works out to

$$\eta = \frac{2\phi^2 e^{\gamma_\mu\tau}}{\phi+\psi},$$

where

$$\phi = \frac{2\gamma_\mu/\sigma^2}{e^{\gamma_\mu\tau}-1}$$

and

$$\psi = \frac{\gamma_\mu}{\sigma^2} + \frac{a}{\sigma^2}.$$

In this notation, again

$$2(\phi+\psi)y(T) \text{ has the distribution of a } \chi^2_{\delta,\eta} \text{ random variable.}$$

Setting $\mu = 1$ yields the distribution of $y(T)$ under the measure $E_{Q_T}[\cdot|\mathcal{F}_t]$.

Setting $\mu = 0$ gives the distribution for the non–discounted measure.

Finally, to find the distribution of $y(t)$ under the measure given by

$$E_{Q_t^*}[\cdot|\mathcal{F}_s] = \frac{E_{Q_t}[P(t,T)\cdot|\mathcal{F}_s]}{E_{Q_t}[P(t,T)|\mathcal{F}_s]},$$

we use the fact

$$\frac{E_{\chi^2_{\delta,\eta}}\left[e^{-\lambda Y} f(Y)\right]}{E_{\chi^2_{\delta,\eta}}\left[e^{-\lambda Y}\right]} = E_{\chi^2_{\delta,\frac{\eta}{1+2\lambda}}}\left[f\left(\frac{Y}{1+2\lambda}\right)\right]$$

Using this it follows that under $E_{Q_t^*}[\cdot|\mathcal{F}_s]$, we have

$2(\phi(t-s)+\psi(t-s)+B(t,T))y(t)$ is a $\chi^2_{\delta,\eta^*}$ random variable,

where

$$\eta^* = \frac{2\phi^2 e^{\gamma\tau}}{\phi(t-s)+\psi(t-s)+B(t,T)}$$

and $\phi$ and $\psi$ are defined in terms of $\gamma = \gamma_1 = \sqrt{a^2+2\sigma^2}$.

## THE MULTIFACTOR GAUSS MODEL

The model equations are

$$r(t) = \alpha_0(t) + \sum_{j=1}^{N} y_j(t) \tag{22.57}$$

where $\alpha_0$ is deterministic and the $y_j$ satisfy the stochastic differential equations

$$dy_j(t) = -a_j y_j dt + \sigma_j dw_j(t) \tag{22.58}$$

where $a_j, \sigma_j > 0$, and the $w_j$ are Brownian motions satisfying

$$dw_j(t)\, dw_k(t) = \rho_{jk}\, dt \tag{22.59}$$

We may assume that each $\rho_{jj} = 1$.

Let

$$f_{\lambda,\mu}(t,y) = E_{Q_0}\left[e^{-\sum_{j=1}^N \mu_j \int_t^T y_j(u)\,du - \sum_{j=1}^N \lambda_j y_j(T)} \middle| y(t) = y\right],$$

where, as usual, $Q_0$ could be replaced with $Q_s$ for any $s \leq t$ without affecting the value of $f_{\lambda,\mu}(t,y)$.

Then, setting,

$$g(t) = e^{-\int_0^t \mu\cdot y(s)\,ds} f(t,y(t)) = E_{Q_0}\left[e^{-\sum_{j=1}^N \mu_j \int_0^T y_j(s)\,ds - \sum_{j=1}^N \lambda_j y_j(T)} \middle| \mathcal{F}_t\right]$$

The process $t \mapsto g(t)$ is a martingale with respect to the measure $Q_0$. By Itô,

$$\begin{aligned} dg(t) &= [\star\star] e^{-\int_0^t \mu\cdot y(s)\,ds} dt \\ &\quad + \star\, dw(t) \end{aligned}$$

where (writing $f$ for $f_{\lambda,\mu}$)

$$\begin{aligned} [\star\star] &= -\mu\cdot y(t) f(t,y(t)) + \frac{\partial f(t,y(t))}{\partial t} \\ &\quad - \sum_{j=1}^N a_j y_j \frac{\partial f(t,y(t))}{\partial y_j} + \frac{1}{2}\sum_{j,k=1}^N \sigma_j\sigma_k\rho_{jk}\frac{\partial^2 f}{\partial y_j\,\partial y_k} \end{aligned}$$

So, because $t \mapsto g(t)$ is a martingale, the drift term is zero:

$$\begin{aligned} &-\mu\cdot y(t) f(t,y(t)) + \frac{\partial f(t,y(t))}{\partial t} - \sum_{j=1}^N a_j y_j \frac{\partial f(t,y(t))}{\partial y_j} \\ &\quad + \frac{1}{2}\sum_{j,k=1}^N \sigma_j\sigma_k\rho_{jk}\frac{\partial^2 f}{\partial y_j\,\partial y_k} = 0 \end{aligned}$$

The boundary condition is

$$f(T,y) = e^{-\lambda\cdot y}$$

We try a solution of the form

$$f(t,y) = e^{\tilde{A}_{\lambda,\mu}(t,T) - \sum_{j=1}^N B_j^{\lambda,\mu}(t,T) y_j}$$

Substituting this into the partial differential equation we get

$$\frac{1}{2}\sum_{j,k=1}^{N}\sigma_k\sigma_k\rho_{jk}B_j^{\lambda,\mu}B_k^{\lambda,\mu}+\sum_{j=1}^{N}a_jy_jB_j^{\lambda,\mu}$$
$$-\sum_{j=1}^{N}\mu_jy_j+\left(\frac{\partial\tilde{A}_{\lambda,\mu}}{\partial t}-\frac{\partial B^{\lambda,\mu}}{\partial t}\cdot y\right)=0$$

Equating to zero the coefficient of $y_j$, and the "constant term", we obtain

$$\frac{\partial B_j^{\lambda,\mu}}{\partial t}=a_jB_j^{\lambda,\mu}-\mu_j$$

and

$$\frac{\partial\tilde{A}_{\lambda,\mu}}{\partial t}=-\frac{1}{2}\sum_{j,k=1}^{N}\rho_{jk}\sigma_j\sigma_kB_j^{\lambda,\mu}B_k^{\lambda,\mu}$$

with boundary conditions

$$\tilde{A}_{\lambda,\mu}(T,T)=0 \qquad B_j^{\lambda,\mu}(T,T)=\lambda_j$$

The differential equation for $B_j^{\lambda,\mu}$ implies

$$\frac{\partial}{\partial t}\left[e^{a_j(T-t)}B_j^{\lambda,\mu}(t,T)\right]=-\mu_je^{a_j(T-t)}$$

and so

$$B_j^{\lambda,\mu}(T,T)-e^{a_j\tau}B_j^{\lambda,\mu}(t,T)$$
$$=-\mu_j\int_t^T e^{a_j(T-s)}\,ds=-\mu_j\int_0^{T-t}e^{a_ju}\,du$$

which gives

$$B_j^{\lambda,\mu}(t,T)=\left(\lambda_j-\frac{\mu_j}{a_j}\right)e^{-a_j\tau}+\frac{\mu_j}{a_j}$$

where

$$\tau = T - t$$

Using the value of $B_j^{\lambda,\mu}$ now in the equation for $\tilde{A}_{\lambda,\mu}$, we obtain

$$\frac{\partial \tilde{A}_{\lambda,\mu}}{\partial t} = -\frac{1}{2}\sum_{j,k=1}^{N} \sigma_j \sigma_k \rho_{jk} \left[\left(\lambda_j - \frac{\mu_j}{a_j}\right)\left(\lambda_k - \frac{\mu_k}{a_k}\right) e^{-(a_j+a_k)\tau} + 2\left(\lambda_j - \frac{\mu_j}{a_j}\right)\frac{\mu_k}{a_k} e^{-a_j\tau} + \frac{\mu_j \mu_k}{a_j a_k}\right]$$

which gives, upon integration and use of $\tilde{A}_{\lambda,\mu}(T, T) = 0$,

$$\tilde{A}_{\lambda,\mu} = \frac{1}{2}\sum_{j,k=1}^{N} \sigma_j \sigma_k \rho_{jk} \, [\star]$$

where

$$[\star] = \left(\lambda_j - \frac{\mu_j}{a_j}\right)\left(\lambda_k - \frac{\mu_k}{a_k}\right) \frac{1 - e^{-(a_j+a_k)\tau}}{a_j + a_k} + 2\left(\lambda_j - \frac{\mu_j}{a_j}\right)\frac{\mu_k}{a_k}\frac{(1 - e^{-a_j\tau})}{a_j} + \frac{\mu_j \mu_k}{a_j a_k}\tau$$

Taking $\lambda = 0$ and each $\mu_j = 1$ we obtain

$$P(t, T) = e^{A(t,T) - B(t,T)\cdot y(t)}$$

where

$$A(t, T) = -\int_t^T \alpha_0(s)\, ds + \frac{1}{2}\sum_{j,k=1}^{N} \sigma_j \sigma_k \rho_{jk} \left[\frac{\left(1 - e^{-(a_j+a_k)\tau}\right)}{a_j a_k (a_j + a_k)} - \frac{2}{a_j a_k}\frac{1 - e^{-a_j\tau}}{a_j} + \frac{1}{a_j a_k}\tau\right]$$

and

$$B_j(t, T) = \frac{1 - e^{-a_j\tau}}{a_j}$$

Returning to the pursuit of the Green's function, we note that

$$\frac{E_{Q_0}\left(e^{-\int_t^T \mu\cdot y(s)\,ds-\lambda\cdot y(T)}\middle|\mathcal{F}_t\right)}{E_{Q_0}\left(e^{-\int_t^T \mu\cdot y(s)\,ds}\middle|\mathcal{F}_t\right)}=e^{\tilde{A}_{\lambda,\mu}-\tilde{A}_{0,\mu}-(B^{\lambda,\mu}-B^{0,\mu})\cdot y(t)}$$

So we determine

$$\begin{aligned}\tilde{A}_{\lambda,\mu} &- \tilde{A}_{0,\mu} - (B^{\lambda,\mu} - B^{0,\mu})\cdot y(t)\\ &= \frac{1}{2}\sum_{j,k=1}^{N}\sigma_j\sigma_k\rho_{jk}[\star\star] - \sum_{j=1}^{N}\lambda_j e^{-a_j\tau}y_j(t)\end{aligned}$$

where

$$[\star\star]=\left\{\lambda_j\lambda_k-2\lambda_j\frac{\mu_k}{a_k}\right\}\frac{\left(1-e^{-(a_j+a_k)\tau}\right)}{a_j+a_k}+2\lambda_j\frac{\mu_k}{a_k}\frac{(1-e^{-a_j\tau})}{a_j}$$

Now if $(X_1,\ldots,X_N)$ is a Gaussian $N$-dimensional variable then, using the Gaussian integration formula $E(e^X)=e^{E(X)+\frac{1}{2}\mathrm{var}(X)}$ (for any Gaussian random variable $X$), we have

$$E\left(e^{-\sum_{j=1}^{N}\lambda_j X_j}\right)=e^{-\sum_{j=1}^{N}E(X_j)\lambda_j+\frac{1}{2}\sum_{j,k=1}^{N}\mathrm{cov}(X_j,X_k)\lambda_j\lambda_k}$$

where

$$\mathrm{cov}(X,Y)\stackrel{\text{def}}{=}E\left[(X-E(X))(Y-E(Y))\right]$$

Putting together all these observations, we conclude that under the measure given by the expectation $F\mapsto\frac{E(e^{-\int_t^T \mu\cdot y(s)\,ds}F\,|\mathcal{F}_t)}{E(e^{-\int_t^T \mu\cdot y(s)\,ds}|\mathcal{F}_t)}$,

the $N$-dimensional random variable $y(T)$ is Gaussian

with

$$\begin{aligned}\text{mean of } y_j(T) &= \frac{1}{2}\sum_{k=1}^{N}\sigma_j\sigma_k\rho_{jk}\frac{\mu_k}{a_k}\left[\frac{1-e^{-(a_j+a_k)\tau}}{a_j+a_k}-\frac{1-e^{-a_j\tau}}{a_j}\right]\\ &\quad + e^{-a_j\tau}y_j(t)\end{aligned}$$

and

$$C_{jk} \stackrel{\text{def}}{=} \text{cov}(y_j(T), y_k(T)) = \rho_{jk}\sigma_j\sigma_k \frac{\left[1 - e^{-(a_j + a_k)\tau}\right]}{a_j + a_k}$$

Setting each $\mu_j$ equal to 1 gives the distribution of $y(T)$ under $E_{Q_T}[\cdot|\mathcal{F}_t]$.

Setting each $\mu_j$ equal to 0 gives the distribution of $y(T)$ under the nondiscounted measure $Q_t$.

With respect to the measure given by $F \mapsto E_{Q_t}[P(t,T)F]/E_{Q_t}[P(t,T)]$, the $N$-dimensional random variable $y(t)$ is Gaussian with mean vector $m^{\text{shifted}}$

$$m^{\text{shifted}} = m - CB(t,T)$$

and variance-covariance matrix $C$. This follows from the formula

$$\frac{E_{Q_0}[e^{-\lambda \cdot X} f(X)]}{E_{Q_0}[e^{-\lambda \cdot X}]} = E_{Q_0}[f(X - \Sigma^2\lambda)]$$

for any $N$-dimensional Gaussian random variable $X$ with variance matrix $\Sigma^2$ and for any vector $\lambda \in \mathbf{R}^N$.

Table 22-1 summarizes some essential facts about Gaussian and $\chi^2$ variables.

**TABLE 22–1**

Properties of the Gaussian and $\chi^2$ Distributions

| | Gauss | Chi-Squared |
|---|---|---|
| Density | The normal random variable $N(m,\sigma^2)$ has density $\frac{1}{\sqrt{2\pi\sigma^2}}e^{-\frac{(x-m)^2}{2\sigma^2}}$ | The $\chi^2_{\delta,\eta}$ random variable has density, for $x>0$, given by: $$\rho_{\chi^2_{\delta,\eta}}(x)=\frac{e^{-\eta/2}}{2\eta^{\frac{\delta}{4}-\frac{1}{2}}}e^{-\frac{x}{2}}x^{\frac{\delta}{4}-\frac{1}{2}}I_{\frac{\delta}{2}-1}(\sqrt{x\eta}),$$ where $$I_\nu(x)=\left(\frac{x}{2}\right)^\nu\sum_{n=0}^{\infty}\frac{\left(\frac{x}{2}\right)^{2n}}{n!\Gamma(\nu+n+1)}$$ |
| Mean | $m$ | $\delta+\eta$ |
| Variance | $\sigma^2$ | $2(\delta+2\eta)$ |
| Sums | If $X_1$ and $X_2$ are independent Gaussians then $X_1+X_2$ is also Gaussian: $$N(m_1,\sigma_1^2)\overset{\text{INDEP.}}{+}N(m_2,\sigma_2^2)\overset{\text{d}}{=}N(m_1+m_1,\sigma_1^2+\sigma_2^2)$$ | $\chi^2_{\delta_1,\eta_1}\overset{\text{INDEP.}}{+}\chi^2_{\delta_2,\eta_2}\overset{\text{d}}{=}\chi^2_{\delta_1+\delta_2,\eta_1+\eta_2}$ |
| Laplace Transforms | If $X$ is $N(m,\sigma^2)$ then $E(e^{-\lambda X})=e^{-\lambda m+\frac{1}{2}\lambda^2\sigma^2}$ for every complex $\lambda$ | $E(e^{-\lambda\chi^2_{\delta,\eta}})=(1+2\lambda)^{-\frac{\delta}{2}}\exp\left[-\frac{\lambda\eta}{1+2\lambda}\right]$ for complex $\lambda$ with real part greater than $-1/2$. |
| Fourier Transforms | If $X$ is $N(m,\sigma^2)$ then $E(e^{ikX})=e^{ikm-\frac{1}{2}k^2\sigma^2}$ for every real $k$ | For any real $k$, $E(e^{ik\chi^2_{\delta,\eta}})=(1-2ik)^{-\frac{\delta}{2}}\exp\left[\frac{ik\eta}{1-2ik}\right]$ |
| 'Shifted' integrals | $$\frac{E_{N(\mu,\sigma^2)}\left[e^{-\lambda X}f(X)\right]}{E_{N(\mu,\sigma^2)}\left[e^{-\lambda X}\right]}=E_{N(\mu-\lambda\sigma^2,\sigma^2)}[f(X)]$$ | $$\frac{E_{\chi^2_{\delta,\eta}}\left[e^{-\lambda Y}f(Y)\right]}{E_{\chi^2_{\delta,\eta}}\left[e^{-\lambda Y}\right]}=E_{\chi^2_{\delta,\frac{\eta}{1+2\lambda}}}\left[f\left(\frac{Y}{1+2\lambda}\right)\right]$$ |

PART FOUR

# Mathematical Tools

In this part we describe the mathematical concepts, definitions, and fundamental results that were used for Parts one through three. We will not, generally, present proofs. The purpose is to provide a summary reference for the mathematical notions used in the previous parts.

CHAPTER 23

# Elements of Measure and Integration

We shall develop the basic framework of measure theory and integration. For proofs we refer to Rudin's standard text [37].

## MEASURES, SIGMA-ALGEBRAS, FUNCTIONS

Measure theory is a framework for measuring the sizes of subsets of a given set. In the financial-probabilistic context, we are concerned with the set $\Omega$ of all market scenarios, and measure theory provides a framework for *probabilities* of market events. In more traditional contexts, measure theory provides the mathematical apparatus for discussing areas and volumes of regions of space.

Consider a set $X$. A *measure* $\mu$ associates to a subset $A$ of $X$ a number $\mu(A) \geq 0$, which measures the size of $A$. Experience shows that in most situations of interest, it is impossible to have a consistent way of measuring *all* subsets of $X$. Thus one has to focus on a certain collection $\mathcal{F}$ of subsets of $X$ that are *measurable*. For sets $A$ that are in $\mathcal{F}$, we should have the measure $\mu(A)$. Of course, some reasonable requirements need to be placed on $\mathcal{F}$ and $\mu$ to get things going.

We work with a set $X$, and a collection $\mathcal{F}$ of subsets of $X$ that has the following properties:

**(i)** $\emptyset \in \mathcal{F}$,
**(ii)** if $A_1, A_2, \ldots \in \mathcal{F}$ then $\cup_{n\geq 1} A_n \in \mathcal{F}$, and
**(iii)** if $A \in \mathcal{F}$ then the complement $A^c$ is also in $\mathcal{F}$.

Such a collection is called a *σ-algebra* of subsets of $X$. The sets in $\mathcal{F}$ are called *measurable*, and the pair $(X, \mathcal{F})$ is called a *measurable space*. It is easy to check that $\mathcal{F}$ contains $X$ and is also closed under countable intersections.

Here are three examples of $\sigma$-algebras of subsets of a set $X$, which can be described with a minimum of mathematical machinery:

**(i)** the trivial $\sigma$-algebra $\{\emptyset, X\}$;
**(ii)** the collection $\mathcal{P}(X)$ of all subsets of $X$;
**(iii)** the collection of all subsets $A \subset X$ for which either $A$ or $A^c$ is countable.

A *measure* $\mu$ associates to each set $A \in \mathcal{F}$ a nonnegative number $\mu(A) \geq 0$ such that:

**(i)** $\mu(\emptyset) = 0$
**(ii)** $\mu(A) \geq 0$ for every $A \in \mathcal{F}$
**(iii)** for any sequence of disjoint sets $A_1, A_2, \ldots \in \mathcal{F}$, we have

$$\mu\left(\bigcup_{n=1}^{\infty} A_n\right) = \sum_{n=1}^{\infty} \mu(A_n)$$

The triple $(X, \mathcal{F}, \mu)$ is called a *measure space*.

Though we have not made it explicit above, the measure of a set may take the value $\infty$. Thus it is useful and necessary to extend the set $\mathbf{R}$ of real numbers to include positive and negative infinity:

$$\overline{\mathbf{R}} = \mathbf{R} \cup \{\infty, -\infty\} \tag{23.1}$$

Addition and multiplication with infinities need to be handled with care, but the rules are all the obvious ones (such as $a + \infty = \infty$ as long as $a \neq -\infty$, while $\infty + (-\infty)$ is not defined) except for one important rule:

$$0 \cdot (\pm\infty) = (\pm\infty) \cdot 0 = 0$$

This is to make integration theory sensible and ensures that a rectangle with zero width has zero area, even if it is infinitely long.

The *indicator function* $1_A$ of a set $A \subset X$ is the function whose value is 1 on $A$, and 0 outside $A$:

$$1_A(x) = \begin{cases} 1 & \text{if } x \in A \\ 0 & \text{if } x \notin A \end{cases} \tag{23.2}$$

In the financial context we have seen that certain basic instruments, the *Arrow-Debreu* instruments, can be understood in terms of indicator functions: the payoff is 1 dollar if the event $A$ happens and is 0 otherwise.

Many financial instruments can be analyzed by viewing them as a combination of indicator functions. A *simple function* is a function that takes only finitely many values. In fact, if $s : X \to \mathbf{R}$ is simple with $c_1, \ldots, c_n$ being the distinct values, then $s$ is a linear combination of indicator functions:

$$s = \sum_{i=1}^{n} c_i 1_{A_i},$$

where $A_i$ is the level set $s^{-1}(c_i)$.

A function $f : X \to \overline{\mathbf{R}}$ is said to be *measurable* with respect to a $\sigma$-algebra $\mathcal{F}$, or $\mathcal{F}$*-measurable*, if for every $a \in \overline{\mathbf{R}}$, the set $\{x \in X : f(x) \leq a\}$ is in $\mathcal{F}$. Sometimes we write

$$f \in \mathcal{F}$$

to indicate that $f$ is $\mathcal{F}$-measurable.

A function $f: X \to S$, where $S$ is any topological space, is said to be *measurable* if $f^{-1}(U)$ is measurable for any open subset $U$ of $S$.

For function $f: X \to \mathbf{R}^n$, given in components by $f = (f_1, \ldots, f_n)$, it can be shown that $f$ is measurable if and only if each component function $f_j$ is measurable.

In particular, this defines measurability for complex-valued functions $X \to \mathbf{C} = \mathbf{R}^2$.

It is often useful to see how a general complex-valued function can be constructed out of simple functions. If $F: X \to \mathbf{C}$ is a function we can write it as

$$F = U + iV,$$

where $U, V$ are real-valued. Next, any function $G: X \to [-\infty, \infty]$ (and, in particular, the functions $U$ and $V$) can be written as

$$G = G^+ - G^-,$$

where $G^+$ and $G^-$ are, of course, nonnegative functions on $X$. Finally, any function $f: X \to [0, \infty]$ can be expressed as

$$f(x) = \lim_{N \to \infty} f_N(x) \quad \text{for all } x \in X$$

where the functions $f_N$ are simple functions given by

$$f_N = \phi_N \circ f,$$

with $\phi_N$ being the simple function on $[0, \infty]$:

$$\phi_N = \sum_{k=1}^{N2^N} \frac{k-1}{2^N} 1_{\left[\frac{k-1}{2^N}, \frac{k}{2^N}\right)} + N 1_{[N,\infty]}$$

Note that

$$0 \le f_1 \le f_2 \le \cdots \le f,$$

with each $f_N$ bounded above by $N$. Note also that each $f_N$ is $f$ composed with the nice simple function $\phi_N$, and so is measurable with respect to any $\sigma$-algebra relative to which $f$ is measurable. Lastly, note that if the function $f$ is bounded above by $N$ on a set, then, on that set $f_k$ approximates $f$ to within $2^{-k}$ for every $k \geq N$.

A property is said to hold *almost everywhere with respect to* $\mu$, in short $\mu$–a.e., if the set of points where the property fails has measure 0. For example, if $f$ and $g$ are measurable functions, then we say that $f = g$ almost everywhere to mean that the set $\{f \neq g\}$ has $\mu$–measure 0.

A sequence of functions $f_1, f_2, \ldots$ is said to *converge pointwise almost everywhere* if $f_n(x)$ converges, as $n \to \infty$, for all $x$ except those constituting a set of measure zero.

## INTEGRATION

Let $(X, \mathcal{F}, \mu)$ be a measure space.

It is readily checked that if $s : X \to \mathbf{R}$ is simple with $c_1, \ldots, c_n$ being the distinct values of $s$, then $s$ is measurable if and only if each of the level-sets $A_i = s^{-1}(c_i)$ is measurable. As noted before, $s = \sum_{i=1}^{n} c_i 1_{A_i}$. In this case, the integral $\int_X s\, d\mu$ is defined as follows

$$\int_X s\, d\mu \stackrel{\text{def}}{=} \sum_{i=1}^{n} c_i \mu(A_i) \tag{23.3}$$

A combinatorial argument shows that this integral depends linearly on $s$. If $f : X \to \overline{\mathbf{R}}$ is a *nonnegative* measurable function then the integral of $f$ is defined to be

$$\int_X f\, d\mu = \sup_{0 \leq s \leq f} \int s\, d\mu \tag{23.4}$$

where the supremum is over measurable simple functions $s$ satisfying $0 \leq s \leq f$.

If $f : X \to \overline{\mathbf{R}}$ is a general function, we can write $f = f^+ - f^-$, where $f^+ = \max\{f, 0\}$ and $f^- = -\min\{0, f\}$. The function $f$ is measurable if and only if $f^+$ and $f^-$ are both measurable.

The integral of such $f$ is defined by

$$\int_X f\,d\mu \stackrel{\text{def}}{=} \int_X f^+\,d\mu - \int_X f^-\,d\mu \tag{23.5}$$

whenever this is meaningful, i.e., when this isn't $\infty - \infty$. Finally, if $f : X \to \mathbf{C}$ is measurable, then define

$$\int_X f\,d\mu \stackrel{\text{def}}{=} \int_X u\,d\mu + i\int_X v\,d\mu \tag{23.6}$$

where $u$ is the real part of $f$ and $v$ the imaginary part, i.e. $u, v : X \to \mathbf{R}$ satisfies $f = u + iv$.

It is often convenient to write

$$\int_X f(x)\,d\mu(x)$$

instead of $\int_X f\,d\mu$. If $A$ is a measurable set, then the integral of $f$ over $A$ is defined to be

$$\int_A f\,d\mu \stackrel{\text{def}}{=} \int_X f\,1_A\,d\mu \tag{23.7}$$

A function $f$ on $X$ is said to be *integrable* if it is measurable and $\int |f|\,d\mu < \infty$. In this case the integral $\int f\,d\mu$ exists as a (finite real or) complex number.

The basic properties of the integral are summarized in:

**Theorem 23.2.1** *Let $(X, \mathcal{F}, \mu)$ be a measure space.*

- *If $f$ and $g$ are measurable functions on $X$ that are equal $\mu$–a.e., then $\int f\,d\mu$ exists if and only if $\int g\,d\mu$ exists, and these values are equal.*
- *For any measurable function $f$ on $X$ with values either in $\overline{\mathbf{R}}$ or in $\mathbf{C}$, the integral $\int_X f\,d\mu$ exists as a finite number if and only if $\int_X |f|\,d\mu < \infty$, and then*

$$\left|\int_X f\,d\mu\right| \le \int_X |f|\,d\mu \tag{23.8}$$

- *If $f, g$ are integrable functions on $X$ and $c_1, c_2 \in \mathbf{C}$ then $c_1 f + c_2 g$ is integrable and*

$$\int_X (c_1 f + c_2 g)\, d\mu = c_1 \int_X f\, d\mu + c_2 \int_X g\, d\mu \quad (23.9)$$

- *If $f$ is a nonnegative measurable function and $\int_X f\, d\mu = 0$ then $f = 0$ almost everywhere, in the sense that the set $\{x \in X : f(x) \neq 0\}$ has measure 0.*

## INTERCHANGING LIMIT AND INTEGRATION

The next result shows when limits can be interchanged with integration.

**Theorem 23.3.1** *Let $f_1, f_2, \ldots$ be a sequence of measurable functions on a measure space $(X, \mathcal{F}, \mu)$ converging pointwise almost everywhere. Let*

$$f(x) = \lim_{n\to\infty} f_n(x)$$

*if the limit is meaningful and set $f(x) = 0$ (or any other constant) otherwise. Then:*

- *$f$ is measurable*
- (MONOTONE CONVERGENCE THEOREM ) *if $0 \leq f_1 \leq f_2 \leq \ldots$ then*

$$\lim_{n\to\infty} \int_X f_n\, d\mu = \int_X f\, d\mu \quad (23.10)$$

- (DOMINATED CONVERGENCE THEOREM) *if there is a measurable function $g$ on $X$ such that $|f| \leq g$ almost everywhere, and if $\int_X |g|\, d\mu < \infty$, then* (23.10) *holds.*

## GENERATED $\sigma$-ALGEBRAS

The intersection of any family of $\sigma$-algebras is readily seen to be a $\sigma$-algebra.

Let $X$ be any nonempty set and $S$ a collection of subsets of $X$. The set of all subsets of $X$ is a $\sigma$-algebra. Thus the family of $\sigma$-algebras that contain the collection $S$ is nonempty. The intersection of this family is thus the smallest $\sigma$-algebra with respect to which each set in $S$ is measurable. This $\sigma$-algebra is denoted $\sigma(S)$, and is called the $\sigma$-algebra *generated* by $S$:

$$\sigma(S) = \sigma\text{-algebra generated by the collection of sets } S \qquad (23.11)$$

If $Y$ is any topological space, then the $\sigma$-algebra generated by all the open sets is called the *Borel $\sigma$-algebra* of $Y$. A map $f : X \to Y$ is measurable if and only if $f^{-1}(B)$ is measurable for every Borel $B \subset Y$.

For $\mathbf{R}^n$, we will denote the Borel $\sigma$-algebra by

$$\mathcal{B}(\mathbf{R}^n)$$

For a measurable space $(X, \mathcal{F})$, a function $f : X \to \mathbf{R}^n$ is measurable if and only if $f^{-1}(\mathcal{B}(\mathbf{R}^n)) \subset \mathcal{F}$.

If $F$ is a family of functions on $X$, then there is a smallest $\sigma$-algebra $\sigma(F)$ of subsets of $X$ such that each $f$ is measurable with respect to this $\sigma$-algebra; this is called the $\sigma$-algebra generated by the family $F$:

$$\sigma(F) = \sigma\text{-algebra generated by a collection of functions } F \qquad (23.12)$$

If the collection $F$ consists of just a map $f : X \to \mathbf{R}^n$, then $\sigma(F)$, also denoted just $\sigma(f)$, is the collection

$$\sigma(f) = \{f^{-1}(B) : \quad B \text{ a Borel subset of } \mathbf{R}^n\}$$

It is useful, especially for the purposes of probability theory, to have an intuitive feel for what it means for a function to be measurable with respect to $\sigma(F)$, where $F$ is a collection of functions. Let us focus just on the case $F = \{f\}$, where $f : X \to \mathbf{R}^n$ is an $n$-component function. Observe first that any function of the form

$$\phi \circ f,$$

with $\phi$ a Borel function on $\mathbf{R}^n$, is $\sigma(f)$-measurable. In the converse direction, first we have:

**Lemma 23.4.1** *Let $f : X \to \mathbf{R}^n$ be any function. Then, no $\sigma(f)$-measurable function can distinguish points within a "level set" of the form $f^{-1}(a)$ for any $a \in \mathbf{R}^n$. More precisely, if $x$ and $y$ are any points in $X$ with $f(x) = f(y)$, then $g(x)$ equals $g(y)$ for every $\sigma(f)$-measurable function $g$ on $X$.*

***Proof.*** Let $a = f(x) = f(y)$. Then $f^{-1}(\{a\})$ is a $\sigma(f)$-measurable subset of $X$. But every set in $\sigma(f)$ is of the form $f^{-1}(A)$ for some Borel subset of $\mathbf{R}^n$. So the only $\sigma(f)$-measurable subsets of $f^{-1}(\{a\})$ are $\emptyset$ and $f^{-1}(\{a\})$ itself. Now consider

$$C = f^{-1}(\{a\}) \cap g^{-1}(\{g(x)\}), \quad \text{and} \quad D = f^{-1}(\{a\}) \cap g^{-1}(\{g(y)\}).$$

These are both in $\sigma(f)$, both are subsets of $f^{-1}(\{a\})$, and $x \in C$, $y \in D$. So,

$$C = D = f^{-1}(\{a\})$$

In particular, $x \in D$, and so the value of $g$ on $x$ is $g(y)$:

$$g(x) = g(y),$$

as desired. QED

We have the following conclusion then:

**Proposition 23.4.2** *Suppose $f : X \to \mathbf{R}^n$ is a mapping, and $g : X \to \mathbf{R}$ a function which is $\sigma(f)$-measurable. Then*

$$g = \phi \circ f$$

*for some function $\phi$ on $\mathbf{R}^n$.*

*Proof.* Just take

$$\phi(a) = g(x) \qquad \text{if } a = f(x) \text{ for some } x \in X$$

and

$$\phi(a) = 0 \qquad \text{if } a \text{ is not in the image of } f$$

The preceding lemma shows that $\phi$ is well defined. Moreover,

$$\phi(f(x)) = g(x),$$

by definition. QED

Thus, in thinking of functions $F$ measurable with respect to $\sigma(\{f_t\}_{t\in J})$, for any family of functions $\{f_t\}_{t\in J}$, it is useful to think of $F$ as a "function of" the values of all the $f_t$.

## PRODUCT SPACES AND FUBINI'S THEOREM

Let $(X_i, \mathcal{F}_i)$, for $i = 1, \ldots, n$, be measurable spaces. On the product space

$$X = \prod_{i=1}^{n} X_i$$

we have the natural "coordinate" projection maps $p_i : X \to X_i$. If $A_1 \subset X_1, \ldots, A_n \subset X_n$ then

$$p_1^{-1}(A_1) \cap \cdots \cap p_n^{-1}(A_n) = \prod_{i=1}^{n} A_i.$$

The *product $\sigma$-algebra*

$$\mathcal{F} = \bigotimes_{i=1}^{n} \mathcal{F}_i$$

is the smallest $\sigma$-algebra of subsets of $X = \prod_{i=1}^{n} X_i$ containing all the measurable boxes $\prod_{i=1}^{n} A_i$, with each $A_i \in \mathcal{F}_i$.

A measure space $(Y, \mathcal{S}, \nu)$ is said to be *σ-finite* if $Y$ is a countable union of sets each of finite measure.

The following is a fundamental theorem of measure theory:

**Theorem 23.5.1, Fubini's Theorem** *Suppose $(X_i, \mathcal{F}_i, \mu_i)$, for $i = 1, \dots, n$, are σ-finite measure spaces. Then there is a unique measure μ on the product σ-algebra $\mathcal{F} = \bigotimes_{i=1}^n \mathcal{F}_i$ such that*

$$\mu\left(\prod_{i=1}^n A_i\right) = \prod_{i=1}^n \mu_i(A_i)$$

*for every $A_i \in \mathcal{F}_i$, and $i = 1, \dots, n$.*

*Suppose $n = 2$. Then for any $\mathcal{F}$-measurable function $f$ on $X = X_1 \times X_2$,*

$$\begin{aligned}\int_X f\,d\mu &= \int_{X_2}\left[\int_{X_1} f(x_1, x_2)\,d\mu_1(x_1)\right] d\mu_2(x_2)\\ &= \int_{X_1}\left[\int_{X_2} f(x_1, x_2)\,d\mu_2(x_2)\right] d\mu_1(x_1)\end{aligned}$$

*holds when either $f \geq 0$ or when at least one of the three terms is defined and finite.*

## COMPLEX MEASURES

A *complex measure* $\nu$ on a σ-algebra $\mathcal{F}$ is a mapping $\nu : \mathcal{F} \to \mathbf{C}$ for which:

$$\nu\left(\bigcup_{n=1}^\infty A_n\right) = \sum_{n=1}^\infty \nu(A_n)$$

holds for any sequence of disjoint sets $A_1, A_2, \ldots \in \mathcal{F}$.

Note that for a complex measure $\mu$, there might well exist measurable sets $A \subset B$ with $\mu(B) = 0$ but $\mu(A) \neq 0$.

A standard way in which a complex measure arises is by integration: if $\mu$ is a(n ordinary) measure on $(X, \mathcal{F})$ and $f : X \to \mathbf{C}$

is an integrable function, then, setting

$$\mu'(A) = \int_A f \, d\mu$$

for all $A \in \mathcal{F}$ yields a complex measure $\mu'$ (the countable additivity condition follows on using the dominated convergence theorem). What is far less clear is that this example pretty much says it all about complex measures.

Let $\nu$ be a complex measure on $(X, \mathcal{F})$. An ordinary measure $|\nu|$ can be generated out of $\nu$ as follows: for any $A \in \mathcal{F}$, define

$$|\nu|(A) = \sup \left\{ \sum_{k \geq 1} |\nu(A_k)| : A = \cup_{k \geq 1} A_k, \text{ each} A_i \in \mathcal{F} \right\} \quad (23.13)$$

It turns out that $|\nu|$ is indeed a measure (in fact, a *finite* measure). Furthermore, there is a measurable function $\phi$ satisfying $|\phi(x)| = 1$ for every $x \in X$, such that

$$\nu(A) = \int_A \phi \, d\, |\nu|$$

It can be shown that $|\nu|(X) < \infty$.

## THE RADON-NIKODYM THEOREM

Let $(X, \mathcal{F})$ be a measurable space. A measure $\alpha$ on $\mathcal{F}$ is said to be *absolutely continuous* with respect to a measure $\beta$ on $\mathcal{F}$ if

$$\alpha(A) = 0 \text{ whenever } A \in \mathcal{F} \text{ and } \beta(A) = 0$$

This is denoted symbolically by

$$\alpha << \beta$$

This notion is also meaningful if $\alpha$ is a complex measure and $\beta$ is an ordinary measure.

**Theorem 23.7.1, Radon-Nikodym Theorem** *Let $\mu$ be a sigma-finite measure on $(X, \mathcal{F})$ and $\nu$ a complex measure or an* *ordinary $\sigma$-finite measure on $\mathcal{F}$. Assume that $\nu << \mu$. Then there is a measurable function $f$ on $X$ such that*

$$\nu(A) = \int_A f\,d\mu$$

*for every measurable set $A$. Moreover, any two such functions are equal $\mu$-almost everywhere.*

## THE DISTRIBUTION MEASURE

Let $(X, \mathcal{F}, \mu)$ be a measure space. A measurable function $f : X \to \mathbf{R}$ induces a *distribution* measure $\mu_f$ on the Borel $\sigma$-algebra of $\mathbf{R}$:

$$\mu_f(A) = \mu(f^{-1}(A)) \tag{23.14}$$

for every Borel set $A \subset \mathbf{R}$.

Using $\mu_f$, the abstract integral $\int_X f\,d\mu$ can be rewritten as a real integral:

$$\int_X f\,d\mu = \int_{\mathbf{R}} x\,d\mu_f(x) \tag{23.15}$$

provided either side exists.

In fact, for any Borel function $\phi$ on $\mathbf{R}$ we have

$$\int_X \phi \circ f\,d\mu = \int_{\mathbf{R}} \phi\,d\mu_f \tag{23.16}$$

if either side exists. The way to prove such a result is to verify it first when $\phi$ is an indicator function $\phi = 1_A$ (in which case the result reduces to the definition of $\mu_f$), then take linear combinations to get the result for simple functions, then take monotone limits to obtain the result for nonnegative functions, and then on, by positive and negative parts and then real and imaginary parts, to general measurable $\phi$.

## LEBESGUE MEASURE AND SOME INTEGRALS

There is a unique measure $\lambda$, called *Lebesgue measure*, on $\mathcal{B}(\mathbf{R}^n)$ such that the measure of any "box" is the product of the lengths of the sides of the box:

$$\lambda([a_1, b_1] \times \cdots \times [a_n, b_n]) = (b_1 - a_1) \ldots (b_n - a_n)$$

This measure is translation invariant:

$$\lambda(C + x) = \lambda(C)$$

for every Borel set $C$ and $x \in \mathbf{R}^n$. Often the term "Lebesgue measure" is used to mean the *completion* of $\lambda$, which is an extension of $\lambda$ to a measure on a $\sigma$-algebra that contains all Borel sets but also contains all subsets of sets of measure 0.

Let $a, b \in \mathbf{R}$, with $a < b$. If $f : [a, b] \to \mathbf{C}$ is continuous then the Lebesgue integral $\int_a^t f(x)\,dx \stackrel{\text{def}}{=} \int_{[a,t]} f\,d\lambda$ is meaningful for every $t \in [a, b]$ and

$$\frac{d}{dt} \int_a^t f(x)\,dx = f(t) \tag{23.17}$$

This simple formula, a version of the fundamental theorem of calculus, allows one to carry out the integration of a vast array of ordinary functions. We shall work out some basic integrals, which will be of use later.

For any $a > 0$, we have

$$\int_0^T e^{-av}\,dv = \frac{1}{a}[1 - e^{-aT}],$$

a formula that can be verified by differentiating the right side with respect to $T$.

Next, for any $u \in \mathbf{R}$,

$$\int_0^T e^{-ux} \sin x\,dx = \frac{1}{1+u^2} - \frac{e^{-uT}}{1+u^2}[u \sin T + \cos T],$$

a formula, obtained by "integration by parts," but verifiable by the differentiation rule.

Similarly,

$$\int_0^T \frac{1}{1+u^2}\,du = \arctan T$$

Taking $T \uparrow \infty$ in this, and using monotone convergence, yields

$$\int_0^\infty \frac{1}{1+u^2}\,du = \frac{\pi}{2}$$

Using these we have

$$\begin{aligned}
\int_0^T \frac{\sin x}{x}\,dx &= \int_0^T \sin x \left(\int_0^\infty e^{-ux}\,du\right) dx \\
&\overset{\text{Fubini}}{=} \int_0^\infty \left(\int_0^T e^{-ux} \sin x\,dx\right) du \\
&= \int_0^\infty \left\{\frac{1}{1+u^2} - \frac{e^{-uT}}{1+u^2}[u \sin T + \cos T]\right\} du \\
&= \frac{\pi}{2} - \int_0^\infty \frac{e^{-uT}}{1+u^2}[u \sin T + \cos T]\,du
\end{aligned}$$

The integrand in the last line is, in absolute value, bounded above by $e^{-u}$ if $T > 1$, and so, because $\int_0^\infty e^{-u}\,du = 1 < \infty$, dominated convergence can be used to determine the $T \to \infty$ limit:

$$\lim_{T\to\infty} \int_0^T \frac{\sin x}{x}\,dx = \frac{\pi}{2} \tag{23.18}$$

In contrast, the Lebesgue integral $\int_0^\infty \frac{\sin x}{x}\,dx$ does not exist. It is also useful to observe that

$$\int_0^T \frac{\sin kx}{x}\,dx = \text{sgn}(k) \int_0^{|k|T} \frac{\sin x}{x}\,dx \tag{23.19}$$

where sgn(k) is 1 if $k > 0$, is 0 if $k = 0$, and is $-1$ if $k < 0$.

## THE $\pi - \lambda$ THEOREM AND UNIQUENESS OF MEASURES

Let $\mu$ and $\nu$ be finite measures on some $\sigma$-algebra. Suppose we know that $\mu(A) = \nu(A)$ for a certain class $P$ of measurable sets $A$. One would like to show that $\mu$ and $\nu$ are equal on the $\sigma$-algebra generated by $P$. The $\pi - \lambda$ theorem does this with one mild assumption on $P$: the collection $P$ should have the property that if $A, B \in P$ then $A \cap B \in P$.

Let $X$ be a set. A $\pi$–system is a set $P$ of subsets of $X$ with the property that $P \neq \emptyset$ and if $A, B \in P$ then $A \cap B \in P$. A $\lambda$-system is a set $L$ of subsets of $X$ with the following properties: (i) $\emptyset \in L$, (ii) if $A \in L$ then $A^c \in L$ and (ii) if $A_1, A_2, \ldots$ are disjoint sets in $L$ then $\cup_{n=1}^{\infty} A_n \in L$.

**Theorem 23.10.1** The DYNKIN $\pi - \lambda$ THEOREM: *Let $X$ be a set, $P$ a $\pi$-system of subsets of $X$, $L$ a $\lambda$–system of subsets of $X$, and $P \subset L$. Then the $\sigma$-algebra generated by $P$ is contained in the family $L$, i.e. $\sigma(P) \subset L$.*

CHAPTER 24

# Probability Theory

In this chapter we develop the standard basic framework of probability theory, focusing mainly on the ideas and results that we have used in the other parts of this book.

## THE FRAMEWORK

A *probability space* is a measure space

$$(\Omega, \mathcal{F}, Q)$$

for which the total mass $Q(\Omega)$ equals 1. An element of $\Omega$ is viewed as a possible *outcome* or *scenario*. A set in $\mathcal{F}$, being a collection of possible scenarios, is viewed as an *event*. The measure $Q(A)$ of an event $A$ is the *probability* of the event. Of course,

$$0 \le Q(A) \le 1$$

Though a probability measure is simply a special type of measure, the intuition in probability is quite different from that of general measure theory. Indeed, general measure theory appears as a tool in probability theory.

A measurable function on $(\Omega, \mathcal{F})$ is called an *$\mathcal{F}$-random variable*, or simply a random variable.

If $Y$ is a random variable then, for any Borel set $A \subset \mathbf{R}$, the event $Y^{-1}(A) = \{\omega : \omega \in \Omega, Y(\omega) \in A\}$ is written as $[Y \in A]$:

$$[Y \in A] = Y^{-1}(A) = \text{the event that } Y \text{ has value in the set } A \tag{24.1}$$

The integral of a random variable $Y$ is called its *expectation* and written $E(Y)$:

$$E_Q(Y) = \int_\Omega Y\, dQ \tag{24.2}$$

When we are working with a particular probability measure, fixed in the given context, we write simply $E$ instead of $E_Q$.

For example, consider a random variable $s$, which has only two possible (distinct) values $a$ and $b$. Thus

$$s = a\mathbf{1}_{[s=a]} + b\mathbf{1}_{[s=b]},$$

where $[s = a]$ and $[s = b]$ are the two disjoint events corresponding to $s$ taking the two values $a$ and $b$. The expected value of this random variable is

$$\int \left(a\mathbf{1}_{[s=a]} + b\mathbf{1}_{[s=b]}\right) dQ = aQ([s = a]) + bQ([s = b]),$$

i.e., the weighted sum of values $a$ and $b$, the weights being the probabilities that $s$ has these values. This is, of course, exactly what we mean by "expected value" in the intuitive sense.

If $X$ is a random variable, then its *distribution measure* is the Borel measure $Q_X$ on $\mathbf{R}$ given by

$$Q_X(A) = Q(X^{-1}(A)) = Q[X \in A] \tag{24.3}$$

for every Borel set $A \subset \mathbf{R}$.

Random variables $X$ and $Y$ are said to have the *same distribution* if $Q_X = Q_Y$.

For any Borel function $\phi$ on $\mathbf{R}$,

$$\int_{\Omega} \phi(X)\,dQ = \int_{\mathbf{R}} \phi\,dQ_X \tag{24.4}$$

whenever either side makes sense. We have seen this in equation (23.16).

The *distribution function* of $X$ is the function $F_X$ on $\mathbf{R}$ given by

$$F_X(x) = Q[X \leq x] \tag{24.5}$$

for all $x \in \mathbf{R}$.

The distribution function determines the distribution measure:

$$Q_X = Q_Y \text{ if and only if } F_X = F_Y \tag{24.6}$$

The proof is a simple application of the Dynkin $\pi - \lambda$–Theorem 23.10.1 (the class of all left-rays $(-\infty, x]$, with $x$ running over all real numbers, is a $\pi$-system, while the collection of all sets on which $Q_X$ and $Q_Y$ agree is a $\lambda$-system).

Suppose $X$ is a random variable such that $Q[X \in A]$ is 0 for every Borel set $A$ of Lebesgue measure 0. Then by the Radon-Nikodym theorem there is a measurable function $\rho_X$ (unique up to measure zero sets) on $\mathbf{R}$ such that

$$Q[X \in B] = \int_B \rho_X(x)\,dx$$

for every Borel set $B \subset \mathbf{R}$. This function $\rho_X$ is called the probability *density* function of (the distribution measure of) $X$. Of course, $\rho_X \geq 0$ almost everywhere.

A random variable $X$ is said to be *Gaussian* if it has a density function of the form

$$\frac{1}{\sqrt{2\pi\sigma^2}} e^{-\frac{(x-m)^2}{2\sigma^2}}.$$

Calculation shows that then

$$m_X \stackrel{\text{def}}{=} E_Q(X) = m, \qquad \sigma_X^2 \stackrel{\text{def}}{=} E_Q[(X-m)^2] = \sigma^2.$$

The variable $X$ is a *standard Gaussian* if the mean $m$ is 0, and the variance $\sigma^2$ is 1. We often use $Z$ to denote a standard Gaussian variable.

Here is a very useful fact about Gaussians:

$$E(e^{\lambda X}) = e^{m_X\lambda + \frac{1}{2}\sigma_X^2\lambda^2} \tag{24.7}$$

## σ-ALGEBRAS

Let $\Omega$ be a nonempty set.

Let $X_1, \ldots, X_n$ be functions on $\Omega$. We are often interested in subsets of $\Omega$ determined by these functions.

For example,

$$[1 \le X_1 < 3, X_2 + X_5 > X_3^2]$$

describes the set of all scenarios in which the value of $X_1$ lies in $[1, 3)$ and the value of $X_2 + X_5$ is greater than $X_3^2$.

The collection of all subsets of $\Omega$ determined in this way constitutes a $\sigma$-algebra. More precisely, we have the smallest $\sigma$-algebra of subsets of $\Omega$ with respect to which all the functions $X_1, \ldots, X_n$ are measurable. This is called the $\sigma$-algebra *generated* by $X_1, \ldots, X_n$ and denoted

$$\sigma(X_1, \ldots, X_n)$$

More generally, for any set $S$ of functions on $\Omega$, the smallest $\sigma$-algebra with respect to which all the functions in $S$ are measurable is the $\sigma$-algebra generated by $S$:

$$\sigma(S)$$

This is the collection of events specified by the values of the random variables in $S$.

If $\Omega$ is the set of all conceivable market scenarios in all times, we are often concerned with the collection of all events defined by means of prices of all instruments up till a given time $t$. This $\sigma$-algebra $\mathcal{F}_t$ essentially describes all market events up till time $t$.

It is useful to recall the discussions in Chapter 23 in this context. In particular, recall that for a function to be measurable with respect to $\sigma(X_1, \ldots, X_n)$ means that it is a function of $(X_1, \ldots, X_n)$.

## INDEPENDENCE

Two concepts special to probability theory are the notions of *independence* and *conditional probability*.

The probability of $A$ *conditional* on an event $B$ is

$$Q(A|B) = \frac{Q(A \cap B)}{Q(B)} \tag{24.8}$$

For this definition we need to assume that $Q(B) > 0$. Thus $Q(A|B)$ measures the "part of $B$ occupied by $A$."

The event $A$ would be independent of $B$ if the knowledge of $B$ happening should have no effect on the probability that $A$ happens, i.e., $Q(A|B)$ should be the same as $Q(A)$. Thus, with $Q(B)$ being positive, $A$ being independent of $B$ means that $Q(A \cap B) = Q(A)Q(B)$. As a matter of definition, events $A$ and $B$ are said to be *independent* if

$$\boxed{Q(A \cap B) = Q(A)Q(B)} \tag{24.9}$$

It is readily checked that if $A$ and $B$ are independent, then so are $A^c$ and $B$, $A$ and $B^c$, and $A^c$ and $B^c$.

Events $A_1, \ldots, A_n$ are independent if for every $i_1 < \ldots < i_k$,

$$Q\left(A_{i_1} \cap \cdots \cap A_{i_k}\right) = Q(A_{i_1}) \ldots Q(A_{i_k}) \tag{24.10}$$

Random variables $X_1, \ldots, X_n$ are independent if for any Borel sets $B_1, \ldots, B_n$ the events $[X_1 \in B_1], \ldots, [X_n \in B_n]$ are independent.

If $X$ and $Y$ are independent random variables, then

$$E_Q[XY] = E_Q[X]E_Q[Y] \tag{24.11}$$

We'll prove this at the end of the next section.

## INDEPENDENCE AND $\sigma$-ALGEBRAS

Consider $\mathcal{G}$, a $\sigma$-algebra with $\mathcal{G} \subset \mathcal{F}$. An event $A$ is said to be *independent of the $\sigma$-algebra $\mathcal{G}$* if $A$ and $B$ are independent events, for every event $B$ in $\mathcal{G}$.

If $\mathcal{G}_1, \ldots, \mathcal{G}_n$ are $\sigma$-subalgebras of $\mathcal{F}$, we say that they are mutually independent if any events $A_1 \in \mathcal{G}_1, \ldots, A_n \in \mathcal{G}_n$ are mutually independent.

Let $S$ and $T$ be sets, each equipped with a $\sigma$-algebra. Random variables $X : \Omega \to S$ and $Y : \Omega \to T$ are independent if for any measurable sets $A \subset S$ and $B \subset T$ the events $[X \in A]$ and $[Y \in B]$ are independent. This is equivalent to saying that $\sigma(X)$ and $\sigma(Y)$ are independent.

Thus, indicator functions $1_A$ and $1_B$ are independent if and only if $A$ and $B$ are independent events. More generally, if the random variables $X$ and $Y$ are of the form

$$X = \sum_{i=1}^{n} c_i 1_{A_i} \text{ and } Y = \sum_{i=1}^{m} d_i 1_{B_i}$$

where the $c_i$'s are all the *distinct* values of $X$, and the $d_i$'s all the *distinct* values of $Y$, then $X$ and $Y$ are independent if and only if each pair of events $A_i$, $B_j$ are independent.

Random variables $X_1, \ldots, X_n$ are independent if the $\sigma$-algebras

$$\sigma(X_1), \ldots, \sigma(X_n)$$

are independent.

In that case the random variables

$$(X_1, \ldots, X_{k_1}), (X_{k_1+1}, \ldots, X_{k_2}), \ldots, (X_{k_{j-1}+1}, \ldots, X_{k_j})$$

are independent for any $1 \le k_1 < k_2 < \cdots < k_j \le n$.

It is clear that if $X_1, \ldots, X_n$ are independent, then for any Borel functions $f_1, \ldots, f_n$, the random variables $f_1(X_1), \ldots, f_n(X_n)$ are independent. Furthermore, $f_1(X_1)$ and $g(X_2, \ldots, X_n)$ are independent for any measurable functions $f$ and $g$ (on the appropriate spaces).

We can now prove (24.11), that if $X$ and $Y$ are independent random variables then

$$E(XY) = E(X)E(Y)$$

This is clear if $X$ and $Y$ are both indicator functions, for then it reduces to the definition (24.9) of independent events. Taking linear combinations, it follows also for $X$ and $Y$ independent simple functions. The case of nonnegative functions follows by recalling that every nonnegative function $f$ is the monotone increasing limit of simple functions of the form $\phi_N \circ f$ and then taking limits, using the monotone convergence theorem. For real-valued $X, Y$, the result follows by decomposing into positive and negative parts, and then finally for complex-valued functions by considering real and imaginary parts.

## CONDITIONAL EXPECTATIONS

In the financial context, it is of fundamental importance to understand what the best estimate of a random variable $X$ is, given the values of all market variables up till a certain time $t$. This best estimate is called the *conditional expectation* of $X$, given the collection of all possible market events till the time $t$.

Moving to a more formal setting, let $(\Omega, \mathcal{F}, Q)$ be a probability space, and $\mathcal{A}$ a $\sigma$-algebra of subsets of $\Omega$ with

$$\mathcal{A} \subset \mathcal{F}$$

We say then that $\mathcal{A}$ is a *sub-$\sigma$-algebra* of $\mathcal{F}$.

Suppose $f$ is an $\mathcal{F}$-measurable function on $\Omega$ with finite expected value (or we could work with $f \geq 0$).

Consider the function $\nu$ on $\mathcal{A}$ given by

$$\nu(A) = \int_A f\,dQ = E_Q(f1_A) \tag{24.12}$$

This is a complex measure on $\mathcal{A}$ (countable additivity follows by using dominated convergence). Moreover, $\nu(A) = 0$ whenever $\mu(A) = 0$. Then the Radon-Nikodym Theorem 23.7.1 shows that there is a unique (up to sets of $Q$–measure 0) $\mathcal{A}$-measurable function $\tilde{f}$ on $\Omega$ with the property that

$$\nu(A) = \int_A \tilde{f}\,dQ, \qquad \text{for every } A \in \mathcal{A}.$$

We can write this as

$$E_Q(f1_A) = E_Q(\tilde{f}1_A) \qquad \text{for every } A \in \mathcal{A}. \tag{24.13}$$

Now taking linear combinations of the functions $1_A$, then monotone limits, positive and negative parts, and, finally, real and imaginary parts, it follows that

$$E_Q(fh) = E_Q(\tilde{f}h) \tag{24.14}$$

for all $\mathcal{A}$-measurable functions $h$ on $\Omega$ for which either side exists.

The function $\tilde{f}$, which is uniquely specified up to sets of $Q$-measure 0, is called the *conditional expectation of $f$ relative to the $\sigma$-algebra $\mathcal{A}$* and is denoted

$$E_Q(f|\mathcal{A})$$

This is, in a sense, the best approximation to the function $f$ if one is forced to stick with $\mathcal{A}$-measurable functions. It is the unique $\mathcal{A}$-measurable random variable $Y$ that solves the minimization problem:

$$\min_{Y \text{ is } \mathcal{A}\text{-measurable}} E_Q\left(|Y - f|^2\right).$$

Here are some of the basic, important properties of conditional expectation:

**Theorem 24.5.1** *Suppose* $(\Omega, \mathcal{F}, Q)$ *is a probability space, and*

$$\mathcal{B} \subset \mathcal{A} \subset \mathcal{F}$$

*are sub-*$\sigma$*-algebras of* $\mathcal{F}$*. Suppose* $f$ *is an* $\mathcal{F}$*-measurable function on* $\Omega$*, with* $E_Q|f| < \infty$*. Then:*

**(i)** *Conditioning first on* $\mathcal{A}$ *and then on* $\mathcal{B}$ *produces the same result as conditioning on* $\mathcal{B}$ *directly:*

$$E_Q[E_Q[f|\mathcal{A}]|\mathcal{B}] = E_Q[f|\mathcal{B}] \qquad (24.15)$$

**(ii)** *If* $h$ *is an* $\mathcal{A}$*-measurable function on* $\Omega$ *with* $E_Q|fh| < \infty$*, then* $h$ *behaves as a constant as far as conditioning on* $\mathcal{A}$ *goes:*

$$E_Q[hf|\mathcal{A}] = hE_Q[f|\mathcal{A}] \qquad (24.16)$$

**(iii)** *If* $g$ *is an* $\mathcal{F}$*-measurable function on* $\Omega$ *with* $E_Q|g| < \infty$*, and is independent of the* $\sigma$*-algebra* $\mathcal{A}$*, then conditioning* $g$ *to* $\mathcal{A}$ *wipes out all but the coarsest information about* $g$*:*

$$E_Q[g|\mathcal{A}] = E_Q[g] \qquad (24.17)$$

**(iv)** *Conditioning* $f$ *on a trivial* $\sigma$*-algebra* $\mathcal{N}$*, i.e., one for which each set has either probability* 0 *or* 1*, produces the ordinary expected value of* $f$*:*

$$E_Q[f|\mathcal{N}] = E_Q f$$

**(v)** *The expected value of the conditional expectation is the expected value:*

$$E_Q[E_Q[f|\mathcal{A}]] = E_Q(f) \qquad (24.18)$$

**(vi)** *If* $f \geq 0$ *then* $E_Q(f|\mathcal{A}) \geq 0$.

All the statements above are fairly direct consequences of the definition of conditional expectation, or of some of the other statements.

Now we can present the proof of Theorem 7.4.1. For ease of reference we repeat the statement of the result:

**Theorem 24.5.2** *Suppose $\mathcal{F}$ is a $\sigma$-algebra of subsets of a nonempty set $\Omega$, suppose $\mathcal{A}$ is a sub-$\sigma$-algebra, and suppose $Q_X$ and $Q_Y$ are probability measures on $\mathcal{F}$ related by*

$$\boxed{Q_X(B) = \frac{E_{Q_Y}\left[v_X^Y 1_B\right]}{E_{Q_Y}\left[v_X^Y\right]}} \tag{24.19}$$

*for all $B \in \mathcal{F}$, where $v_X^Y$ is an $\mathcal{F}$-measurable positive function on $\Omega$. Then*

$$E_{Q_X}[f|\mathcal{A}] = \frac{E_{Q_Y}\left[f v_X^Y|\mathcal{A}\right]}{E_{Q_Y}\left[v_X^Y|\mathcal{A}\right]} \tag{24.20}$$

*for all $\mathcal{F}$-measurable functions $f$ for which either side exists.*

***Proof.*** Let

$$g = \frac{v_X^Y}{E_{Q_Y}(v_X^Y)}$$

Then the conversion formula (24.19) reads:

$$E_{Q_X}(1_B) = E_{Q_Y}(1_B g) \tag{24.21}$$

Taking linear combinations, monotone limits, and the usual procedure, we have then

$$E_{Q_X}(f) = E_{Q_Y}(fg) \tag{24.22}$$

valid for all measurable functions $f$ for which either side exists.

We will show that

$$E_{Q_X}[f|\mathcal{A}] = \frac{E_{Q_Y}[fg|\mathcal{A}]}{E_{Q_Y}[g|\mathcal{A}]}, \tag{24.23}$$

from which (24.20) follows by substituting in $g = \frac{v_X^Y}{E_{Q_Y}(v_X^Y)}$.

We may and will assume that $f$ is nonnegative, because the general case can be broken down to this case.

Now consider any $\mathcal{A}$-measurable nonnegative function $h$. Then, using the properties of conditional expectations repeatedly, we have:

$$\begin{aligned}
E_{Q_X}\left[h\frac{E_{Q_Y}[fg|\mathcal{A}]}{E_{Q_Y}[g|\mathcal{A}]}\right] &= E_{Q_Y}\left[gh\frac{E_{Q_Y}[fg|\mathcal{A}]}{E_{Q_Y}[g|\mathcal{A}]}\right] \quad \text{by (24.22)} \\
&= E_{Q_Y}\left[E_{Q_Y}\left[gh\frac{E_{Q_Y}[fg|\mathcal{A}]}{E_{Q_Y}[g|\mathcal{A}]}\Big|\mathcal{A}\right]\right] \\
&= E_{Q_Y}\left[h\frac{E_{Q_Y}[fg|\mathcal{A}]}{E_{Q_Y}[g|\mathcal{A}]}E_{Q_Y}[g|\mathcal{A}]\right] \\
&= E_{Q_Y}\left[E_{Q_Y}[hfg|\mathcal{A}]\right] \\
&= E_{Q_Y}[ghf] \quad \text{using (24.18)} \\
&= E_{Q_X}(hf) \quad \text{again by (24.22)}
\end{aligned}$$

Thus, we have

$$E_{Q_X}(hf) = E_{Q_X}\left[h\frac{E_{Q_Y}[fg|\mathcal{A}]}{E_{Q_Y}[g|\mathcal{A}]}\right]$$

valid for all nonnegative $\mathcal{A}$-measurable functions $h$. This proves that the conditional expectation $E_{Q_X}(f|\mathcal{A})$ is given by (24.23). QED

## THE CHARACTERISTIC FUNCTION

The *characteristic function* $\phi_X$ of a random variable $X$, on a probability space $(\Omega, \mathcal{F}, Q)$, is the function on $\mathbf{R}$ given by

$$\boxed{\phi_X(t) = E_Q[e^{itX}]} \tag{24.24}$$

Because $\omega \mapsto e^{itX(\omega)}$ is bounded and measurable, $\phi_X(t)$ exists for every real $t$ and :

**(i)** $\phi_X(0) = 1$ and

**(ii)** $\phi_X$ is continuous (this follows by dominated convergence).

Because

$$\phi_X(t) = \int_{\mathbf{R}} e^{itx}\, dQ_X(x)$$

where $Q_X$ is the probability distribution measure for $X$, $\phi_X$ is determined by $Q_X$, and so we we will often write $\phi_\mu$ to denote the characteristic function of a random variable whose distribution is $\mu$.

If $X$ is Gaussian, then

$$E(e^{\lambda X}) = e^{\lambda E(X) + \lambda^2 \sigma_X^2/2} \tag{24.25}$$

for all $\lambda \in \mathbf{C}$. In particular, the characteristic function of a standard Gaussian variable $Z$ is given by

$$\boxed{\phi_Z(t) = e^{-t^2/2}} \tag{24.26}$$

If $X_1, \ldots, X_n$ are independent random variables then

$$\phi_{X_1+\cdots+X_n} = \phi_{X_1} \cdots \phi_{X_n}$$

This follows from the formula (24.11), which says that the expected value of products of independent variables is the product of the expected values.

Perhaps the most important fact about the characteristic function is that it specifies the distribution of the random variable uniquely. Indeed, the distribution measure $Q_X$ can be recovered from the characteristic function, as we shall see in the next section.

## RECOVERING Q FROM ITS CHARACTERISTIC FUNCTION

We turn now to the inversion formula, which recovers a probability measure from its characteristic function.

As initial preparation, let us note the inequality

$$|e^{i\theta} - 1| = |2\sin(\theta/2)| \leq |\theta|$$

(for all real $\theta$) and its consequence

$$|e^{ix} - e^{iy}| \leq |x - y| \text{ for all } x, y \in \mathbf{R}.$$

Geometrically, this says that the arc length along a circle from $e^{ix}$ and $e^{iy}$ is greater or equal to the chord length $|x - y|$.

Moreover,

$$\frac{e^{ikx} - e^{iky}}{x - y} \to ik, \text{ as } |x - y| \to 0,$$

and so we define the expression $\frac{e^{ikx}-e^{iky}}{x-y}$ to mean $ik$ if $x = y$. With this understanding,

$$\frac{e^{ikx} - e^{iky}}{x - y} \text{ is a continuous function of } (x, y), \text{ bounded by } |k|.$$

**Theorem 24.7.1** *Let $X$ be a random variable on a probability space $(\Omega, \mathcal{F}, Q)$. Let $a, b \in \mathbf{R}$, with $a < b$. Then*

$$Q[a < X < b] + \frac{1}{2}(Q[X = a] + Q[X = b]) = \lim_{T\to\infty} \frac{1}{2\pi} \int_{-T}^{T} \frac{e^{-iat} - e^{-ibt}}{it} \phi_X(t)\, dt \tag{24.27}$$

*If $\int_{\mathbf{R}} |\phi_X(t)|\, dt < \infty$, then $X$ has a continuous density function $\rho_X$ given by*

$$\rho_X(x) = \frac{1}{2\pi} \int_{\mathbf{R}} e^{-ixt} \phi_X(t)\, dt \tag{24.28}$$

*and*

$$Q[a < X < b] = \frac{1}{2\pi}\int_{-\infty}^{\infty}\frac{e^{-iat}-e^{-ibt}}{it}\phi_X(t)\,dt \qquad (24.29)$$

***Proof.*** Using $\phi_X(t) = E_Q(e^{itX})$ and $e^{i\theta} - e^{-i\theta} = 2i\sin\theta$, we have

$$\int_{-T}^{T}\frac{e^{-iat}-e^{-ibt}}{it}\phi_X(t)\,dt = \int_{-T}^{T}E_Q\left[\frac{e^{it(X-a)}-e^{it(X-b)}}{it}\right]dt$$

$$\overset{\text{Fubini}}{=} E_Q\left[\int_{-T}^{T}\frac{e^{it(X-a)}-e^{it(X-b)}}{it}\,dt\right]$$

Using the simple identity

$$\int_{-T}^{T}g(t)\,dt = 2\int_{0}^{T}\frac{g(t)+g(-t)}{2}\,dt$$

we then have

$$\int_{-T}^{T}\frac{e^{-iat}-e^{-ibt}}{it}\phi_X(t)\,dt$$

$$= 2E_Q\left[\int_{0}^{T}\frac{\sin t(X-a)}{t}\,dt - \int_{0}^{T}\frac{\sin t(X-b)}{t}\,dt\right]$$

$$= 2E_Q(Y_T)$$

Here, recalling (23.19),

$$Y_T = \operatorname{sgn}(X-a)S(T\,|X-a|) - \operatorname{sgn}(X-b)S(T\,|X-b|),$$

and

$$S(t) = \int_{0}^{t}\frac{\sin x}{x}\,dx$$

Now, as seen earlier in (23.18),

$$\lim_{T\to\infty} S(T) = \pi/2$$

So $Y_T$ is bounded by the finite constant $2\sup S$. Furthermore,

$$\lim_{T\to\infty} Y_T = \left[-\frac{\pi}{2}1_{[X<a]} + \frac{\pi}{2}1_{[X>a]}\right] - \left[-\frac{\pi}{2}1_{[X<b]} + \frac{\pi}{2}1_{[X>b]}\right]$$
$$= \pi 1_{[a<X<b]} + \frac{\pi}{2}\left(1_{[X=a]} + 1_{[X=b]}\right)$$

Note that we do use the hypothesis that $a<b$. Applying the dominated convergence theorem, we have:

$$\lim_{T\to\infty}\int_{-T}^{T}\frac{e^{-iat}-e^{-ibt}}{it}\phi_X(t)\,dt$$
$$= \lim_{T\to\infty} 2E_Q(Y_T)$$
$$= 2\pi E_Q\left(1_{[a<X<b]} + \frac{1}{2}\left(1_{[X=a]} + 1_{[X=b]}\right)\right)$$

and this yields the first inversion formula (24.27).

If $\int_{\mathbf{R}}|\phi_X(t)|\,dt<\infty$, then in (24.27) we can use dominated convergence to replace $\lim_{T\to\infty}\int_{-T}^{T}$ by the integral $\int_{\mathbf{R}}$. Then, letting $b\to a$ we see that $Q[X=a]$, and similarly, $Q[X=b]$, is zero, thus yielding the inversion formula (24.29). Finally, by writing $\frac{e^{-iat}-e^{-ibt}}{it}$ as $\int_a^b e^{-ixt}\,dx$ and using Fubini's theorem in (24.29), we see that $Q[a<X<b]=\int_{[a,b]}\rho_X(x)\,dx$, where $\rho_X(x)=\frac{1}{2\pi}\int_{\mathbf{R}}e^{-ixt}\phi_X(t)\,dt$, thus proving that $\rho_X$ is indeed a density function for $X$. Dominated convergence again implies that $\rho_X$ is continuous. QED

## CONVERGENCE NOTIONS

There are several different, useful notions of convergence in probability theory.

Consider a sequence $(X_n)_{n\geq 1}$ of random variables on a probability space $(\Omega, \mathcal{F}, Q)$. We write

$$X_n \to X \quad \text{w.p. } 1 \tag{24.30}$$

to mean that $X_n(\omega)\to X(\omega)$, as $n\to\infty$, *with probability* 1, i.e.

that

$$Q[X_n \to X] = 1$$

Next, we have the notion of *convergence in probability*: we say the sequence $(X_n)_{n\geq 1}$ converges in probability to $X$ if

$$\lim_{n\to\infty} Q\big[|X_n - X| > \epsilon\big] = 0 \text{ for all } \epsilon > 0 \qquad (24.31)$$

Another standard measure-theoretic notion of convergence is $L^p$–convergence:

$$\lim_{n\to\infty} E_Q[|X_n - X|^p] = 0. \qquad (24.32)$$

Finally, there is a much more probabilistic notion of convergence. For this, consider a sequence of random variables $X_n$, and a random variable $X$, possibly all on different probability spaces. The sequence $(X_n)_{n\geq 1}$ is said to *converge in distribution* to $X$ if

$$\lim_{n\to\infty} F_{X_n}(t) = F_X(t) \qquad \text{at all points } t \text{ where } F_X \text{ is continuous.}$$

We write this as

$$X_n \xrightarrow{\text{d}} X$$

Note that *this is really a statement about distributions*, not random variables.

It can be proven that

$$X_n \xrightarrow{\text{d}} X \text{ if and only if } \phi_{X_n}(t) \to \phi_X(t) \text{ for all } t \in \mathbf{R}$$

For a proof see, for instance, [5, Theorem 2.63].

A frequent application of the preceding fact is in proving *central limit theorems*. A basic instance of such a theorem says that *if $Y_1, Y_2, \ldots$ are independent identically distributed random variables with finite variance,* and

$$S_n = \sum_{j=1}^{n} Y_j$$

*then the sequence of normalized partial sums*

$$Z_n \stackrel{\text{def}}{=} \frac{S_n - E(S_n)}{\sigma_{S_n}},$$

*converges, in distribution, to the standard Gaussian:*

$$Z_n \xrightarrow{d} Z, \qquad \text{as } n \to \infty,$$

where $Z$ is a standard Gaussian variable (mean 0, variance 1).

We give a very brief sketch of the proof. Let $\sigma = \sigma_{Y_1}$, $m = E(Y_1)$, and $Y = Y_1 - m$. Then, because the variables $Y_j$ are independent and identically distributed, the characteristic function of $Z_n$ works out to:

$$\phi_{Z_n}(t) = \left[\phi_Y\left(\frac{t}{\sigma\sqrt{n}}\right)\right]^n$$

Now,

$$\phi_Y(s) = E(e^{isY}) = 1 + isE(Y) - \frac{s^2}{2}[\sigma^2 + h_s] = 1 - \frac{s^2}{2}[\sigma^2 + h_s],$$

where $h_s \to 0$ as $s \to 0$. Then,

$$\phi_{Z_n}(t) = \left[1 - \frac{t^2}{2\sigma^2 n}\left(\sigma^2 + h'_n\right)\right]^n,$$

where $h'_n \to 0$ as $n \to \infty$. Thus, we have

$$\lim_{n\to\infty} \phi_{Z_n}(t) = e^{-t^2/2},$$

which is, indeed, the characteristic function of the standard Gaussian, as noted in (24.26).

CHAPTER 25

# Stochastic Processes

Throughout this chapter we work with a probability space

$$(\Omega, \mathcal{F}, Q)$$

In our applications, $\Omega$ describes the set of all possible market scenarios, $\mathcal{F}$ is the set of all possible market events, and $Q$ a pricing measure.

## SOME BASIC NOTIONS

Let $T$ be a set whose elements correspond to time instants. Typically, $T$ will be an interval of real numbers, or $T$ may be the set of all positive (or nonnegative) integers. In any case, we require that $T$ be equipped with an order relation $<$, where we interpret $s < t$ to mean that time $s$ is prior to time $t$.

A *filtration* on $(\Omega, \mathcal{F})$ is a family of $\sigma$-algebras

$$\mathcal{F}_t$$

for $t \in T$, such that

$$\mathcal{F}_s \subset \mathcal{F}_t$$

for all $s \leq t$.

In the situations of interest to us, $\mathcal{F}_t$ is the set of all possible market events up till time $t$. Then $\mathcal{F}_s \subset \mathcal{F}_t$ is clear.

A *stochastic process* on $(\Omega, \mathcal{F})$ with values in a topological space $S$ is a family of $\mathcal{F}$-measurable maps

$$X_t : \Omega \to S$$

for $t \in T$. This process is *adapted* to the filtration $\{\mathcal{F}_t\}_{t \in T}$ if each $X_t$ is $\mathcal{F}_t$-measurable.

Sometimes, even when $T$ is an interval in the real line, it is convenient to adjoin $\infty$ to it.

A *stopping time*, relative to a filtration $\{\mathcal{F}_t\}_{t \in T}$, is a random variable $\tau$, with values in the set $T$, with the property that,

$$[\tau \leq t] \in \mathcal{F}_t, \tag{25.1}$$

for every $t \in T$. Thus, whether $\tau$ is $\leq t$ or not is decidable in terms of the knowledge available in $\mathcal{F}_t$. A typical example (with appropriate hypotheses) of a stopping time is the first time a stochastic process exits some given set.

## PROCESSES AND FILTRATIONS: THE USUAL CONDITIONS

We work in this section with the continuum case, i.e., with the time index set $T$ being $[0, \infty)$.

The not(at)ion

$$\mathcal{F}_{t+} \stackrel{\text{def}}{=} \bigcap_{s>t} \mathcal{F}_s \tag{25.2}$$

appears useful in studying some problems concerning stochastic processes.

Many results of interest are proved under the following additional conditions on a filtration, called *the usual conditions*:

$$\mathcal{F}_t = \bigcap_{s>t} \mathcal{F}_s \text{ for all } t \in T, \text{ and } \mathcal{F}_0 \text{ contains all subsets of sets of } Q\text{-measure } 0. \tag{25.3}$$

The first condition is *right continuity*, and can be restated as

$$\mathcal{F}_{t+} = \mathcal{F}_t \text{ for all } t \in T$$

Most processes $t \mapsto X_t$ of interest also satisfy the following conditions:

**(i)** For $Q$–almost-every $\omega$, the map $t \mapsto X_t(\omega)$ is left continuous;

**(ii)** For $Q$–almost-every $\omega$, the map $t \mapsto X_t(\omega)$ has right limits, i.e. $\lim_{s \downarrow t} X_s(\omega)$ exists.

Most processes of interest also have a stronger measurability property: *For any $t \geq 0$, the mapping*

$$[0, t] \times \Omega \to S : (s, \omega) \mapsto X_s(\omega)$$

*is measurable with respect to the product $\sigma$–algebra*

$$\mathcal{B}_{[0,t]} \otimes \mathcal{F}_t,$$

*where $\mathcal{B}_{[0,t]}$ is the Borel $\sigma$–algebra on* $[0, t]$.

## MARTINGALES

A *martingale* is a stochastic process $t \mapsto X_t$, adapted to a filtration $\{\mathcal{F}_t\}_{t \in T}$, for which the following hold:

**(i)** $E|X_t| < \infty$ for each $t$

**(ii)** $E[X_t|\mathcal{F}_s] = X_s$ for all $s < t$

Thus, for a martingale, the best estimate of its time-$t$ value at a prior time $s$, is the time-$s$ value itself. This is a feature of asset prices as judged by the market pricing measure (see Chapter 7).

For example, consider any random variable $Y$ for which $E|Y| < \infty$, and set

$$Y_t = E[Y|\mathcal{F}_t]$$

Then the stochastic process $t \mapsto Y_t$ is a martingale for the filtration $\{\mathcal{F}_t\}_{t \geq 0}$.

## CONSTRUCTION OF STOCHASTIC PROCESSES

A stochastic process $X$ is often described through its *finite dimensional distributions*, i.e., the distributions of $(X_{t_1}, \ldots, X_{t_n})$ for time instants $t_1, \ldots, t_n$. These distribution measures $Q_{X_{t_1},\ldots,X_{t_n}}$ satisfy a natural consistency condition:

$$Q_{X_{t_1},\ldots,X_{t_n},X_{t_{n+1}}}(A \times \mathbf{R}) = Q_{X_{t_1},\ldots,X_{t_n}}(A)$$

for any instants $t_1, \ldots, t_{n+1}$, and any Borel set $A \subset \mathbf{R}^n$.

A fundamental result in probability theory is *Kolmogorov's theorem*, which says that given a consistent family of putative finite-dimensional distributions, a stochastic process with these finite-dimensional distributions does exist.

The first form of Kolmogorov's theorem that we examine says that if a family of probability measures $\mu_n$ on $\mathbf{R}^n$, for all $n \geq 1$, is given, and these measures satisfy a natural consistency condition, then these measures fit together to form a measure $\mu$ on the infinite product $\mathbf{R}^\infty$. The infinite product $\mathbf{R}^\infty$ consists of all sequences $(x_1, x_2, \ldots)$ of real numbers $x_n$, and has the *product $\sigma$-algebra*, which is the smallest $\sigma$-algebra containing all sets of the form $E \times \mathbf{R} \times \mathbf{R} \times \cdots$ with $E$ running over all Borel sets in $\mathbf{R}^n$ and $n$ running over $\{1, 2, 3, \ldots\}$.

**Theorem 25.4.1** *Suppose that for each $n \geq 1$, $\mu_n$ is a Borel probability measure on $\mathbf{R}^n$ such that the Kolmogorov consistency condition*

$$\mu_{n+1}(A \times \mathbf{R}) = \mu_n(A) \text{ for every } n \geq 1 \text{ and every Borel set } A \subset \mathbf{R}^n \tag{25.4}$$

*holds. Then there is a unique probability measure $\mu$ on the product $\sigma$-algebra of $\mathbf{R}^\infty$ such that for any $n \geq 1$ and any Borel subset $A$ of $\mathbf{R}^n$, the measure $\mu(A \times \mathbf{R} \times \mathbf{R} \times \cdots)$ equals $\mu_n(A)$.*

Notice that if $\mu$ does exist, satisfying the conclusion of the theorem, then the consistency condition must necessarily hold.

Kolmogorov's theorem leads to the construction of stochastic processes in the following way. Consider the case where $T$, the set of time instants is countable:

$$T = \{t_1, t_2, \ldots\}$$

Suppose that for any $t_1, \ldots, t_n$, we are given a probability measure $Q_{t_1,\ldots,t_n}$ on the Borel sigma–algebra of $\mathbf{R}^n$, satisfying the natural consistency conditions. Then, by the theorem, there is a probability measure $Q$ on the product $\sigma$-algebra of $\Omega = \mathbf{R}^\infty$ such that

$$Q(A \times \mathbf{R} \times \mathbf{R} \times \cdots) = Q_{t_1,\ldots,t_n}(A) \tag{25.5}$$

for every Borel subset $A$ of $\mathbf{R}^n$, and every $n$. Now let $X_{t_j}$ be the random variable on $\Omega$ given by

$$X_{t_j}(x) = x_{t_j}$$

for all $x \in \Omega$, where $x_{t_j}$ is the $t_j$–component of $x$. The defining property (25.5) of the measure $Q$ then shows that

$$\begin{aligned} Q[(X_{t_1}, \ldots, X_{t_n}) \in A] &= Q(A \times \mathbf{R} \times \mathbf{R} \times \cdots) \\ &= Q_{t_1,\ldots,t_n}(A) \end{aligned}$$

Thus, the stochastic process $\{X_t\}_{t \in T}$ has the specified finite-dimensional distributions.

To handle the case of stochastic processes with a general indexing set $T$, a more general version of Kolmogorov's theorem is needed. To this end, let us bring in some notation.

Let $T$ be a nonempty set. Instead of $\mathbf{R}^\infty$, we use

$$\mathbf{R}^T = \{\text{all maps } x : T \to \mathbf{R}\} \tag{25.6}$$

An element $x \in \mathbf{R}^T$ may be also denoted $(x_t)_{t \in T}$, and can be viewed as a path

$$t \mapsto x_t$$

We shall denote nonempty finite subsets of $T$ by greek letters $\alpha, \beta, \ldots$.

We have the coordinate projection maps

$$\pi_t : \mathbf{R}^T \to \mathbf{R} : x \mapsto x_t$$

A *cylinder set* is a subset of $\mathbf{R}^T$ of the form

$$\pi_{t_1,\ldots t_n}^{-1}(A)$$

for $t_1, \ldots, t_n \in T$ and $A \subset \mathbf{R}^n$. This is the set of all $(x_t)_{t \in T}$ for which the coordinates $(x_{t_1}, \ldots, x_{t_n})$ lie in the set $A$, respectively. We will call this a *measurable* cylinder set if $A$ is a Borel set.

If $I$ and $K$ are any nonempty subsets of $T$ with $I \subset K$, then we have a natural projection map

$$p_{IK} : \mathbf{R}^K \to \mathbf{R}^I : x = (x_t)_{t \in K} \mapsto (x_t)_{t \in I} = x|I$$

where $x|I$ is just the restriction of $x$ to $I$.

The projection map $p_{IT} : \mathbf{R}^T \to \mathbf{R}^I$ will be denoted simply by $p_I$.

Thus, a measurable cylinder set is a subset of $\mathbf{R}^T$ of the form

$$p_\alpha^{-1}(A)$$

for some nonempty finite subset $\alpha$ of $T$ and a Borel set $A \subset \mathbf{R}^\alpha$.

The collection $\mathcal{F}$ of all measurable cylinder sets fails to be a $\sigma$-algebra (unless $T$ is finite) only in countable additivity.

The *product* $\sigma$*-algebra* on $\mathbf{R}^T$ is the $\sigma$-algebra generated by all the projections $\pi_t$. Equivalently, it is the $\sigma$-algebra $\sigma(\mathcal{F})$ generated by all measurable cylinder sets.

**Theorem 25.4.2** *Suppose that for every nonempty finite subset $\alpha \subset J$ we are given a Borel probability measure $\mu_\alpha$ on $\mathbf{R}^\alpha$. Suppose also that the Kolmogorov consistency condition*

$$\mu_\beta\big(p_{\alpha\beta}^{-1}(A)\big) = \mu_\alpha(A) \tag{25.7}$$

*holds for every nonempty finite subsets $\alpha \subset \beta$ of $J$ and every Borel* *set* $A \subset \mathbf{R}^{\alpha}$. *Then there is a unique probability measure* $\mu$ *on* $\sigma(\mathcal{F})$ *such that*

$$\mu\big(p_{\alpha}^{-1}(A)\big) = \mu_{\alpha}(A)$$

*for every nonempty finite subset* $\alpha$ *of* $J$ *and every Borel set* $A \subset \mathbf{R}^{\alpha}$.

Construction of a stochastic process from given finite dimensional distributions proceeds then as follows. Suppose we are given a probability measure $Q_{\alpha}$ on $\mathbf{R}^{\alpha}$ for every finite subset $\alpha$ of $T$, and assume these measures satisfy the natural consistency condition. Then the preceding theorem produces a probability measure $Q$ on $\mathbf{R}^{T}$ with the $Q_{\alpha}$ as finite-dimensional distributions. Then the process

$$T \times \mathbf{R}^{T} \to \mathbf{R} : (t, x) \mapsto X_t(x) \stackrel{\text{def}}{=} x_t$$

has finite-dimensional distributions given by

$$\begin{aligned} Q\big[(X_{t_1}, \ldots, X_{t_n}) \in A\big] &= Q\left(\pi^{-1}_{\{t_1,\ldots,t_n\}}(A)\right) \\ &= Q_{t_1,\ldots,t_n}(A) \end{aligned}$$

Observe that what this theorem provides is a stochastic process defined on the space $\mathbf{R}^{T}$, not on any particular given probability space. Secondly, if $T$ is an interval of real numbers, such as $[0, \infty)$, the process constructed above need not have any continuity properties. However, the following theorem of Kolmogorov addresses the question of continuity:

**Theorem 25.4.3** *Asssume that a stochastic process* $\{X_t\}_{t\geq 0}$, *on some given probability space* $(\Omega, \mathcal{F}, Q)$, *satisfies the following Kolmogorov Continuity Condition: for any* $T \in [0, \infty)$ *there are positive constants* $\alpha, \beta, L > 0$, *such that*

$$E_Q\left[|X_t - X_s|^{\alpha}\right] \leq L|t - s|^{1+\beta}, \qquad \textit{for all } s, t \in [0, T]$$

*Then there exists a stochastic process* $\{X'_t\}_{t\geq 0}$, *defined on the same probability space, which is a continuous version of* $\{X_t\}_{t\geq 0}$, *in the sense that*

$$Q[X_t = X'_t] = 1 \text{ for every } t \in [0, \infty),$$

*and*

$$t \mapsto X'_t(\omega) \text{ is continuous for every } \omega \in \Omega.$$

Notice that if processes $\{X_t\}_{t\in T}$ and $\{X'_t\}_{t\in T}$ are *versions* of each other, in the sense that $X_t = X'_t$ almost certainly for every $t$, then

$$(X_{t_1}, \ldots, X_{t_n}) \text{ and } (X'_{t_1}, \ldots, X'_{t_n}) \text{ have the same distribution}$$

for every finite subset $\{t_1, \ldots, t_n\} \subset T$.

## BROWNIAN MOTION

Consider, as usual, a probability space $(\Omega, \mathcal{F}, Q)$. A standard *Wiener process* on this space is a stochastic process $\{W_t\}_{t\geq 0}$:

$$[0, \infty) \times \Omega \to \mathbf{R} : (t, \omega) \mapsto W_t(\omega)$$

such that:

**(i)** $W_0 = 0$ almost surely

**(ii)** The process $t \mapsto W_t$ has *independent increments*, i.e., for any $0 \leq t_1 < t_2 < \cdots < t_n$ the increments $W_{t_2} - W_{t_1}, \ldots, W_{t_n} - W_{t_{n-1}}$ are mutually independent;

**(iii)** For any $t > s \geq 0$, the increment $W_t - W_s$ is Gaussian with mean 0 and variance $t - s$; thus it has the characteristic function

$$E[e^{i\lambda(W_t - W_s)}] = e^{-\frac{\lambda^2}{2}(t-s)}$$

For a detailed treatment of the construction of a Wiener process, see, for instance, [5]; later in this section we give a short sketch.

It can be shown that if a Wiener process as above exists on $(\Omega, \mathcal{F}, Q)$ then this process can be modified to produce a Wiener process $\{W_t\}_{t\geq 0}$ on the same space for which the path

$$t \mapsto W_t(\omega)$$

is continuous for every $\omega \in \Omega$, and $W_0(\omega) = 0$ also for every $\omega \in \Omega$. Such a process is a *Brownian motion*, and we will often use the notation $B_t$ in place of $W_t$.

A Wiener process with values in $\mathbf{R}^n$ is a stochastic process with values in $\mathbf{R}^n$ whose components are mutually independent Wiener processes.

The typical Brownian path $t \mapsto B_t(\omega)$ is very jagged. Since $B_t - B_s$ is Gaussian with mean 0 and variance $t - s$, a rough idea of the behavior of the Brownian increment is given by

$$B_t - B_s \sim |t-s|^{1/2}$$

This leads to a correct estimate for the *quadratic variation* of a Brownian path: for a partition $a = t_0 < t_1 < \cdots < t_n = b$ of an interval $[a, b]$,

$$\sum_{j=1}^{n} \left(B_{t_j} - B_{t_{j-1}}\right)^2 \to b - a,$$

as one shrinks the partition size $\max_j (t_j - t_{j-1})$ to 0. Note that the quadratic variation being finite, it seems unlikely that the Brownian path will be differentiable. Indeed, with probability 1, a Brownian path is never differentiable.

A precise measure of the behavior of the typical Brownian path is given by Lévy's result: for small values of $\delta = t_2 - t_1$, the maximum increment $B(t_2) - B(t_1)$ approaches, in magnitude,

$$[2\delta \log(1/\delta)]^{1/2}$$

More precisely,

$$\limsup_{0\leq t_1<t_2\leq 1, t_2-t_1\downarrow 0} \frac{|B(t_2) - B(t_1)|}{[2(t_2-t_1)\log(t_2-t_1)^{-1}]^{1/2}} = 1 \quad \text{with probability 1} \quad (25.8)$$

Let us examine the construction of a Wiener process. The definition of a Wiener process essentially specifies the finite-dimensional distributions of the process. If $0 < t_1 < t_2 < \cdots < t_n$, then the variables

$$W_{t_1}, W_{t_2} - W_{t_1}, \ldots, W_{t_n} - W_{t_{n-1}}$$

are independent, with $W_{t_j} - W_{t_{j-1}}$ being Gaussian of mean 0 and variance $t_j - t_{j-1}$. So,

$$W_0 = 0,$$

and, for $0 < t_1 < \cdots < t_n$, the distribution measure $Q_{t_1,\ldots,t_n}$ of $(W_{t_1}, W_{t_2}, \ldots, W_{t_n})$ on $\mathbf{R}^n$ has density function

$$p_{t_1}(x_1)p_{t_2-t_1}(x_2 - x_1)\cdots p_{t_n-t_{n-1}}(x_n - x_{n-1}), \tag{25.9}$$

where

$$p_t(x) = \frac{1}{\sqrt{2\pi t}} e^{-\frac{x^2}{2t}}$$

is the density of a Gaussian of mean 0 and variance $t$.

The consistency condition for Kolmogorov's theorem follows from the fundamental fact that the sum of two independent Gaussians is Gaussian. This is expressed through the convolution identity

$$\int_{\mathbf{R}} p_t(x - y)p_s(y - z)\,dy = p_{t+s}(x - z)$$

Integrating the density function in (25.9) over $x_j$ thus has the effect of removing the $j$-th term in the product. Therefore, Kolmogorov's theorem yields a stochastic process

$$X : [0, \infty) \times \mathbf{R}^{[0,\infty)} \to \mathbf{R} : (t, x) \mapsto X_t(x) = x(t)$$

which has the required finite-dimensional distributions.

The process constructed above is, however, not continuous. But Kolmogorov's theorem on continuous versions comes to the rescue. The random variable $X_t - X_s$ is Gaussian, with mean 0 and variance $t-s$, and is thus $|t-s|^{1/2}$ times a standard Gaussian $Z$. It follows that

$$E|X_t - X_s|^3 = |t-s|^{1+\frac{1}{2}} E|Z|^3$$

Then Kolmogorov's theorem produces a new stochastic process

$$t \mapsto W_t$$

with the same finite-dimensional distributions, but now with each path

$$t \mapsto W_t(x)$$

continuous. Thus, this process is a Brownian motion.

## MARKOV PROCESSES

A Markov process is a stochastic process $\{X_t\}_{t \in T}$ which has "no memory of the past." What this means is that for any time instant $s$, and any future moment $t$, the behavior of $X_t$ depends on the period at times $\leq s$ only through the value $X_s$.

For example, consider Brownian motion $\{B_t\}_{t \geq 0}$ with values in $\mathbf{R}^n$. The probability that $B_t$ lies in a Borel set $A \subset \mathbf{R}^n$, given that at an earlier time $s$ the motion was at the point $B_s = x$, is given by

$$Q[B_t \in A | B_s = x] = \int_A (2\pi)^{-\frac{n}{2}} e^{-\frac{(y-x)^2}{2(t-s)}} \, dy$$

The distribution of $B_t$, conditional on information available till time $s$, is entirely determined by its value at any given earlier time $s$.

As another example, consider symmetric *random walk* in $\mathbf{R}$. This process starts at time 0 at some given point, say the origin in $\mathbf{R}$. Then, at each time instant $t \in \{0, 1, 2, \ldots\}$, the process moves one unit to the right or to the left, with equal probability. Then the distribution of the location at time $t$ can be worked out entirely in terms of the location at any given earlier time $s$.

To set this up more generally and precisely, let $T$ be an ordered set representing time; thus, there is a relation $<$ on $T$, with $s < t$ signifying that "time" $s$ is earlier than time $t$. Consider a probability space $(\Omega, \mathcal{F}, Q)$, and a family of $\sigma$-algebras $\mathcal{F}_t$, for $t \in T$, with

$$\mathcal{F}_s \subset \mathcal{F}_t \subset \mathcal{F} \text{ for all } s < t.$$

Consider now a process $t \mapsto X_t$, given by a map

$$X : T \times \Omega \to \mathbf{R}^n : (t, \omega) \mapsto X_t(\omega)$$

such that $X_t$ is $\mathcal{F}_t$-measurable for each $t \in T$. We shall say that this is a *Markov process* if

$$E[f(X_t)|\mathcal{F}_s] \text{ is } \sigma(X_s)\text{–measurable}$$

for any bounded measurable function $f$, and time instants $s < t$.

In particular, taking $f$ to be the indicator function of a set $A$ we see that the conditional probability

$$Q[X_t \in A|\mathcal{F}_s] \text{ is a function of } X_s.$$

Of course, $Q[X_t \in A|\mathcal{F}_s]$ will also depend on the set $A$ and the time instants $s, t$. Thus

$$Q[X_t \in A|\mathcal{F}_s] = Q(s, X_s; t, A)$$

for some function $Q(s, x; t, B)$ of $s, t \in T$, with $s \leq t$, $x \in \mathbf{R}^n$, and $B$ running over Borel subsets $B$ of $\mathbf{R}^n$. The number

$$Q(s, x; t, B)$$

is the *transition probability*, the probability that, starting at time $s$ at the point $x$, the process will reach a value in the set $B$ at time $t$.

We shall concentrate on processes for which there is a transition probability *density*

$$p(s, x;\ t, y),$$

a function, nonnegative and measurable in $y$, satisfying

$$Q(s,x;t,B) = \int_B p(s,x;t,y)\,dy \tag{25.10}$$

for all relevant $s, x, t, B$. Then for any measurable function $f$ on $\mathbf{R}^n$,

$$E[f(X_t)|\mathcal{F}_s] = \int f(y)p(s,X_s;t,y)\,dy \tag{25.11}$$

whenever either side exists. This reduces to (25.10) if $f$ is the indicator function $1_B$.

Suppose now that we are given a well-behaved function $p$ satisfying the consistency condition

$$\int_{\mathbf{R}} p(s,x\,;u,z)p(u,z\,;t,y)\,dz = p(s,x\,;t,y) \tag{25.12}$$

for all $0 \leq s < u < t$, and $x, y \in \mathbf{R}^n$.

Our objective is to construct a Markov process $\{X_t\}_{t\geq 0}$ with $p$ as the transition density function. For convenience, let $T = [0,\infty)$ be the time indexing set, and, choose any arbitrary point $x_0 \in \mathbf{R}$ as the initial point of the process

$$X_0 = x_0$$

Then, for $0 < t_1 < t_2 < \cdots < t_n$, we have putative finite-dimensional distributions $Q_{t_1,\ldots,t_n}$ with density given by

$$p(0,x_0\,;t_1,x_1)p(t_1,x_1\,;t_2,x_2)\cdots p(t_{n-1},x_{n-1}\,;t_n,x_n)$$

The condition (25.12) ensures that the measures $Q_{t_1,\ldots,t_n}$ satisfy the consistency condition of Kolmogorov's theorem, and then the theorem produces a probability measure $Q$ on the product $\mathbf{R}^T$ such that the stochastic process

$$T \times \mathbf{R}^T \to \mathbf{R} : (t,x) \mapsto X_t(x) = x(t)$$

has the finite-dimensional distributions given by the measures $Q_{t_1,\ldots,t_n}$, and with $X_0 = x_0$. It follows that this process has $p$ as transition density.

## THE STOCHASTIC INTEGRAL

Let us first examine the overall idea. Consider a stochastic processes $t \mapsto X_t$ and $t \mapsto Y_t$. We would like to define an integral

$$\int_a^b Y_t \, dX_t$$

A natural definition, based on the Riemann sum idea, is to take

$$\int_a^b Y_t \, dX_t = \lim_{\max_j \Delta t_j \downarrow 0} \sum_{j=1}^{n} Y_{t_{j-1}} (X_{t_j} - X_{t_{j-1}}),$$

where $\Delta t_j = t_j - t_{j-1}$, and $a = t_0 < t_1 < \cdots < t_n = b$ is a partition of $[a, b]$. Of course, it is necessary to specify in what sense the above limit is taken. Such an integral was constructed by Itô [24], and it became the foundation for virtually all of modern stochastic analysis. We shall not develop the theory of the Itô integral, but shall indicate in the following section a very useful algebra of differentials it gives rise to.

Let us simply note that the limit in consideration above is the limit in probability.

## THE ALGEBRA OF STOCHASTIC DIFFERENTIALS

The algebra of stochastic differentials was created by Itô in his short, but beautiful, paper [25]. We give a very brief sketch here, following [25].

For a stochastic process $X$ define the *differential* $dX$ to be the function that associates to each interval $I = (a, b]$ the random variable

$$dX(I) \stackrel{\text{def}}{=} X(b) - X(a) \tag{25.13}$$

On the set of all such differentials we introduce three operations: (i) addition, (ii) multiplication by processes, and (iii) product. Moreover, there is the Itô integral itself, a linear functional on differentials, associated to each interval $[a, b]$:

$$\int_a^b dX = X(b) - X(a)$$

Addition is defined simply by

$$(dX + dY)(I) \stackrel{\text{def}}{=} dX(I) + dY(I)$$

Multiplication of $dX$ by a process $Y$ is specified by

$$Y\,dX(I) \stackrel{\text{def}}{=} \lim_{\max_j \Delta t_j \downarrow 0} \sum_{j=1}^{n} Y_{t_{j-1}} dX\big((t_{j-1}, t_j]\big), \qquad (25.14)$$

where the limit is limit in probability, and $t_0 < t_1 < \cdots < t_n$ is a partition of the interval $I$. Of course, the product is meaningful only if the processes $X$ and $Y$ are good enough.

The product $dXdY$ is defined through

$$(dXdY)(I) \stackrel{\text{def}}{==} \lim_{\max_j \Delta t_j \downarrow 0} \sum_{j=1}^{n} dX\big((t_{j-1}, t_j]\big) dY\big((t_{j-1}, t_j]\big), \quad (25.15)$$

with the same notation and comments as for $Y\,dX$. Again, the product is meaningful only for good-enough processes, and it is only such processes that Itô calculus is concerned with.

The usual product rule of calculus gets modified in Itô calculus by inclusion of a product of differentials:

$$\boxed{d(XY) = XdY + Y\,dX + (dX)(dY)} \qquad (25.16)$$

This is, in essence, a consequence of the simple algebraic identity

$$AB - ab = a(B - b) + b(A - a) + (A - a)(B - b)$$

Next, consider appropriate processes $X_1, \ldots, X_n$, and a $C^2$ function $f$ on $\mathbf{R}^n$. Then, writing $X = (X_1, \ldots, X_n)$, the differential of the process $f(X)$ is given by

$$df(X) = \sum_{i=1}^{n} \partial_i f(X) + \frac{1}{2} \sum_{i,j=1}^{n} \partial_i \partial_j f(X)\, dX_i\, dX_j \tag{25.17}$$

This is the celebrated *Itô formula*.

Consider, for example, standard Brownian motion

$$t \mapsto B_t$$

The square of the Brownian differential $dB_t$ works out to be

$$(dB_t)^2 = dt \tag{25.18}$$

In more precise, though less suggestive, notation,

$$dB\,dB((a,b]) = b - a \qquad \text{for all } b > a \geq 0,$$

which, when spelt out in more detail, says

$$\lim_{\max_j \Delta t_j \downarrow 0} \sum_{j=1}^{n} (B(t_j) - B(t_{j-1}))^2$$
$$= b - a, \text{ for partitions } a = t_0 < t_1 \cdots < t_n = b$$

Moreover,

$$dB_t\, dt = 0$$

**TABLE 25-1**

Itô Multiplication Table

| · | $dB_t$ | $dt$ |
|---|---|---|
| $dB_t$ | $dt$ | 0 |
| $dt$ | 0 | 0 |

Thus, we have the multiplication table for Itô calculus given in Table 25.1.

If

$$t \mapsto B(t) = \big(B_1(t), \ldots, B_n(t)\big)$$

is Brownian motion in $\mathbf{R}^n$, then

$$\boxed{dB_j(t)\,dB_k(t) = \delta_{jk}dt} \qquad (25.19)$$

where $\delta_{jk}$ is 1 if $j = k$, and 0 otherwise.

Application of Itô's formula to Brownian motion gives, for example,

$$d\left(B_t^2\right) = 2B_t dB_t + \frac{1}{2}2(dB_t)^2 = 2B_t dB_t + dt,$$

which can also be deduced from the product rule:

$$d(B_t B_t) = B_t dB_t + B_t dB_t + (dB_t)(dB_t) = 2B_t dB_t + dt$$

Another useful example is:

$$d(e^{B_t}) = e^{B_t}dB_t + \frac{1}{2}e^{B_t}(dB_t)^2 = e^{B_t}dB_t + \frac{1}{2}e^{B_t}dt.$$

A typical *stochastic differential equation* (sde) is of the form

$$\boxed{dX_t = a(t, X_t)dt + b(t, X_t)dB_t} \qquad (25.20)$$

where $\{X_t\}_{t\geq 0}$ is the "unknown" stochastic process to be solved for in terms of the given Brownian motion $\{B_t\}_{t\geq 0}$.

The original reason for examining stochastic differential equations is as follows. As we have seen, a nice enough Markov process $\{X_t\}_{t\geq 0}$ is described by its transition density function

$$p(s, x; t, y)$$

Assume that the process has a "drift" described through

$$E(X_t - X_s|\mathcal{F}_s) = \int_{\mathbf{R}} (y - X_s)p(s, X_s\,; t, y)\,dy \simeq a(s, X_s)(t - s)$$

and a fluctuation part described by

$$E\big((X_t - X_s)^2|\mathcal{F}_s\big) = \int_{\mathbf{R}} (y - X_s)^2 p(s, X_s; t, y)\,dy \simeq b(s, X_s)^2(t - s)$$

The transition density function $p$ satisfies a certain second-order partial differential equation (due to Kolmogorov) whose coefficients are determined by $a$ and $b$. Kolomogorov's extension theorem then provides a stochastic process on $\mathbf{R}^{[0,\infty)}$, with the given transition density function.

In contrast, Itô's method constructs such a stochastic process as "a function of" *a given* Brownian motion, by solving the stochastic differential equation (25.20) with the functions $a$ (drift) and $b$ ('volatility') specified by means of the coefficients of the partial differential equation satisfied by the transition density function.

CHAPTER 26

# Probability and Differential Equations

In the context of pricing formulas, we have seen how a price, given as an expectation value—an integral over the space of Brownian paths—can be obtained by solving a partial differential equation. This was the essence of the Feynman-Kac formula.

At first it seems magical that the solution of a partial differential equation might have something to do with an integral over a space of paths. In this chapter we work through an example that should resolve some of the mystery.

The key idea we will explore is summarized schematically as:

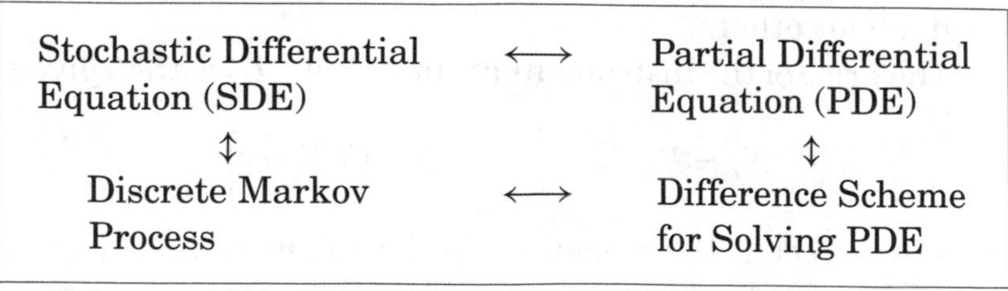


To illustrate the ideas, we work with a relatively simple example, the one-factor Hull-White model.

## THE SDE AND THE PDE

Let us review briefly the framework of the one-factor Gaussian Hull-White model. The state of the market, at any instant of time, is determined by one factor $y$. The interest rate $r(t)$, at time $t$, is expressed as

$$\boxed{r(t) = \alpha_0(t) + y(t)} \tag{26.1}$$

where $\alpha_0$ is a deterministic function, and $y$ is a stochastically varying factor. The evolution of $y$ is described by the stochastic differential equation

$$\boxed{dy(t) = -ay(t)dt + \sigma dB(t)} \tag{26.2}$$

with respect to the pricing measure $Q_0$.

As usual, we denote by $\mathcal{F}_t$ the $\sigma$-algebra of all market events until time $t$. For our purposes, $\mathcal{F}_t$ is $\sigma(\{B_s : 0 \leq s \leq t\})$.

Consider then an instrument whose payoff, or worth, at time $T \geq 0$ is $F(y)$ in state $y$:

instrument is worth $F(y)$ in state $y$, at time $T$

For instance, for a bond maturing on date $T$, the value of $F(y)$ is 1 in all states. For an option that pays amount 1 in certain states and nothing in other states, $F(y)$ would be 1 for certain values of $y$ and 0 for others.

The price of the instrument at time $t \in [0, T]$ is then given by

$$X_t = E_{Q_t}\left[e^{-\int_t^T r(s)ds} F(y(T)) \Big| \mathcal{F}_t\right]$$

As we have seen, the measure can be taken to be $Q_0$ instead of $Q_t$, without altering the value of the expectation. Also, note that we are working with a good enough function $F$ so that all expectations are finite.

Then, converting to time-0 cash, i.e., discounting back to time 0, we have the price

$$M_t = e^{-\int_0^t r(s)\,ds} X_t = E_{Q_0}\left[ e^{-\int_0^T r(s)\,ds} F(y(T)) \Big| \mathcal{F}_t \right],$$

which is a martingale relative to the filtration of $\sigma$–algebras $\{\mathcal{F}_t\}_{t\geq 0}$.

Fundamental properties of stochastic differential equations dictate that $X_t$ is, in fact, a function of $t$ and $y(t)$:

$$X_t = f(t, y(t))$$

Then, working out $dM_t$ we have:

$$\begin{aligned} dM_t &= -r(t)e^{-\int_0^t r(s)\,ds} f\big(t, y(t)\big)dt + e^{-\int_0^t r(s)\,ds} \\ &\quad \times \left[ \frac{\partial f}{\partial t} dt + \frac{\partial f}{\partial y} dy(t) + \frac{1}{2}\frac{\partial^2 f}{\partial y^2} dy(t)^2 \right] \end{aligned}$$

Because $M_t$ is a martingale, the $dt$ term on the right above has to be 0. Then, using (26.2) to determine the $dt$ term, we obtain the partial differential equation

$$\boxed{\frac{\partial f}{\partial t} = -\frac{\sigma^2}{2}\frac{\partial^2 f}{\partial y^2} + ay\frac{\partial f}{\partial y} + (\alpha_0(t) + y) f} \tag{26.3}$$

The function $f$ satisfies also the terminal condition

$$f(T, y) = F(y) \qquad \text{for all } y \in \mathbf{R} \tag{26.4}$$

We have thus shown that, *starting with a stochastic process*, the expectation value

$$f(t, y) = E_{Q_0}\left[ e^{-\int_t^T r(s)\,ds} F(y(T)) \Big| y(t) = y \right] \tag{26.5}$$

is the solution of the partial differential equation (26.3) with terminal condition (26.4).

In the next two sections, we reverse the procedure and show how, *starting with the partial differential equation, we can generate a stochastic process* that yields the solution of the partial differential equation as an expectation value over all paths of the process.

The way we generate the stochastic process is by creating a discretization scheme for the numerical solution of the partial differential equation.

## DISCRETIZING THE PDE: A NUMERICAL SCHEME

Let us now approximate the solution of the partial differential equation (26.3) by discretizing space and time.

First, let us focus on a finite region of space, i.e., values of $y$ in some interval $[-L, L]$, where $L > 0$ is finite. Divide up this interval into $2N$ intervals of size $h$:

$$y_{-N} = -L, \ldots, y_{-1} = -h, y_0 = 0, y_1 = h, \ldots, y_N = L$$

where

$$h = \frac{L}{N}$$

and $N$ is some large positive integer.

Next discretize time by dividing $[0, T]$ into $M$ little steps of size $k > 0$ each:

$$0 = t_0 < t_1 = k < t_2 = 2k < \cdots < t_M = Mk = T$$

Now let us write

$$f_i(j) = f(t_i, y_j)$$

Thus $f_i$ itself may be thought of as a vector:

$$f_i = \begin{pmatrix} f_i(N) \\ \vdots \\ f_i(0) \\ \vdots \\ f_i(-N) \end{pmatrix}$$

The vector $f_M$ is known through the given terminal value function $F(y)$:

$$f_M = \begin{pmatrix} F(L) \\ \vdots \\ F(0) \\ \vdots \\ F(-L) \end{pmatrix}$$

The objective now is to create a procedure that would work systematically *backward* from $f_M$, producing the vectors $f_{M-1}$, $f_{M-2}, \ldots, f_0$. The entry $f_0(0)$ would be the time-0 price of the instrument, setting the factor $y$ equal to 0 initially, by matching $\alpha_0(0)$ to the prevailing rate at time 0.

To generate the scheme, we need first to discretize the partial derivative operators. There is no unique choice, but one natural scheme is:

$$\left.\frac{\partial f}{\partial t}\right|_{(t_i,y_j)} \simeq \frac{1}{k}[f(i+1,j) - f(i,j)]$$

and symmetric choices for the spatial partials:

$$\left.\frac{\partial f}{\partial y}\right|_{(t_i,y_j)} \simeq \frac{1}{2h}[f_i(j+1) - f_i(j-1)],$$

and

$$\left.\frac{\partial^2 f}{\partial y^2}\right|_{(t_i,y_j)} \simeq \frac{1}{h^2}[f_i(j+1) - 2f_i(j) + f_i(j-1)]$$

With these discretizations, the partial differential equation can be (and this is one of several choices) discretized to

$$\begin{aligned}\frac{1}{k}[f_{i+1}(j) - f_i(j)] &= -\frac{\sigma^2}{2}\frac{1}{h^2}[f_{i+1}(j+1) - 2f_{i+1}(j) + f_{i+1}(j-1)] \\ &\quad + ay_j\frac{1}{2h}[f_{i+1}(j+1) - f_{i+1}(j-1)] \\ &\quad + (\alpha_0(t_i) + y_j)f_{i+1}(j)\end{aligned}$$

We can solve for $f_i(j)$, expressing it as a linear combination of the values of $f_{i+1}$ at $j-1$, $j$, and $j+1$:

$$\boxed{\begin{aligned}f_i(j) = p_i^{j\to j+1} & f_{i+1}(j+1) \\ &+ \left[p_i^{j\to j} - k(\alpha_0(t_i) + y_j)\right] f_{i+1}(j) \\ &+ p_i^{j\to j-1} f_{i+1}(j-1)\end{aligned}} \tag{26.6}$$

where

$$p_i^{j\to j+1} = \sigma^2 \frac{k}{2h^2}(1 - ay_j h), \quad p_i^{j\to j-1} = \sigma^2 \frac{k}{2h^2}(1 + ay_j h), \tag{26.7}$$

and

$$p_i^{j\to j} = 1 - \frac{\sigma^2 k}{h^2} \tag{26.8}$$

The equation (26.6) can be expressed in matrix notation:

$$f_i = T_i f_{i+1}$$

where

$$T_i = P_i - k\begin{pmatrix} \alpha_0(t_i) + y_N & 0 & \cdots & 0 & 0 \\ 0 & \alpha_0(t_i) + y_{N-1} & 0 & \cdots & 0 \\ \vdots & \vdots & \vdots & \vdots & \vdots \\ 0 & \cdots & \cdots & 0 & \alpha_0(t_i) + y_{-N} \end{pmatrix}$$

which, as is $P_i$, is a matrix whose entries, except those along and adjacent to the diagonal, are zeros.

The process for numerically solving the partial differential equation is now clear: start with the given "terminal vector" $f_M$ and keep applying the matrices $T_i$:

$$f_0 = T_0 T_1 \ldots T_{M-1} f_M$$

The central entry of the column vector $f_0$ gives the required value

$$f(0,0)$$

which would be the appropriate price of the instrument at time 0.

The procedure we have carried out is just one of many possible discretization schemes, and it is not necessarily the most efficient.

## THE DIFFERENCE SCHEME: A PROBABILISTIC INTERPRETATION

Let us look back at (26.6) and understand it from a different point of view. Observe that

$$p_i^{j \to j+1} + p_i^{j \to j} + p_i^{j \to j-1} = 1$$

With $k, h$ chosen appropriately, we make these transition terms all $\geq 0$.

We can reformulate the difference scheme as:

$$\boxed{\begin{aligned} f_i(j) = e^{-(\alpha_0(t_i)+y_j)k}\big[&p_i^{j\to j+1} f_{i+1}(j+1) \\ &+p_i^{j\to j} f_{i+1}(j) \\ &+p_i^{j\to j-1} f_{i+1}(j-1)\big] \end{aligned}} \tag{26.9}$$

where we see a glimpse of the "discounting" factor.

To be sure, the difference scheme (26.9) here is not exactly the same as the one given earlier (26.6) But the two schemes are identical up to first order in $k$ and $h$, and that is all that matters for our purposes. Let us for the moment proceed with the discussion, postponing till a bit later in this section the task of checking that the scheme (26.9) is equivalent, in first order, to the scheme given earlier in (26.6).

In view of the noted facts about the terms $p_i^{j\to k}$, we can view the terms

$$p_i^{j\to j'}$$

as transition *probabilities*, governing a process

$$t \mapsto y_{h,k}(t)$$

of values of $y$, which runs through the discrete values $y_j$, and $t$ runs over $t_0, t_1, \ldots, t_M$. Thus, *the difference scheme constructed in the preceding section has a probabilistic interpretation.*

With this interpretation, we see that $(t_i, y_{h,k}(t_i))$ is the *expected value* as follows:

$$f(t_i, y) = E\left[e^{-(\alpha_0(t_i)+y)\delta t} f\left(t_{i+1}, y_{h,k}(t_{i+1})\right)\Big| y_{h,k}(t_i) = y\right], \quad (26.10)$$

where

$$\delta t = k$$

Having worked back one time step, from $t_{i+1}$ to $t_i$, let us see what happens when we put all the little steps together to generate the initial value $f(t_0, y_0)$ in terms of terminal values $f(t_M, y) = F(y)$:

$$f(t_0, y_0) = E\left[e^{-\sum_{i=0}^{M-1}(\alpha_0(t_i)+y)\delta t} F(y_{h,k}(T))\Big| y_{h,k}(0) = y_0\right] \quad (26.11)$$

where now the expectation is over *all the random paths* $y_{h,k}$ initiating at $y_0$. We have written $f$ now to denote the discrete approximation to the solution of the original partial differential equation (26.3).

The rule governing the evolution of the stochastic process $y_{h,k}$ has been described above:

$$P\left[y_{h,k}(t_{i+1}) = y_l | y_{h,k}(t_i) = y_j\right] = p_i^{j\to l}$$

Now let us check that the scheme (26.9) is equivalent, in first order, to the scheme given earlier in (26.6).

Keeping only terms of first order, we have

$$e^{-(\alpha_0(t_i)+y_j)k} \simeq 1-(\alpha_0(t_i)+y_j)k$$

and

$$p_i^{j\to j+1} f_{i+1}(j+1)+p_i^{j\to j} f_{i+1}(j) \\ +p_i^{j\to j-1} f_{i+1}(j-1) \simeq 1\cdot f_{i+1}(j)-2\sigma^2 a y_j k \left.\frac{\partial f}{\partial y}\right|_{(t_{i+1},y_j)}$$

where we used

$$p_i^{j\to j+1}+p_i^{j\to j}+p_i^{j\to j-1}=1$$

and

$$f_{i+1}(j\pm 1) \simeq f_{i+1}(j) \pm h\left.\frac{\partial f}{\partial y}\right|_{(t_{i+1},y_j)},$$

along with the value of $p_i^{j\to j+1}-p_i^{j\to j-1}$ deduced from (26.7).

Putting together the preceding expressions, it becomes clear that

$$e^{-(\alpha_0(t_i)+y_j)k}\left[p_i^{j\to j+1} f_{i+1}(j+1)+p_i^{j\to j} f_{i+1}(j) \right. \\ \left. +p_i^{j\to j-1} f_{i+1}(j-1)\right] \\ \simeq p_i^{j\to j+1} f_{i+1}(j+1)+\left[p_i^{j\to j}-k(\alpha_0(t_i)+y_j)\right] f_{i+1}(j) \\ +p_i^{j\to j-1} f_{i+1}(j-1)$$

again, by keeping only terms up to first order in $k$ and $h$. This is just what we needed to check.

## FROM THE DIFFERENCE SCHEME TO THE SDE

Let us we examine this stochastic process for $y$ in more detail. Observe that the expected value of the change

$$\delta y = y_{h,k}(t_{i+1}) - y_{h,k}(t_i)$$

is

$$E[\delta y] = p_i^{j\to j+1}h + p_i^{j\to j}\cdot 0 + p_i^{j\to j-1}(-h) = -ay_jk = -ay\delta t$$

and

$$E[(\delta y)^2] = p_i^{j\to j+1}h^2 + p_i^{j\to j}\cdot 0^2 + p_i^{j\to j-1}(-h)^2 = \sigma^2 k = \sigma^2\delta t$$

Comparing with our original stochastic differential equation (26.2)

$$dy(t) = -ay(t)dt + \sigma dB(t)$$

we see (since $dB(t)^2 = dt$) a complete consistency!

Indeed, we can simulate the process $y_{h,k}$ by generating a sequence of independent random numbers $\delta B_i$, with mean 0 and variance $\delta t$:

$$E(\delta B_i) = 0, \qquad E[(\delta B_i)^2] = \delta t$$

and generate the random path $y_{h,k}$ by using the generating scheme

$$y_{h,k}(t_{i+1}) = y_{h,k}(t_i) - ay_{h,k}(t_i)\delta t + \sigma\delta B_i$$

The manner of choosing $\delta B_i$ ensures that $y_{h,k}$ is a process with the right mean and variance. We can make an exact match by choosing the $\delta B_i$ having three discrete values, corresponding to up/straight/down for $y_{h,k}$.

Thus, *the numerical scheme for solving the PDE, interpreted in the probabilistic way, provides a discrete stochastic process that is a discretization of the process whose SDE is associated to the PDE.*

Moreover, as seen in (26.11), *the value of the approximation to the solution of the PDE is obtained as an integral (expected value) over the set of all random paths* $y_{h,k}$ *from the given initial point to the terminal time instant T.*

*Taking the continuum limit* of this discrete formulation in an appropriate way, should then lead to the expression of the solution of the original partial differential equation in terms of an integral over Brownian paths, i.e., it would *give the Feynman-Kac formula.*

We have used the discretization of the partial differential equation to sketch a numerical procedure. One can use the stochastic differential equation as the starting point for discretization and then generate approximations to prices. The discrete stochastic process generated in this approach often has the form of a "tree", with up/straight/middle branches from each node. This leads to the method of *interest rate trees*.

CHAPTER 27

# The Hahn-Banach Theorem

In Chapter 6 we saw how the existence of a pricing measure satisfying the requirements of no-arbitrage could be shown through a max-min argument. As mentioned in that context, this core max-min argument is enshrined formally in a central result in functional analysis called the Hahn-Banach theorem. In this chapter we examine several formulations of the theorem and its proof.

In this chapter $V$ is a real vector space.

## THE GEOMETRIC SETTING

In this section we set up general terminology concerning some geometric concepts: hyperplanes and convex sets.

The *translate* of a set $A \subset V$ by a vector $x \in V$ is the set

$$x + A = \{x + a : a \in A\}$$

If $A$ and $B$ are subsets of $V$, and $t$ any real number, we use the notation

$$tA = \{ta : a \in A\} \qquad \text{and} \qquad A + B = \{a + b : a \in A, b \in B\}$$

If $x, y \in V$, then the *segment* $xy$ is the set of all points on the line running from $x$ to $y$:

$$xy = \{tx + (1-t)y : 0 \leq t \leq 1\}$$

A subset $C$ of $V$ is *convex* if for any two points $P, Q \in C$, the segment $PQ$ is contained in $C$. Equivalently, $C$ is convex if

$$\lambda C + (1-\lambda)C \subset C$$

for every $\lambda \in [0, 1]$.

It is clear that the translate of any convex set is convex, and indeed if $C$ is a convex set, then so is $a + tC$ for any $a \in V$ and $t \in \mathbf{R}$.

A subspace $W$ of $V$ has *codimension* 1 if there is a vector $x \in V \setminus W$ such that $W + \mathbf{R}x = V$. This is equivalent to saying that the quotient space $V/W$ has dimension 1.

A *hyperplane* is a set of the form $W + x$ where $W$ is any codimension one subspace and $x$ is any vector.

Let $W$ be a codimension 1 subspace of $V$, and $v$ any vector outside $W$. Then $V$ can be expressed as the union of $W$ with two open half-spaces:

$$V = W \cup (W + \{tv : t > 0\}) \cup (W - \{tv : t > 0\})$$

If $x$ is any vector in $V$, then the hyperplane $W + x$ specifies two *closed half-spaces*:

$$W + x + \{tv : t \geq 0\} \text{ and } W + x - \{tv : t \geq 0\}$$

whose intersection is the hyperplane $W + x$ and whose union is all of $V$. We refer to these closed half-spaces as the two *sides* of the hyperplane.

It will be convenient to use the infinities $\infty$ and $-\infty$. We require that $-\infty < \infty$, and $-\infty < x < \infty$ for all real numbers $x$. The following arithmetic operations with $\infty$ will be defined:

$$t + \infty = \infty + t = \infty, \qquad k\infty = \infty k = \infty, \qquad 0\infty = \infty 0 = 0$$

for all $k > 0$ and all $t \in \mathbf{R} \cup \{\infty\}$.

## THE ALGEBRAIC FORMULATION

Our first objective now is to construct and study properties of a function $p_C$, called the Minkowski functional, which encodes much of the essential information about a convex set $C$.

Let $C$ be a nonempty convex subset of $V$. Because $C$ is nonempty, we can translate $C$ appropriately to ensure that $0 \in C$. For this section, we assume that the origin 0 belongs to the convex set $C$, i.e. $0 \in C$.

The "size" of a vector $v \in V$ relative to $C$ is the "smallest" nonnegative number $t \geq 0$ such that $v$ lies in the $tC$; more precisely, define

$$\boxed{p_C(v) = \inf\{t \geq 0 : v \in tC\}} \tag{27.1}$$

where the infimum of the empty set is taken to be $\infty$. The function

$$p_C : V \to [0, \infty]$$

is the *Minkowski functional* for the set $C$.

Note that

$$p_C(0) = 0$$

However, it might be the case that $p_C(v)$ is 0 for some nonzero $v$. Suppose, for instance, that $v$ is a nonzero vector and that the entire ray

$$\{tv : t \geq 0\}$$

lies in the set $C$. In this case, clearly, $p_C(v)$ is 0. Thus, if the convex set extends to "infinity" in any one direction, then it isn't a good measure of size of vectors in that direction.

At the other extreme, suppose that the only nonnegative multiple of a vector $v$ that lies in $C$ is 0. In this case, the set

$$\{t \geq 0 : v \in tC\}$$

is empty, and so its infimum, by definition, is $\infty$. Thus, for such directions $p_C$ is also not a good measure of size, having the value $\infty$.

**Proposition 27.2.1** *Let $C$ be a convex set containing* 0. *Then*

**(i)** *For any $v \in V$, the set $\{t \geq 0 : v \in tC\}$ is an interval, either equal to $[p_C(v), \infty)$ or $(p_C(v), \infty)$*

**(ii)** $p_C(tv) = tp_C(v)$ *for every $v \in V$ and $t \geq 0$*

**(iii)** *If $x, y \in V$ then*

$$p_C(x+y) \leq p_C(x) + p_C(y)$$

*This is the "triangle inequality."*

***Proof.*** (i) Suppose $s$ is a real number $> p_C(v)$. We want to show that $v$ lies in $sC$. The definition of $p_C(v)$ implies that there is some $t \in [0, s)$ such that $v \in tC$ and so $v = tx$ for some $x \in C$. Hence

$$v = s\left[\frac{t}{s}x + \left(1 - \frac{t}{s}\right)0\right] \in sC$$

by convexity of $C$.

(ii) For any real $s > 0$ we have

$$\{t \geq 0 : sv \in tC\} = \{sr : r \geq 0, \text{and } v \in rC\} = s\{r \geq 0 : v \in rC\}$$

which implies

$$p_C(sv) = sp_C(v).$$

If $s = 0$, then this equality is clear, using the convention $0\infty = 0$ for the case where $p_C(v)$ is $\infty$.

(iii) If either $p_C(x)$ or $p_C(y)$ is $\infty$ then $p_C(x+y)$ is automatically $\leq p_C(x) + p_C(y)$. So suppose $p_C(x) < \infty$ and $p_C(y) < \infty$. Let $t, s$ be real numbers with $t > p_C(x)$ and $s > p_C(y)$. Then $x \in tC$ and $y \in sC$ and so

$$x + y \in tC + sC = (t+s)\left(\frac{t}{t+s}C + \frac{s}{t+s}C\right) \subset (t+s)C,$$

the last subset relation following from convexity of $C$. So $p_C(x+y) \leq t + s$. Taking inf over $t$ and then over $s$ gives $p_C(x+y) \leq p_C(x) + p_C(y)$. QED

The definition of the Minkowski functional $p_C$ implies that $p_C(x) \leq 1$ for every $x \in C$, i.e.

$$C \subset \{v \in V : p_C(v) \leq 1\}$$

but $C$ may not actually be equal to the "closed ball" $\{v \in V : p_C(v) \leq 1\}$.

The following result shows how to construct a convex set from a function $p$, satisfying the essential properties of a Minkowski functional:

**Proposition 27.2.2** *Suppose $p : V \to [0, \infty]$ is a map satisfying the following conditions:*

**(a)** $p(0) = 0$

**(b)** $p(tx) = tp(x)$ *for all $x \in V$ and real $t \geq 0$*

**(c)** $p(x + y) \leq p(x) + p(y)$ *for every $x, y \in V$*

*Let*

$$C = \{v \in V : p(v) \leq 1\}$$

*Then $C$ is a convex set containing 0 and the Minkowski functional of $C$ is $p$:*

$$p_C = p$$

***Proof.*** Using (a), (b), (c), it is readily checked that $C$ is a convex set and contains 0.

Now for any real $t > 0$ we have:

$$x \in tC \qquad \text{if and only if} \qquad p(x) \leq t$$

So

$$\{t \in \mathbf{R} : t > 0, x \in tC\} = \{t : p(x) \leq t\} = [p(x), \infty)$$

Taking the infimum gives

$$p_C(x) = p(x) \quad \boxed{\text{QED}}$$

Next we formulate an algebraic equivalent of a hyperplane.

Let $W$ be a codimension 1 subspace of $V$. Then there is a vector $n \notin W$ such that

$$V = W + \mathbf{R}n$$

This sum is a direct sum, for if $x \in W \cap \mathbf{R}n$, then $x = tn \in W$ for some real number $t$, and so $t$ must be zero, for otherwise $n = t^{-1}x$ would be in $W$.

Thus, the map

$$W \oplus \mathbf{R}n \to V : (w, tn) \mapsto w + tn$$

is a linear isomorphism.

Consequently, the function

$$L : V \to \mathbf{R} : w + tn \mapsto t$$

is linear and its kernel is exactly the subspace $W$.

Conversely, if $f : V \to \mathbf{R}$ is a nonzero linear map, then the kernel $\ker f$ is a codimension 1 subspace of $V$, for

$$\ker f + \mathbf{R}n = V,$$

where $n$ is any vector for which $f(n) = 1$. If $f$ and $g$ are two nonzero linear maps $V \to \mathbf{R}$, then $\ker f = \ker g$ if and only if $f$ is a nonzero multiple of $g$.

A hyperplane in $V$ is specified by the level set of a linear functional, i.e., if $H$ is a hyperplane then there is a nonzero linear functional $L : V \to \mathbf{R}$ and a real number $t \in \mathbf{R}$ such that $L^{-1}(t) = H$.

Thus we have found algebraic equivalents for the geometric notions of convex sets and hyperplanes:

| | | |
|---|---|---|
| Convex set $C$ | $\longleftrightarrow$ | Minkowski functional $p_C$ |
| Hyperplane | $\longleftrightarrow$ | Level set $L^{-1}(t)$ of a linear functional $L$ |

## THE HAHN-BANACH THEOREM

We can now finally state and prove a form of the Hahn-Banach theorem.

Here is a very rough sketch of how the theorem can be brought to bear on a financial context (see also Chapter 6). The vector space $V$ consists of a space of functions on the set $\Omega$ of all market scenarios, each function $\phi$ representing the worths $\phi(x)$ of an instrument in various market scenarios $x \in \Omega$. In this context, $p$ is the maximum value of a function, i.e., $p(\phi)$ is the supremum of $|\phi(x)|$, with $x$ running over all market scenarios. The subspace $W$ corresponds to a class of instruments, say all those that are obtainable from combinations of market-traded instruments. The no-arbitrage condition, that the *a priori* price cannot exceed the maximum worth in all scenarios, is encoded in the condition

$$g(\phi) \leq p(\phi) \quad \text{for all } \phi \in W$$

The theorem below would then extend the pricing functional $g$ to the entire space $V$, i.e., "all possible" instruments. With the right framework for $V$, this would then lead to a probability measure, the pricing measure $Q$, such that the price of an asset is the expected value of the worth of the asset in all scenarios:

$$f(\phi) = \int \phi \, dQ$$

**Theorem 27.3.1** *Let $V$ be a real vector space. Suppose $p : V \to [0, \infty]$ is a mapping satisfying the following conditions:*

**(a)** $p(0) = 0$

**(b)** $p(tx) = tp(x)$ *for all* $x \in V$ *and real* $t \geq 0$

**(c)** $p(x + y) \leq p(x) + p(y)$ *for every* $x, y \in V$

*Assume, furthermore, that for each $x \in V$, either both $p(x)$ and $p(-x)$ are $\infty$ or that both are finite.*

*Let $a \in V$ and $\alpha$ a real number with $0 \le \alpha \le p(a)$. Then there is a linear functional*

$$f : V \to \mathbf{R}$$

*such that $f(a) = \alpha$ and*

$$f(x) \le p(x)$$

*for all $x \in V$.*

*More generally, if $W$ is a subspace of $V$ and $g : W \to \mathbf{R}$ a linear mapping satisfying $g(x) \le p(x)$ for all $x \in W$, then there is a linear mapping $f : V \to \mathbf{R}$ such that $f \le p$ and $f|W = g$.*

***Proof.*** Let us first show that the second statement is indeed more general than the first, i.e., that the first statement follows from the second. To this end, consider the subspace $W_1 = \mathbf{R}a$, and on $W$ define $g : W \to \mathbf{R} : ta \mapsto t\alpha$. This is a linear map and satisfies

$$g(ta) = t\alpha \le \begin{cases} tp(a) = p(ta) & \text{for } t \ge 0, \\ 0 \le p(ta) & \text{for } t < 0. \end{cases}$$

Thus, $g \le p$ on $W_1$. So the second statement produces a linear functional $f$ on $V$, which satisfies $f \le p$ and agrees with $g$ on $W_1$. In particular, $f(a) = g(a) = \alpha$. This demonstrates the first statement.

Now we proceed to the general statement. Assume then that $W$ is a subspace of $V$, and $g$ a linear functional on $W$ bounded above by $p$.

If $W$ were equal to $V$, then there would be nothing to prove. So suppose there is a vector $v \in V$ that is not in $W$. The major step is to show how to extend $g$ to a subspace $W + \mathbf{R}v$, where $v$ is any vector outside $W$, preserving the condition of being bounded above by $p$.

Note that each element of $W + \mathbf{R}v$ can be expressed uniquely in the form $w + tv$ with $w \in W$ and $t \in \mathbf{R}$.

If $p$ is finite-valued, then the proof proceeds smoothly, but taking into account points where $p$ is $\infty$ makes the argument complicated.

The linear map $h: W + \mathbf{R}v \to \mathbf{R} : w + tv \mapsto g(w)$ restricts to $g$ on $W$. If it so happens that $p(x) = \infty$ for all $x \in W + \mathbf{R}v$ outside $W$, then $h \leq p$ holds automatically on $W + \mathbf{R}v$. So we may and shall assume that the particular vector $v$ outside $W$ is chosen such that $p(v) < \infty$.

Define $h: W + \mathbf{R}v \to \mathbf{R}$ by

$$h(w + tv) = g(w) + th(v)$$

for all $w \in W$ and $t \in \mathbf{R}$, where $h(v)$ is a real number chosen to satisfy

$$h(w - sv) = g(w) - sh(v) \leq p(w - sv) \quad \text{for all } w \in W \text{ and real } s \geq 0 \tag{27.2}$$

and

$$h(w + tv) = g(w) + th(v) \leq p(w + tv) \quad \text{for all } w \in W \text{ and real } t \geq 0 \tag{27.3}$$

That such a choice of $h(v)$ is possible will be shown below. Note that $h(w) = g(w)$ for all $w \in W$. The preceding inequalities together imply

$$h(x) \leq p(x) \qquad \text{holds for all } x \in W + \mathbf{R}v.$$

Thus $h$ gives the desired extension of $g$.

To complete the preceding argument, we need to show that a real number $h(v)$ can be chosen which is $\geq \frac{g(w) - p(w - sv)}{s}$ and $\leq \frac{p(w + tv) - g(w)}{t}$ for every $w \in W$, and all real numbers $s, t > 0$. This means that we have to prove the max-min condition:

$$\sup_{s>0, w\in W} \frac{g(w) - p(w - sv)}{s} \leq \inf_{t>0, w\in W} \frac{p(w + tv) - g(w)}{t} \tag{27.4}$$

and check that this inequality isn't reading $\infty \leq \infty$ or $-\infty \leq -\infty$.

The inequality (27.4) is equivalent to

$$\frac{g(w) - p(w - sv)}{s} \leq \frac{p(w' + tv) - g(w')}{t} \tag{27.5}$$

holding for all $w, w' \in W$ and all $s, t > 0$. If either $p(w - sv)$ or $p(w' + tv)$ is $\infty$, then (27.5) holds automatically. So suppose both $p(w - sv)$ and $p(w' + tv)$ are finite. Then, after rearranging terms, (27.5) is *equivalent* to

$$g(tw + sw') \leq p(sw' + stv) + p(tw - tsv)$$

and this is indeed true because

$$g(tw + sw') \leq p(tw + sw') \leq p(sw' + stv) + p(tw - tsv)$$

The infinities don't occur: for (i) the right side of (27.4) is seen, upon taking $w = 0$, to be bounded above by $p(v)$, which has been assumed to be finite; and (ii) the left side of (27.4) is bounded below by $-p(-v)$.

So we may choose a real number $h(v)$ satisfying:

$$\sup_{s>0, w\in W} \frac{g(w) - p(w - sv)}{s} \leq h(v) \leq \inf_{t>0, w\in W} \frac{p(w + tv) - g(w)}{t} \tag{27.6}$$

This proves the existence of a linear function

$$h : W + \mathbf{R}v \to \mathbf{R}$$

which restricts to $g$ on $W$ and which satisfies $h \leq p$ on $W + \mathbf{R}v$.

There is now a routine procedure, the method of *Zorn's lemma*, that finishes off the task of producing a functional $f$ on the entire space $V$.

Let $X$ be the set of all pairs

$$(S, h)$$

where $S$ is a subspace of $V$ with $W \subset S$ and $h : S \to \mathbf{R}$ is a linear mapping satisfying $h|W = g$ and $h \leq p|S$. Define the relation $<$ on $X$ by

$$(S_1, h_1) < (S_2, h_2)$$

to mean $S_1 \subset S_2$ and $h_2|S_1$.

This is a partial ordering with the property that any totally ordered subset has a maximal element.

Zorn's lemma says then that $X$ has a maximal element $(S_*, h_*)$. If $S_*$ were a proper subspace of $V$, i.e., $S_* \neq V$, then the argument given before produces an extension of $h$ to a larger subspace $S_* + \mathbf{R}v$, contradicting the maximality of $(S_*, h_*)$. QED

It is possible to extend the theorem to the case of complex vector spaces, but that is not relevant to our context and so we omit this.

## A GEOMETRIC INTERPRETATION

In earlier sections, we saw that the notions of linear functional and convex functional had geometric meanings in terms of hyperplanes and convex sets. Using this, it is possible to view the Hahn-Banach theorem in a geometric way.

Let us consider, for simplicity, a convex set $C \subset V$ containing the origin 0 in its interior, in the sense that every line through 0 contains points of $C$ on both of the rays emanating away from 0. This implies that the Minkowski functional $p_C$ is finite-valued.

Now consider a point $a \in V$ that is in the exterior of $C$, in the sense that the ray from 0 through $a$ contains no points of $C$ in a neighborhood of $a$. This implies that

$$p_C(a) > 1 \tag{27.7}$$

Then, by the Hahn-Banach theorem, there is a linear functional

$$L : V \to \mathbf{R}$$

such that

$$L(x) \leq p_C(x) \qquad \text{for all } x \in V$$

and

$$L(a) = p_C(a)$$

Consider then a hyperplane given as the level set

$$H = L^{-1}(t)$$

where $t$ is any real number satisfying

$$1 < t < p_C(a)$$

If $x$ is a point in $C$, then

$$L(x) \leq p_C(x) \leq 1 < t$$

Thus, the convex set $C$ lies on one side of the hyperplane $H$:

$$C \subset \{v \in V : L(v) < t\}$$

On the other hand, for the point $a$ we have

$$p_C(a) > t$$

and so $a$ lies on the opposite side of $H$:

$$a \in \{v \in V : L(v) > t\}$$

Thus,

- *For the convex set $C$ and the point $a$ in the exterior of $C$, there is a hyperplane that passes between $a$ and $C$, in the sense that $a$ and $C$ are on opposite sides of the hyperplane.*

We can obtain other, similar geometric conclusions. For instance, going back to the condition (27.7) that $a$ lies exterior to $C$, we could instead look at a point $b$ "on the boundary" of $C$, i.e. for which

$$p_C(b) = 1$$

Then, the Hahn-Banach theorem produces a linear functional

$$L : V \to \mathbf{R}$$

for which

$$L(x) \le p_C(x) \qquad \text{for all } x \in V$$

and

$$L(b) = 1$$

Thus, now every point $x$ of $C$ satisfies

$$L(x) \le p_C(x) \le 1$$

and so the hyperplane

$$S = L^{-1}(1)$$

is such that the convex set $C$ lies on one side of $S$, and $S$ contains the point $b$:

$$C \subset \{v \in V : L(v) \le 1\} \qquad \text{and} \qquad b \in S$$

This hyperplane $S$ is a *supporting hyperplane* to the convex set $C$ at the boundary point $b$.

# ENDNOTES

## CHAPTER 1

Prices of instruments of the type $I_B$ are called *Arrow-Debreu prices*. Though such instruments are rarely available in real markets, they are of great theoretical value.

## CHAPTER 3

A caveat is necessary at this stage. Though it does appear to be perfectly reasonable and rational that the price of an instrument should be its expected value, it is known that human behavior is not always governed by this principle. In the celebrated *St. Petersburg paradox*, which goes back to Gabriel Cramer and Nicholas Bernoulli in the early 1700s, a game of chance has an infinite possible payoff. But in reality no one would, or could, bet an infinite amount on such a game. Pursuing this paradox, Daniel Bernoulli developed *utility theory*, based upon the idea that agents seek to maximize expected utility, as opposed to simply expected profit. In the twentieth century, utility theory saw extensive further growth after a new set of ideas were brought in by von Neumann and Morgenstern [40].

## CHAPTER 5

Geman, El Karoui, and Rochet's paper [16] has had considerable influence on the use of change-of-numeraire in understanding prices. The notion of change of numeraire goes back to longstanding actuarial practice of transferring cash flows from one point in time to another.

## CHAPTER 6

In the financial mathematics literature, the term *arbitrage* is given a number of technical definitions. In the first paragraphs of Chapter 6, we are using the term in its broadest sense.

We use the Arrow-Debreu instruments $\delta_\omega$ in our discussion of the no-arbitrage condition and pricing measures. The definition of market *completeness* given in Chapter 6 is also in a very broad sense. The technical literature in financial mathematics contains more particularly formalized definitions.

The concepts of utility function, preference, economic equilibrium, and pricing measure form a fundamental and interconnected set of ideas. The reader familiar with thermodynamics/statistical-mechanics (or see Lieb and Yngvason [30]) may observe analogies with the concepts of entropy, adiabatic accessibility of states, thermodynamic equilibrium, and thermodynamic state measures.

For a development of the economic theory relevant to the financial concepts of this Chapter, see Duffie [14] or Huang and Litzenberger [21].

## CHAPTER 7

That the discounted price process is a martingale is the cornerstone of standard approaches in mathematical finance. Indeed, the market equilibrium measure is generally called an *equivalent martingale measure*. The qualifier "equivalent" indicates that the measure is equivalent to the "real life" probability measure, in the sense that any event that has zero probability according to one measure should also have zero probability measure according to the other. Proving existence of an equivalent measure, under various theoretical and technical hypotheses, is a small industry in the mathematical finance literature (see, for instance, the works of F. Delbaen and W. Sachermeyer such as [13] for such a theory relating the existence of the martingale measure to certain formalizations of the no-arbitrage principle. Some of the original ideas and and terminology was developed by Harrison and Kreps [17] and Harrison and Pliska [18]).

Samuelson's paper [38] explains randomness of prices within economic theory. For a study of "real life" probability in the market in the context of complex systems theory, see Sornette's book [39].

## CHAPTER 11

See also the exposition of option price inequalities in Arditti's book [2].

## CHAPTER 13

As with many other topics concerning derivatives, the reader will find it useful to consult the Web site of the International Swaps and Derivatives Association (ISDA), which sets the specifications of many derivative instruments.

The floating rate used in swaps is often the *Libor rate* ("Libor" stands for London Interbank Offered Rate).

## CHAPTER 16

We have given only the bare basic ideas of hedging. This is a popular topic in mathematical finance texts. See, for instance, Björk's book [6].

## CHAPTER 18

Without the hypothesis that the distribution of $Y_t - Y_s$ is the same as that of $Y_v - Y_u$ after rescaling, one is led to an infinitely divisible law. Asset models with jumps are also a popular field of inquiry (see, for example, Chapter 7 of Lamberton and Lapeyre's book [29]).

For an exposition of the case of assets paying dividends see, for instance, [6].

For an analysis of several interacting assets (as opposed to a single isolated one), see Albeverio and Steblovskaya's paper [1].

## CHAPTER 19

Our use of the term "Green's function" is closer to that of quantum physics than probability theory (where the term has a related, but different, meaning).

There is an important model for interest rate dynamics that we do not study here. This is the Heath-Jarrow-Morton model [19] based on dynamics of forward rates.

## CHAPTER 20

For a detailed study of volatility and correlation matters, see Rebonato's work [35].

## CHAPTER 21

The stochastic process that underlies the chi-squared model was studied by Feller in [15]. We have followed Feller's method of using the Laplace transform to determine transition densities.

## CHAPTER 22

For two–factor CIR model prices, see Chen and Scott [9].

## CHAPTER 24

For a deep study of causality and conditional probability, see [33].

## CHAPTER 25

Some of the significant basic mathematical properties of Brownian motion were discovered, in a financial context, by Bachelier [4].

Though the generic Brownian path is never differentiable, a mathematically rigorous meaning can be given to the "derivative" of the Brownian path, in a generalized sense, within the calculus of infinite-dimensional distribution theory known as white noise analysis. See the book by Hida et al. [20] or by Kuo [27].

For a deep investigation of Brownian motion and diffusion processes, see Itô and McKean [26]. For a vast array of facts about such processes, see Borodin and Salminen's book [8].

For more details on the Markov property of solutions of stochastic differential equations, see, for instance, Øksendal's book [32, Chapter 7]. For Itô calculus and more on stochastic differential equations, see Kuo's book [28].

## CHAPTER 26

For more on numerical methods, see, for instance, [29, Section 5.2]. For an introduction to the interest-rate tree method see [22, Section 19.8].

## CHAPTER 27

For more on the Hahn-Banach theorem, see, for example, Rudin [36].

# BIBLIOGRAPHY

1. Albeverio, S., and V. Steblovskaya. 2002. "A model of financial market with several interacting assets. Complete market case." *Finance and Stochastics* **6** Number 3 (July): 383–396.
2. Arditti, F.D. 1996. *Derivatives: A Comprehensive Resource for Options, Futures, Interest Rate Swaps, and Mortgage Securities.* Harvard Business School Press.
3. Arrow, K. 1964. "The role of securities in the optimal allocation of risk bearing." *Review of Economic Studies* 31: 91–96.
4. Bachelier, L. 1900. "Théorie de la spéculation." *Ann. Sci. École Norm. Sup.* **17**: 21–86.
5. Billingsley, P. 1995 (Third Edition) *Probability and Measure.* John Wiley & Sons.
6. Björk, T. 1998. *Arbitrage Theory in Continuous Time.* Oxford University Press.
7. Black, F., and M. Scholes. 1973. "The Pricing of Options and Corporate Liabilities." *Journal of Political Economy* **81** (May/June): 637–659.
8. Borodin, A.N., and P. Salminen. 1996. *Handbook of Brownian Motion: Facts and Formulae.* Birkhäuser.
9. Chen, R.-R., and L. Scott. 1992. "Pricing Interest Rate Options in a Two-Factor Cox-Ingersoll-Ross Model of the Term Structure." *The Review of Financial Studies* **5**: 613–636.
10. Cox, J.C., J.E. Ingersoll and S.A. Ross. 1985. "An Intertemporal General Equilibrium Model of Asset Prices." *Econom.* **53**: 363–384.
11. Cox, J.C., J.E. Ingersoll and S.A. Ross. 1985. "A Theory of the Term Structure of Interest Rates." *Econom.* **53**: 385–407.
12. Debreu, G. 1976 (Seventh printing) *Theory of Value: An Axiomatic Analysis of Economic Equilibrium.* Yale University Press.
13. Delbaen, F., and W. Schachermayer. 1994. "A general version of the fundamental theorem of asset pricing." *Math. Ann.* **300**, 463–520.
14. Duffie, D. 1996. *Dynamic Asset Pricing Theory.* (2nd Edition) Princeton University Press.

15. Feller, W. 1951. "Two singular diffusion problems." *Ann. Math.* **54**: 173–182.
16. Geman, H., N. El Karoui, and J.C. Rochet. 1995. "Changes of Numéraire, Changes of Probability Measure, and Option Pricing." *Journal of Applied Probability* **32**: 443–458.
17. Harrison, M., and D. Kreps. 1979. "Martingales and Arbitrage in Multiperiod Securities Markets." *Journal of Economic Theory* **20**: 381–408.
18. Harrison, M., and S. Pliska. 1981. "Martingales and Stochastic Integrals in the Theory of Continuous Trading." *Stochastic Processes and Their Applications* **11**: 215–260.
19. Heath, D., A. Jarrow, and A. Morton. 1992a. "Bond Pricing and the Term Structure of Interest Rates: A New Methodology for Contingent Claims Valuation." *Econometrica* **60**: 77–106.
20. Hida, T., H.-H. Kuo, J. Potthoff, and L. Streit. 1993. *White Noise : An Infinite Dimensional Calculus*, Kluwer Academic Publishers.
21. Huang, C.-F., and R. Litzenberger. 1988. *Foundations for Financial Economics*. Amsterdam: North-Holland.
22. Hull, J.C. 1997. *Options, Futures, and Other Derivatives*, 3rd edition, Prentice Hall International Inc.
23. Hull, J.C., and A. White. 1990. "Pricing Interest–Rate–Derivative Securities." *Review of Financial Studies* 3: 573–592.
24. Itô, K. 1946. "Stochastic Integral." *Proc. Imp. Acad. Tokyo* **20**, 519–524. Reprinted in *Kiyosi Itô, Selected Papers*, 1987, Ed. Stroock, D.W., and S.R.S. Varadhan. Springer-Verlag.
25. Itô, K. 1974. "Stochastic Differentials." *Appl. Math. and Opt.* **1**, 374–381. Reprinted in *Kiyosi Itô, Selected Papers*, 1987, Ed. Stroock, D. W., and S.R.S. Varadhan. Springer-Verlag.
26. Itô, K., and H.P. McKean. 1974 (Second Printing, Corrected.) *Diffusion Processes and their Sample Paths*. Springer-Verlag.
27. Kuo, H.-H. 1996. *White Noise Distribution Theory*, CRC Press.
28. Kuo, H.-H. *Introduction to Stochastic Integration*, Springer-Verlag, 2005.
29. Lamberton, D., and B. Lapeyre. 1996. *Introduction to Stochastic Calculus Applied to Finance*. (Transl. N. Rabeau and F. Mantion). Chapman & Hall.
30. Lieb, E.H., and J. Yngvason. 1999. "The Physics and Mathematics of the Second Law of Thermodynamics." *Phys. Rep.* **310**: 1–96. (Erratum in **314**:669.)

**31.** Merton, R.C. 1973. "Theory of Option Pricing." *Bell J. Economics and Management Science* **4** (Spring): 141–183.
**32.** Øksendal, B. 1998. *Stochastic Differential Equations. An Introduction with Applications.* (Fifth Edition) Springer-Verlag.
**33.** Pearl, J. 2000. *Causality*. Cambridge University Press.
**34.** Rebonato, R. 1998. *Interest Rate Option Models.* John Wiley & Sons.
**35.** Rebonato, R. 1999. *Volatility and Correlation.* John Wiley & Sons.
**36.** Rudin, W. 1991. *Real and Complex Analysis.* (3rd Edition) McGraw-Hill.
**37.** Rudin, W. 1991. *Functional Analysis.* (2nd Edition) McGraw-Hill.
**38.** Samuelson, P.A. 1965. "Proof that Properly Anticipated Prices Fluctuate Randomly." *Industrial Management Review* **6**: 13–31.
**39.** Sornette, D. 2003. *Why Stock Markets Crash. Critical Events in Complex Finanical Systems*. Princeton University Press.
**40.** von Neumann, J., and O. Morgenstern. 2004 (60th anniversary edition). *Theory of Games and Economic Behavior* (Commemorative Edition). Princeton University Press.

# INDEX

NOTE: Boldface numbers indicate illustrations; (*t*) indicates a table.


American call option, 81–84
American option, 68
arbitrage, 9, 23–37, 264
  Hahn-Banach theorem and, 24, 30–37
  Martingale principle and, 41–43
  min-max argument and, 24–37
  no-arbitrage and pricing measure in, 24–29
  options and no-arbitrage in, 67, 80
  uniqueness/non-uniqueness of Q in, 29–30
Arrow-Debreu prices, 187, 263, 264
at-the-money options, 76

Bernoulli, Nicholas, 263
Black, Fischer, 117. *See also* Black-Scholes model
Black-Scholes model, 7, 112, 117–123
  Central Limit Theorem and, 120–121
  parameters of, 122–123
  Q and, 117
  stochastic differential equations (SDEs) and, 117, 121–122
  volatility and "smile effect" of, 122
bond price, 18
bonds, 47–54
  coupons and, 47, 48
  credit default swaps (CDSs) and, 53–54
  default density function in, 53
  default risk in, 48–49, 50–53
  discount factor and, 50, 57–59, 136
  exchange rates and, 48
  face value of, 47
  forward price in, 57–59
  forward rate, forward rate agreement in, 85–89
  interest rate calculations and, 49–50
  intertemporal equilibrium and, 48
  maturity date of, 47, 48
  sources for (municipal, state, etc.), 47–48
  spot rate and, 136
  yield curves and, 135
  zero-coupon, 45, 48–50, 106(*t*)
Borel measure, 51
Borel subset and sigma-algebra, 192–194, 197
  stochastic processes and, 221, 222–226
Brownian motion, 128, 130, 133, 226–227, 237, 266–267
  Gaussian models and, 138, 141
  Green's function and, 163
  quadratic variation in, 227
  stochastic processes and, 226–229, 235, 236

call option, 5–7, 106–107(*t*)
calls and puts, 67–84. *See also* options
causality, 266
central limit theorem, 216
  Black-Scholes model and, 120–121
characteristic function, 211–215
  chi-squared models and, 153
  probability and, 211–215
  Q from, 213–215

chi-squared models, 109, 151–157, 266
  characteristic function in, 153
  Cox-Ingersoll-Ross (CIR) model (one-factor) and, 151–152, 169–176
  degrees of freedom and, 153
  density, 182
  Fourier transform in, 182
  Green's function and, 153, 154–157, 169–176
    forward, 154–155
    nondiscounted, 155–156
    shifted, 156–157
  Laplace transform in, 153, 165, 182
  mean in, 182
  one-factor, 169–176
  properties of, 182(*t*)
  shifted integrals in, 182
  stochastic differential equations (SDEs) and, 152
  sums in, 182
  variance in, 182
closed half-spaces, Hahn-Banach theorem and, 250
codimension, Hahn-Banach theorem and, 250
completeness, of market, 30, 264
complex measures, 195–196
complex systems, 265
conditional expectations, 207–211
conditional price and Martingale principle, 39–44
conditional probability, 205–207, 266
consistent pricing, 1, 23
constant maturity swaps, 98
continuity, right, 221
continuum limits, 247
convergence, 215–217
  probability and, 215–217
convergence theorem, 191
  dominated, 191
  monotone, 191
convexity, Hahn-Banach theorem and, 250, 254
convexity adjustment
  forward rates and, 97–98
  Gaussian models and, 148–149
correlation, 266
  Gaussian models and, 144–148
coupons, bond, 47, 48
Cox-Ingersoll-Ross (CIR) (one-factor) model, 151–152. *See also* chi-squared model
  Green's function and, 169–176
Cramer, Gabriel, 263
credit default swaps (CDSs), 53–54
cylinder sets, stochastic processes and, 224–226

default density function, 53
default risk, bond, 48–49, 50–53
degrees of freedom, chi-squared models and, 153
delta, in hedging, 104–105
density function, probability and, 203
density property, Gaussian and chi-squared models, 182
density, transition, 127
differential equations, 237–247
  continuum limits in, 247
  difference scheme in, probabilistic interpretation in, 243–245
  Feynman-Kac formula in, 247
  Hull-White (one-factor) Gaussian models and, 237
  interest rate trees and, 247
  Markov processes and, **237**
  partial (PDE), 237, 238–240
    discretizing, numerical scheme for, 240–243
  probability and, difference scheme in, 243–245
  stochastic (SDE), **237**, 238–240, 246–247, 246
differentials, stochastic. *See* stochastic differentials, algebra of
diffusion processes, 267
  Markov processes and, 127

discount factors, 16–18, 136
bond, 50
forward price and, 57–59
Martingale principle and, 41–43
distribution function, probability and, 203
distribution measure
probability and, 202–203
dominated convergence theorem, 191
Dynkin pi-lambda theorem, 203
probability and, 203
sigma-algebra and, 200

economic equilibrium, 264
equilibrium, 9–11
economic, 264
Markov evolution (processes) and, 126–128
equivalent martingale measure, 264
European call options, 5–7, 67
European put option, 67
exchange rates, 48
bonds and, 48
fixed, 19–20
exercising of options, 67, 68
expectation
conditional expectations and, 207–211
conditional probability and, 39–41
price and, 13–14
probability and, 202
expiration date, option, 69–72

face value, 47
factors, in modeling, 109
Feynman-Kac formula, 109, 129–132, 133, 237, 247
Green's function and, 129–132, 129
filtration, 219–221
finite dimensional distribution, stochastic processes and, 222
floating leg of swap, 92–93
fluctuation and Markov processes, 127
forward agreement, 55, 106(*t*)
forward Green's function, 163–166
chi-squared models and, 154–155
forward measure, 56–59
forward price, 7, 45, 55–59
discount factor and, 57–59
forward agreement and, 55
forward measure and, 56–59
forward rate and, 88
options, 73–75
swap rates and, 95–96
forward rate, 85–89
Gaussian models and, 144
natural time lag and convexity adjustment in, 97–98
forward spot rate, Gaussian models and, 144
Fourier transform
chi-squared models, 182
Gaussian models, 182
freedom. *See* degrees of freedom
Fubini's theorem, 194–195
futures agreement, 62
futures prices, 61–65
futures agreement and, 62
long position in, 62
futures, 108(*t*)

gamma, in hedging, 105
Gaussian distributions, 20–21
Definition of, 203–204
Gaussian models, 109, 135–150
Brownian motion and, 138, 141
calibration of, 138
convexity adjustment and, 148–149
density, 182
forward rate, forward spot rate and, 144
Fourier transform in, 182
Green's function and, 136–137, 139, 163, 176–181

Gaussian models (*Cont.*):
Hull-White (one-factor), 137–141, 237
Laplace transform in, 182
log-normal cases and, 140
mean in, 182(*t*)
mean-reversion in, 138, 141
multifactor, 141–144, 176–181
N factors and, 135–136
N-factor models and, 135
one-factor, 137–141
one-factor, Green's function and, 163
properties of, 182(*t*)
shifted integrals in, 182
state space in, 135–136
stochastic differential equations (SDEs) and, 136–137
summary of, 150(*t*)
sums of, 182
variance in, 182
volatility and correlations with, 144–148
yield curves and, 135
geometry, in Hahn-Banach theorem, 249
Greeks, in hedging formula, 104–105
Green's function, 109, 125, 127, 128–132, 133, 159–182, 266
Brownian motion and, 130
chi-squared models and, 153, 154–157
derivation of
Brownian motion and, 163
derivation of, 159–182
forward Green's function and, 163–166
Ito's stochastic differential equation in, 164
Laplace transform in, 162, 165
multi-factor Gaussian model and, 176–181
nondiscounted Green's function in, 167
one-factor chi-squared Cox-Ingersoll-Ross model and, 169–176
one-factor Gaussian model and, 163
Ornstein-Uhlenbeck equation in, 163
probability and, 159–160
shifted Green's function, 167–169
Feynman-Kac formula and, 129–132
forward, 154–155, 163–166
Gaussian models and, 136–137, 139
Ito stochastic differential equation (SDE) and, 132
Laplace transform in, 131, 162
Markov models and, 128
nondiscounted, 155–156, 167
Schrodinger equation and, 129
shifted, 156–157, 167–169

Hahn-Banach theorem, 24, 30–37, 249–261, 267
algebraic formulation in, 251–254
closed half-spaces in, 250
codimension in, 250
convex of set in, 250, 254
geometric interpretation of, 259–261
geometric setting for, 249–250
hyperplane in, 250, 254
Minkowski functional in, 251–254
proof of, 255–259
half-spaces, closed, Hahn-Banach theorem and, 250
Heath-Jarrow-Morton model, 266
hedging, 100–108, 265
delta in, 104–105
gamma in, 105
Greeks in , 104–106

rho in, 105
theta in, 105
vega in, 105
holder or owner, option, 67, 68
Hull-White (one-factor) Gaussian models, 137–141, 237. *See also* differential equations
hyperplane, Hahn-Banach theorem and, 250, 254

in-the-money options, 70
independence, 205–207
probability and, 205–207
sigma-algebra and, 206–207
indicator functions, 187
infinities, 186–187
integral, stochastic, 232
integrals, in modeling, 133
integration, 189–191
dominated convergence theorem and, 191
interchanging limit and, 191
monotone convergence theorem and, 191
interchanging limit and integration, 191
interest rate swaps, 91
interest rate trees, 247, 267
interest rates, 133
bond, 49–50
Heath-Jarrow-Morton model, 266
International Swaps and Derivatives Association (ISDA), 54, 265
intertemporal equilibrium, 48
Itô formula, 234
Itô integral, 232
Itô stochastic differential equation, 109, 128, 232–236, 234(*t*)
Green's function and, 132, 164

Kolmogorov's theorem stochastic processes and, 222–226, 228–229, 236

Laplace transform, 133, 266
chi-squared models and, 153, 182
Gaussian models, 182
Green's function and, 131, 162, 165
Lebesgue measure, 198–199
probability and, 203
Libor rate, 265
Libor set in arrears swap, 98
Lieb, G., xiv
log-normal cases
Gaussian models and, 140
probability, numeraires and, 20–21, 20
log-normal pricing in options, 111–116
London Interbank Offered Rate. *See* Libor rate
long position in futures, 62

market, 1
market equilibrium, 9–11, 32
arbitrage and, 9, 23–37
bonds and, 48
common price in, 9
intertemporal equilibrium and, 48
min-max argument and, 23–37
numeraire in, 10
probability and, 10
risk-neutral measure in, 10
market equilibrium measure 10
Markov processes, 126–128, 228–231, 267
Brownian motion and, 128
differential equations and, **237**
diffusion processes and, 127
fluctuation and, 127
Green's function and, 127, 128–132
Ito stochastic differential equation, 128
Kolmogorov SDEs and, 127
random walk processes and, 128

Markov processes (*Cont.*):
  stochastic differential equation (SDEs) and, 128
  stochastic processes and, 229–231, 235
  transition density in, 127
  transition probabilities and, 125. *See also* Green's functions
  tree models and, 128
  Wiener process and, 128
martingales, 38–44, 64, 221–222
  equivalent, 264
mathematical tools, 183
maturity date, bond, 47, 48
mean, Gaussian and chi-squared models, 182
mean-reversion, Gaussian models and, 138, 141
measurable space, 186
measure space, 186
measures, 185–189
Merton, Robert, 117. *See also* Black-Scholes model
min-max argument, 23–37
Minkowski functional, 251–254
model prices, 109
modeling concepts, summary of, 133(*t*)
monotone convergence theorem, 191
multifactor Gaussian models, 141–144

N factors, in Gaussian models, 135–136
N-factor models, 109, 135. *See also* Gaussian models
natural time lag, convexity adjustment, and forward rates, 97–98
no-arbitrage and pricing measure in, 24–29
nondiscounted Green's function, 167
  chi-squared models and, 155–156
numeraires, 4–5, 10, 15–21, 43–44
  change in, and probability, 15–21, 43–44
  discount factors and, 16–18
  fixed exchange rate and, 19–20
  log-normal case and, 20–21

one-factor Gaussian models, 137–141
options, 5–7
  American call type, 81–84
  American type, 68
  arbitrage and, 67
  at-the-money, 76
  Black-Scholes formula in, 7, 117–123
  call, 5–7, 67
  call price in, 72–75
  calls and puts on, 67–84
  delta in, 104–105
  European call type, 67
  European put type, 67
  exercise of, 67, 68
  expiration date of, 69–72
  forward price in, 7, 45, 55–59, 73–75
  futures agreement and, 62
  futures prices in, 61–65
  gamma in, 105
  holder or owner in, 67, 68
  in-the-money, 70
  inequalities in price of, 77–81
  log-normal, pricing in, 111–116
  long position in, 62
  no-arbitrage and, 80
  out-of-the-money, 70
  premium of, 67
  pricing formula for, 5–7, 68
  pricing of, 76–81, 106–107(*t*)
  probability in, 73–75
  put, 67
  put price in, 75
  put-call parity in, 76
  rho in, 105
  stopping times in, 82
  strike price in, 69–72
  swaption price in, 99–100
  theta in, 105
  time value of, 70

vega in, 105
writer in, 67, 68
Ornstein-Uhlenbeck equation, 163
out-of-the-money options, 70
owner, option, 67, 68

parity, put-call, in options, 76
partial differential equation (PDE), **237**, 238–240. *See also* differential equations; stochastic differential equation
discretizing, numerical scheme for, 240–243
pi-lambda theorem, sigma-algebra and, 200
preference, 264
premium, 1
premium, option, 67
pricing, 2, 45–46
arbitrage and, 23–37
Black-Scholes formula in, 7
bond price in, 18
common price in, 9, 32
conditional price and Martingale principle in, 39–44
consistency in, 1, 23
discount factors and, 16–18
expectation and, 13–14
futures, 61–65
Hahn-Banach theorem and, 249–261
log-normal pricing in options, 111–116
min-max argument and, 23–37
model prices in, 109
no-arbitrage and pricing measure in, 24–29
option, 5–7, 68, 76–81, 106–107(*t*)
pricing measures in, 4
probability and, 3–7
Q (probability) and, 4, 15–18
swaption, 99–100, 99
pricing measure, 4, 264
probability, 2, 3–7, 201–217
characteristic function in, 211–215
from characteristic function, 213–214
conditional expectations and, 207–211
conditional price and Martingale principle in, 39–44
conditional, 205–207, 266
convergence and, 215–217
default density function and, 53
default risk and, 50–53
density function in, 203
differential equations and, 237–247
discount factors and, 16–18
distribution function in, 203
distribution measures in, 202–203
Dynkin pi-lambda theorem and, 203
expectation and, 202
random variables and, 202
fixed exchange rate and, 19–20
forward price and, 55–59
Gaussian distributions in, 203–204
Green's function and, 125, 159–160
independence and, 205–207
Lebesgue measure and, 203
log-normal case and, 20–21
market equilibrium and, 10
no-arbitrage and pricing measure in, 24–29
numeraire in, 4–5, 15–21, 43–44
option pricing formula and, 5–7
options and, 73–75
pricing and, 3–7
pricing measures and, 4
probability space in, 201
Radon-Nikodym theorem and, 203, 208
random variables and, 202
risk-neutral measure in, 10
sigma-algebra and, 40, 204–205
stochastic processes and, 219–236

probability (*Cont.*):
  transition, 125, 230. *See also* Green's functions
  uniqueness/non-uniqueness of Q in, 29–30
  weighting in, 202
probability space, 201
product spaces, 194–195
protection buyer/seller, 54. *See also* credit default swaps (CDSs)
puts. *See* calls and puts

Q in pricing probability, 4
  Black-Scholes model and, 117
  characteristic function and, 213–215
  forward price and, 55–59
  Martingale principle and, 41–43
  no-arbitrage and pricing measure in, 24–29
  numeraire change and, 15–18
  options and, 73–75
  uniqueness/non-uniqueness of, 29–30
  volatility and, 100
quadratic variation in Brownian motion, 227

Radon-Nikodym theorem, 203, 208
  probability and, 203, 208
  sigma-algebra and, 196–197
random variables and probability, 202
random walk processes, 128
randomness, 265
reference entity, 54. *See also* credit default swaps (CDSs)
reset dates, swaps and, 91
rho, in hedging, 105
right continuity, 221
risk, 1–2
  bond, 48–53
  risk-neutral measure in, 10

Scholes, Myron, 117. *See also* Black-Scholes model
Schrödinger equation, 129
segment of set, Hahn-Banach theorem and, 250
shifted Green's function, 167–169
  chi-squared models and, 156–157
shifted integrals, Gaussian and chi-squared models, 182
sigma-algebra, 40, 185–189, 191–194
  Borel function/subset in, 192–194, 197
  complex measures and, 195–196
  conditional expectations and, 207–211
  distribution measure in, 197
  Dynkin pi-lambda theorem and, 200
  filtration in, 219–221
  Fubini's theorem and, 194–195
  generated, 191–194
  independence and, 206–207
  Lebesgue measure and integrals in, 198–199
  pi-lambda theorem and, 200
  probability and, 204–205
  product spaces and, 194–195
  Radon-Nikodym theorem and, 196–197
  stochastic processes and, 221
  uniqueness of measures and, 200
simple functions, 187
simple instruments, 13
"smile effect," 122
spot rate, 136
spread, 54. *See also* credit default swaps (CDSs)
St. Petersburg paradox, 263
state space, 109, 125–132, 133
  Gaussian models and, 135–136
  Green's function and, 127, 128–132
  market factors and, 126

Markov evolution of, 126–128
stochastic differential equations (SDEs) and, 126
transition density in, 127
transition probabilities and, 125. *See also* Green's functions
variables in, 126
state variables, 126
stochastic differential equation (SDE), 117, 133, 235–236, **237**, 238–240, 246–247. *See also* differential equations; partial differential equations
Black-Scholes model and, 117, 121–122
chi-squared models and, 152
continuum limits in, 247
Feynman-Kac formula in, 247
Gaussian models and, 136–137
interest rate trees and, 247
Itô, 232–236, **234**
Markov processes and, 128
state space and, 126
stochastic differentials, algebra of, 232–236
stochastic processes, 219–236, 266
Brownian motion and, 226–229, 235, 236
construction of, 222–226
cylinder sets in, 224–226
filtration in, 219–221
finite dimensional distribution in, 222
integral in, 232
Ito stochastic differential equation (SDE) and, 232–236, **234**
Kolmogorov's theorem in, 222–226, 228–229, 236
Markov processes in, 229–231, 235
martingales and, 221–222
right continuity in, 221
stochastic differential equations (SDEs) and, 235–236
stopping times and, 220
transition probability and, 230
usual conditions in, 220–221
Wiener process in, 226–229
stopping times, 220
option, 82
stochastic processes and, 220
strike price in options, 69–72
swap rate, 91, 93–95, 108($t$)
forward prices and, 95–96
swaps, 91–96, 108($t$)
constant maturity, 98
credit default swaps (CDSs) and, 53–54
fixed vs. floating rate of interest in, 91
floating interest rate in, 93
floating leg of, 92–93
forward prices and swap rates in, 95–96
interest rate type, 91
legs of, 91
Libor set in arrears, 98
reset dates in, 91
swap rate in, 91, 93–95
swaption price in, 99–100
swaption price, 99–100
swaption, 108($t$)

theta, in hedging, 105
time lag, convexity adjustment, and forward rates, 97–98
time value of option, 70
trading, 1, 9
transition density, 127, 133
transition probabilities, 125, 230. *See also* Green's functions
tree models, 128

utility function, 264
utility theory, 263

variance, 204
Gaussian and chi-squared models, 182(*t*)
vega, in hedging, 105
volatility, 100–108, 266
  Black-Scholes model and, 122
  Gaussian models and, 144–148
  "smile effect" of, 122

Wiener process, 128, 133, 226–229
  stochastic processes and, 226–229
World Bank, 47–48
writer, option, 67, 68

yield curves, 135
  Gaussian models and, 135

zero-coupon bonds, 45, 48–50, 106(*t*)
  yield curves and, 135
Zorn's lemma, 35

# ABOUT THE AUTHOR

Ambar N. Sengupta is Professor of Mathematics at Louisiana State University, Baton Rouge. He has been consultant to AIG Trading Corporation and Dresdner Kleinwort Wasserstein. His work appears regularly in a variety of academic journals.